With Love Beyond All Telling

A Biblical Approach to Adult Spiritual Formation

Maureen Abbott, S.P.
and
Joseph M. Doyle, S.S.J.

PAULIST PRESS
New York/Mahwah

Library of Congress Cataloging-in-Publication Data

Abbott, Maureen.
    With love beyond all telling: a biblical approach to adult spiritual formation / Maureen Abbott and Joseph Doyle.
        p.   cm.
    Includes bibliographical references.
    ISBN 0-8091-3209-5
    1. Spiritual life—Biblical teaching. 2. Spiritual exercises. I. Doyle, Joseph, 1938–   . II. Title.
    BS680.S7A33   1991
    268'.434—dc20   90-24768
                                                                               CIP

Published by Paulist Press
997 Macarthur Boulevard
Mahwah, New Jersey 07430

Printed and bound in the
United States of America

Contents

PART II
Spiritual Formation through the Life of Grace in the Church

Acknowledgments

We would like to express our gratitude to the following people, who helped make this book possible:

A great debt of thanks is owed to Mary Frances Hession, former Director of Religious Education for the Diocese of Corpus Christi, who came up with the original design of the course and contributed many of its sessions.

Those who had the greatest impact on the formation of the book were the ministry candidates in the Diocese of Corpus Christi, who took the class during 1984–85 and helped us gain a clearer understanding of lay spirituality, as well as the teachers of these classes who gave us feedback about what was helpful and/or difficult.

Bishop Rene Gracida's sponsorship of the Pastoral Institute of the Diocese of Corpus Christi made it possible for the class to be offered throughout the diocese in a variety of settings.

A number of persons have helped with typing and preparation of the manuscript: Patricia Abbott Ashton in Tustin, CA, Eva Carlos in New Orleans, Anna de Leon in Corpus Christi, and Lou Driver in Houston.

Several women who have had experience in parish programs and discussion groups commented on the readability of the text and the clarity of our directions: Kathy Dietro, Peg Peramble, and Patricia Ashton.

Finally, we are most grateful to our religious congregations who provided us not only with our own spiritual formation and with opportunities for ministry which have continued that formation, but also allowed us the time to pursue this project.

Introduction

HOW THIS BOOK CAME TO BE

The germ of this book came to us in 1984 when we were working in the Diocese of Corpus Christi, Texas—Joe as pastor of Holy Cross Parish and Maureen as Director of Lay Ministries for the Diocese. Our aim was to develop a course of studies for training lay ministers. We had spent quite a lot of time and energy in researching what was being done elsewhere and in prioritizing what we felt was important.

Most of us taking the leadership in the project were priests and sisters who had the advantage of a structured spiritual formation in the seminary and/or novitiate. Our work in parishes and adult religious education convinced us that people became excited when they participated in retreats and workshops and realized that in the midst of their ordinary lives, they were living an active spiritual life. They were delighted to meet and talk with others on a deeper level. Our objective became clearer—to prepare a course which would provide a structure for such people to identify and describe their spiritual formation.

We collaborated with the Diocesan Director of Religious Education, Sr. Mary Frances Hession, S.P., to develop such a course, combining scriptural figures with basic Christian themes common to the spiritual life. During 1984–85 the course was taught at ten centers across the diocese, in both English and Spanish. The response of instructors and participants was enthusiastic, testifying to the validity of our assumptions. The course continues to be used as the first year of the diocese's Pastoral Institute three-year preparation for the commissioning of lay ministers. Because we wanted to share this opportunity with more people, we contacted Paulist Press and reworked the basic outline and course into this book.

THE BASIC ASSUMPTION—
GOD'S COVENANT LOVE

As Christians, our lives are guided by the revelation we have received in the scriptures about God's covenant with humanity. Our God is the One who says to us, "I will be your God and you will be my people." God takes the initiative and issues the call, while we listen and respond. God intends that every human being who is placed on earth will come to a sense, within the ordinary circumstances of life, that he or she has a destiny as a child of God. We are all on a journey during which God forms us "from our mother's womb" (Ps 139). We can rest assured that God will fulfill the covenant and bring us home, but we can also enjoy our journey to the fullest by studying the signposts, by entering into dialogue and communion with our savior.

The title of this book is drawn from the eucharistic liturgy for the Advent season, where we reflect on the fact that Mary nurtured Jesus "with love beyond all telling." Our own spiritual nurturing has been accomplished by a God who, "with love beyond all telling," places in our lives the persons, environment, and events which make us realize that our deepest spiritual longings are an invitation to participate in the life-stream of God's continuing creative action. We **have** received spiritual gifts, and these gifts are for the upbuilding of the kingdom.

THE OVERALL STRUCTURE OF THE BOOK

This book is not intended as a formal study of scripture. Rather, we have selected scripture passages which have special significance for us as Christians. We have tried to provide some minimal background information regarding the formation of the texts—the author and the times when they were written—simply to relate the text to the context. We recommend that anyone who is serious about the spiritual life take time at some point to do an intensive scripture study to deepen his or her own background, but that is not the purpose of this study.

Neither is the book intended to be a formal study of the areas of spirituality or of doctrine. Again, we necessarily touch upon areas of spirituality such as prayer and self-emptying, and areas of doctrine such as incarnation and redemption, but we do not dwell on them in a descriptive or formal way. Rather, we assume that the interested participant will pursue particular questions on his or her own.

What we do attempt to provide is a series of reflections and exercises which will awaken the interest and questions of ordinary people in such a way that they can explore deeper issues with companions on the journey. Rather than an original contribution to the literature of spirituality, we are proposing a very basic framework for identifying one's own personal development. Because the framework is supported by scripture, it will be necessary for each participant to have a Bible. It will also be extremely helpful for the participant to keep a journal during the course of the study sessions, and even to seek out a spiritual director afterwards to continue serious attention to the spiritual life.

Our "definition" of spirituality is the ability to look at life not simply from our limited human perspective, but with a firm conviction that we are created and loved by a God who calls us to a fuller life. Spirituality serves as a mirror that reflects back not only our physical appearance, but our precious appearance before God. We believe that God reveals God's own self to the world through a human being, Jesus, who continues to reach out to us through the lives of other human beings. It is through us that the face of God is seen in the world.

WHO CAN USE THIS BOOK?

The book could be used with profit by an individual who has a desire to deepen his or her spiritual life, since it provides a format for enriching one's own insights. Simply reading the text, along with the suggested scripture passages, as well as taking time for the prayer and responding to the follow-up activity and questions in one's journal, will provide an impetus for attending to the action of God in one's life.

The book could be used with great advantage by **a group** since the text material is further enriched by the real-life contributions of others in one's community. Persons who have already participated in such groups as Renew, or the R.C.I.A., will find this a convenient vehicle to continue the growth they have learned to appreciate. Persons responsible for adult religious education groups could use the sessions as starters to develop a number of themes. Since the course was originally intended for lay ministers, such groups could use the book as a text for a preparation course, or as a means of continued growth.

THE PROCESS OF THE SESSIONS

We have set up the sessions as though they would be used by a small group meeting in a home for about an hour and a half. Each session has five parts:

1. Scripture-centered prayer
2. Lesson/discussion
3. An activity or questions designed to raise deeper issues
4. Fellowship among participants
5. Wrap-up

1. The **scripture-centered prayer** is designed to connect the specific "call" or theme of Christian life to a scripture passage and text which highlight God's revelation about that topic. This includes:

a) "Scripture Passage"—a citing of the section of scripture which has been chosen to highlight the CALL
b) "An Introduction to the Text"—a brief explanation of the background of the passage and how it relates to the CALL
c) "Call to Prayer"—words and/or gesture to focus attention
d) "Reading"—a short passage of the actual passage which is to be read aloud to bring God's word to life for the participants
e) "Individual Reflection"—brief comments or questions to lead into silent reflection
f) "Prayer"—a summary imploring the assistance of God

2. The **lesson/discussion** is the meat of the book. This usually consists of two parts:

a) an explanation of how the scriptural "hero" or topic provides divine direction for human growth; and
b) a presentation of how the participant can think about or act on the CALL

3. The **activity or questions** are designed to apply the theoretical concepts of the lesson to practical aspects of living a spiritual life. These are usually intended to be done as a group, but could be adapted to private use. **Note:** Chapter 1 is designed to explain the rationale for a group-based approach to developing the spiritual life and to help a

group establish "rules" and procedures. Directions for group leaders are provided on pages 7–8.

4. Time is allotted for **fellowship,** usually in the context of hospitality and refreshments, because informal sharing among Christians has always been a key ingredient of satisfaction and motivation, a precursor of our sharing in the heavenly banquet.

5. The **wrap-up** is a transitional moment to provide movement out of the actual session, forward into the follow-up and future session. Participants can:

a) Look over the "During the Week" activities to see what is suggested as a follow-up. These are considered optional, depending on the amount of time available to each participant.
b) Look ahead to the next session for:
    (1) the scripture passage which is suggested, locating it and marking his/her Bible;
    (2) the CALL topic—we recommend that each participant decide on a convenient time during the upcoming week to read the lesson so as to be prepared to discuss the contents.
c) The brief closing prayer can take whatever form the leader suggests.

We have also included a bibliography to give credit to those authors who have helped us in formulating our ideas.

It is our hope that through use of this book, many people will come to a greater appreciation of how precious we are to our God, who loves us "beyond all telling."

Sr. Maureen Abbott, S.P.
Rev. Joseph Doyle, S.S.J.
Feast of the Sacred Heart, June 2, 1989

Procedures for Groups

STARTING A GROUP

1. Someone needs to take the leadership to **recruit** a group of people who are interested in meeting regularly to work through the sessions together. Approach your pastor to work out a plan, possibly putting announcements in the church bulletin and sign-up sheets in the vestibule.
2. **Form groups** of six to eight persons who agree to a regular day of the week. Decide on a meeting place and notify the participants.
3. **Order books,** one per participant. You will also want to find out if anyone needs a Bible, and may also want to make notebooks (journals) available.
4. Recruit persons for two **leadership roles:**
   a) Hospitality (possibly the person in whose home you are meeting): This person provides refreshments and arranges the serving.
   b) Group leader: This person takes responsibility to move the group through the session.

PROCEDURES FOR GROUP LEADER

1. Read through the entire chapter to get an overview.
2. Look up and read the biblical passage cited at the beginning of the chapter.
3. Estimate the time to be allotted to the sections in order to finish in about an hour and a half:
   a) Prayer
   b) Discussion of content
   c) Activity or sharing questions

    d) Hospitality

    e) Wrap-up

4. Gather needed materials for the prayer (tape, song sheet, candle, flowers, etc.)

5. Decide on a form for the closing prayer. For example, you could ask participants to join hands and say the Our Father, to sing a familiar hymn, to recite the Memorare, etc.

6. Look over the topic of the following week's session and locate the Bible passage.

7. Prepare to lead the discussion of content. You may select one of these methods for handling the discussion:

    a) "Teach" the lesson by giving a presentation of the main ideas.

    b) Assume that participants have read the chapter and rephrase the subheadings into questions in order to encourage them to explain what they got out of the reading. Example from page 29:

    Subheading: *Progressive levels of listening*

    Question: What three levels of listening do the authors describe?

    Possible response: First, we pay attention to the person. Second, we rephrase what they say to test if we heard correctly, and third, we go on to tell the other person how we feel about it.

    c) Read the text material aloud in the group, paragraph by paragraph, pausing to summarize the main ideas, such as the "possible response" given for method (b).

    d) Take 10–15 minutes of quiet time for group members to read through the text material. Then proceed with method (b) above.

Note that any of these methods requires you to make sure you have read the material and have a good understanding of it.

8. Prepare to lead the activity or sharing questions. Be sure you understand what is expected and are prepared to give the necessary directions. For example, if small groups of three are required, suggest moving to the kitchen, the dining room, and the living room. If written responses are called for, make sure pencils and pads are available.

PART I

Spiritual Formation through Covenant Love

1. Call To Listen

Scripture Passage

Isaiah, chapters 42–43: **Promises to the Servant of the Lord.**

PRAYER

Introduction: A Note on the Text

Leader: As we begin our journey through the scriptures, keep in mind that our first selection, from the book of Isaiah, is generally regarded by scholars to actually be not one, but three books. The first "book" (chapters 1–39, or "First Isaiah") was written by Isaiah of Jerusalem in the 8th century B.C. to all the people and kings of Judah, urging them to stand firm in their spiritual heritage during a time of war and destruction. The second "book" (chapters 40–55, or "Second Isaiah") was written by an unnamed prophet who was in exile in Babylon in the 6th century so that he might give comfort to a refugee people bereft of their homeland. The prophet's message is one of hope and restoration on the part of a Creator who saves, so his style is lyrical and solemn. A later "book" (chapters 55–66, or "Third Isaiah") retains many of the themes of the earlier books, but has a more somber and liturgical tone.

The passage we will use for our prayer today is taken from the second of these three books. It seems appropriate for us to begin our scriptural approach to our spiritual formation by plunging into the heart of the Old Testament, into what is sometimes called the "Book of Consolation." Some commentators even believe that this book was written for small groups like the one we are forming today! The words we will hear in a few moments were probably first read in Babylon between 550–539 B.C., as a group of Jews gathered on the Sabbath to

11

praise God and to celebrate their call to covenant. The prophet is convinced of God's "love beyond all telling" and makes it clear to us as well.

Call to Prayer

Leader: Let us allow the cares and concerns of daily life to fall away so that we may be attentive to the voice of our God within. (Music, song, or gathering gesture may be used.)

Reading

Reader: A reading from the book of Isaiah (42:5-9; 43:1b-7).

Thus says God, the LORD,
  who created the heavens and stretched them out,
  who spreads out the earth with its crops,
Who gives breath to its people
  and spirit to those who walk on it;
I, the LORD, have called you for the victory of justice,
  I have grasped you by the hand;
I formed you, and set you
  as a covenant of the people,
  a light for the nations.
To open the eyes of the blind,
  to bring out prisoners from confinement,
  and from the dungeon, those who live in darkness.
I am the LORD, this is my name;
  my glory I give to no other, nor my praise to idols.
See, the earlier things have come to pass,
  new ones I now foretell;
Before they spring into being,
I announce them to you. . . .
Fear not, for I have redeemed you;
  I have called you by name; you are mine.
When you pass through the water, I will be with you;
  in the rivers you shall not drown.
When you walk through fire, you shall not be burned;
  the flames shall not consume you.
For I am the LORD, your God,
  the Holy One of Israel, your savior . . .
Because you are precious in my eyes
  and glorious, and because I love you, . . .

Fear not, for I am with you;
    from the east I will bring back your descendants;
    from the west I will gather you.
I will say to the north: Give them up!
    and to the south: Hold not back!
Bring back my sons from afar,
    and my daughters from the ends of the earth:
Everyone who is named as mine,
    whom I created for my glory,
    whom I formed and made.

Individual Reflection

Leader: What is spirituality? Somehow, we realize that there is more to life than what is apparent on a merely human level. We sense an extra dimension which our faith tells us is God's mysterious presence. We hear within ourselves the words, "I have called you by name —you are mine." Some of us find ourselves more and more conscious of that presence, more and more needing to pay attention to it, to trace its movements. Take a moment now to reflect on how God has given you "breath and spirit." (All pause for silent reflection.)

Prayer

All: God our Creator, I trust in you. I thank you for setting my feet on this journey. Help me to put aside my fears as I grasp your hand. It is you who have formed me, named me, and called me. Help me to echo with confidence the words of Isaiah: "Yes! I am precious in your eyes." Amen.

LESSON

A Scriptural Approach to Spiritual Formation

We who are Christians have as our heritage the whole of the Bible. While all of us cannot claim as much familiarity with these "books" as we would like, we are aware of the two major divisions, the Old Testament and the New Testament. What our Christian Bibles call the Old Testament are actually the Jewish scriptures, those texts which were mostly written in Hebrew over a very long period of time, between the eleventh and second centuries before Christ. We today find spiritual nourishment in these scriptures for many reasons: they speak to us of God's covenant love, the tradition that was the basis for Jesus' spirituality, and that Christians have made them their own through liturgy and writings. We believe that God speaks to us through these texts in a special manner because God **inspired** (enspirited) the writer with a particular message.

A major message was that of **covenant,** God's active seeking of the human spirit. God offers to be the God of a particular people, the Israelites, so we can trace the divine search in actual historical people. In the first centuries (2000–1800 B.C.), God initiated the call to Abraham's family. Then there was a long quiet period when the people were exiled in Egypt (1800–1300 B.C.). Around 1300, God inspired Moses to lead the exodus from Egypt and gave the people the Book of the Covenant to guide them. The saga of the judges and the conquest tells us of God's care that this people would have a land to call their own. The centuries of the kings (1100–600 B.C.) were times when the social structure and the church structure were combined, a situation not always helpful to spiritual growth; this was a time when the prophets flourished, calling the people to live more faithful lives.

A renewed period of covenant came during the Exile (598–539 B.C.), when it must have appeared to be all over for this people. They had been conquered by the Assyrians and then by the Babylonians, and physically displaced from the promised land. They were faced with the question of who they were before the Lord. Who was their God? How were they a "people"? This time of soul-searching was the time during which much of the Hebrew scriptures took form. The people came to realize that they were still very much loved by God. How did they come to this realization?

After settling in Babylonia, the exiles received a letter from Jeremiah, writing from Jerusalem. He told them to accept their situation: "Build houses to dwell in. Plant gardens and eat their fruits. Take wives and beget sons and daughters. . . . For I know well the plans I have in mind for you, says the LORD, plans for your welfare, not for woe! Plans to give you a future full of hope" (Jer 29:5–6; 11). So, far from their homeland, deprived of their temple, they did as Jeremiah said. They gathered in each other's homes and reread the scrolls which told them the stories of God's love. In this way God formed them through their scriptures. They came to understand that they had an active part to play in God's plans.

Today we are also called to gather and to ponder the scriptures and to discover the part we have to play in God's plans. Our first task is to develop a listening heart so that we can hear the God within ourselves and the God who comes to us through other seekers.

Our "Spiritual Streak"

Scripture reveals to us that God has formed us, so we should not be surprised at the "spiritual streak" we find in ourselves. A spiritual sense is not that uncommon, even though most people don't talk much about it. We're aware of our "spiritual self" at unexpected times. Perhaps it's a fleeting sensation that comes at moments of waiting—for the children to come out of school, for the traffic light to change, for the toast to pop up, or for mass to start. But it's persistent, like the Hound of Heaven in Francis Thompson's poem: "from those strong feet that followed, followed after. But with unhurrying chase,/ and unperturbed pace." We know we can't get away. We know we must turn and look into those eyes, and acknowledge our mysterious but ever-present God.

Because this search is frightening at times, we want to join with others who sense the same movement and who want to train themselves to be more welcoming of God's presence. All our lives we have been influenced by people who have helped us to notice the God-dimension. Some people stand out in our memories as persons who have had a great impact on our spiritual development. When we choose to join a group such as the one being formed to study this book, we invite further growth.

The "Johari Window" Personality Model

Back in the 1950s, when psychology was gaining in popularity, a great deal of study went into describing the process of human interaction. Joseph Luft and Harold Ingham popularized a model that they named by combining their first names to call it the "Johari window." Why a window? Like the traditional four-paned window, their model had four sections. Each section showed a different aspect of a person, as is seen in this diagram:

THE "JOHARI WINDOW"

	Known to self	Not known to self
Known to others	1 **OPEN** area	2 **BLIND SPOT**
Not known to others	3 **PRIVATE** life	4 **UNKNOWN** area

The diagram is intended to show that the part of our personality which is known to both our self and also to others (1) is "open." The part of our personality which is known to ourself but not to others (3) is "private." The part of our personality that is known to others but not known to ourself (2) is a "blind" spot, while that part of our personality which is not known either by others or by ourself (4) is truly "unknown" to anyone but God.

This model explains a great deal about why we feel comfortable or uncomfortable in sharing personal matters with someone else. Unlike windowpanes, which stay the same size, the four areas can become larger or smaller. In social situations we adjust the size of the "open" area to fit our comfort level, much as the eye adjusts to the amount of light in a room. With close friends who know details of our private life (3) and also some of our blind spots (2), our OPEN area is wide. With strangers the situation is just the opposite: they don't know either our private life or our blind spots, so the OPEN area is small.

With friends

1	2
3	4

With strangers

1	2
3	4

This model is useful to us as we begin a formal study of spirituality. In our discussion group, as we get to know one another better and to trust the fact that God often leads us through our human interactions, we have less reason to hide our true selves. We tend to be more tolerant of our "blind spots," more willing to share our private lives with sympathetic listeners. We spend more time in reflection, so our hidden self grows stronger and more able to engage in life. As a consequence, we become more open.

Group Rules: 1. Respect for Privacy

The model provides us with a useful framework for rules to govern our group discussion. Even though in most social situations we are too polite to let out our negative feelings, we nevertheless recognize that God can use even negative emotions such as anger or impatience to form us. There may be times when it is appropriate to express such negative emotions in order to foster spiritual growth, times when we allow them to move from "private" to "open."

Likewise we recognize that a group setting is not the best place to bring out family skeletons, so normally we're sensitive and respect a certain privacy. Yet, in the group, when we or another person feel moved to share something which would normally be held private, we pledge ourselves to respect that confidence, and not to repeat it. Just as the church has always guarded confessional matter with the seal of secrecy, we too foster healing and reconciliation by a like obligation. While such private areas are allowed to be "open" in the group, they are respectfully and steadfastly considered "private" outside the group setting.

Group Rules: 2. Truthful Feedback

A second insight we can gain from this model is in reference to the "blind" area. One of the biggest blocks to spiritual growth is our inability to see the total picture. Among the "woes" of Matthew's gospel we find these harsh words of Jesus: "Blind guides! You strain out the gnat and swallow the camel! Woe to you scribes and Pharisees, you frauds!" (Mt 23:24–25). We see that those who held ministry leadership positions within the Jewish community were considered blind by Jesus.

People who take religion seriously seem more likely than most people to get off track, to emphasize areas that are really of secondary importance, to resent people who don't have the same values or priorities. If we're going to make a conscious effort in spiritual formation, we have to be able to listen to those who give us feedback about our negative side. On the other hand, we have to learn how to speak the truth in love to others who may be detrimental to the group effort toward spiritual growth. In the church, the viewpoint of the group has always had a special place in clearing up the blind spots of individuals.

Group Rules: 3. Honest to Self and to God

And finally, the "unknown" area is very influential for our spirituality because God our Creator is already within us at our deepest self. From within, it is God who invites us both to seek and to find our Source. Little by little, our unknown area opens up and our "best self" is released. Although many people shy away from self-reflection because they are afraid of what they might find, from a spiritual standpoint, this inward growth is the whole purpose of our existence—it is our real life's work. Outwardly we may show signs of aging, but inwardly, spiritually, we are growing stronger and stronger (1 Cor 4:16). We must trust the words of Isaiah which we read in our prayer above: "Fear not, I have redeemed you" (43:1).

So the "Johari window" becomes a useful way of describing our spirituality in process. Our light shines more clearly as the open area becomes larger when our trust allows us to take our fears from hiding (which shrinks section 3), when our humility allows us to listen to the honest words of spiritual friends (which shrinks section 2), and when our listening heart enables us to allow the unknown God to be revealed (which shrinks section 4).

If we are working through this book as part of a group, we are counting on the group members to walk our spiritual journey with us. In order to do this, we need to start out with a little orientation to one another. We can't expect to listen well to God if we can't listen well to one another. Psychology describes three levels of presence when we "listen." First, we **pay attention** to the other person. We nod in agreement or raise a quizzical eyebrow. The speaker is made to feel that he or she is getting through. Such signs of attention encourage a preacher or teacher to keep going, and they do the same for us when we're trying to say something of importance. When we're in the role of listener, it's important to give visible signs of interest and attention. However, such signs are only the first step, because the communication so far is one-sided.

We need first to listen with attention, but secondly, we need to make sure we understand what is being said. So we **test** it out by repeating it in our own words, or by asking clarifying questions. For example, when your child babbles on about how the other kids pick on her, you say, "it sounds to me like you're pretty upset." This gives her an opening to say some more. Pretty good communication, right? Yes and no. Yes because the child knows you're listening and trying to understand. No, because it's still one-sided. So we move on to the third level.

Here I not only pay attention and test out what I'm hearing, but I also **tell you how I feel.** This is mutual sharing, which is appropriate when we're trying to communicate on a deeper level with someone we trust. "If I heard you right, you're upset that your daughter is marrying the wrong man, but it seems to me that she's thought it through pretty well." We don't get to this stage with strangers because mutuality requires trust. Once trust is established, we're more likely to open up our "hidden" area or to question the other's "blind" spot.

Group Rules: 4. Aim for Redemptive Listening

In her book, *Parish Life: Manual for Spiritual Leadership Formation,* Sister Nancy Westmeyer, O.S.F., describes these three levels but goes beyond them to a fourth level, what she calls **redemptive listening.** Because we are Christians, we look at each other in a new way. Most people automatically size up others from their own cultural frame of reference. People who work at listening try to put aside their personal agenda in order to tune in to the speaker.

When we listen as Christians, we try to do even more. We look past the facade or "filter" of appearance, body language, and voice quality to recognize the hidden or unknown self trying to grow strong. We draw on the strength of our own Christ-life to be more sensitive, more careful about our own "filter" or appearance, body language, and voice quality. We moderate these aspects of ourselves in order to encourage the other person to speak. We listen at a deeper level in order to pick up what lies beneath the surface, trying to come out.

As Christians, we try to make the right moment happen. When it does, our partner is able to say out loud thoughts about the underlying momentum which he or she feels beneath the surface of everyday life. The very act of speaking has the potential for bringing out the inner self which was christened (made Christ-like) at baptism. Because Christ is in the picture, listening takes on the power of redemption. Isaiah's prophecy is fulfilled: "Fear not, for I have redeemed you."

LISTENING EXERCISE

Not everybody is a good listener. Listening is easier for some people than for others, but any Christian who is called to spiritual formation is necessarily called to become a better listener. It's hard work and requires practice, but like any skill, it can be improved. Take some time while the ideas are fresh in your head to practice listening.

1. Form groups of three persons.
2. Everyone in the group writes out a brief completion of either sentence:
   The most important thing a work group should have is . . .
   The most important thing a parish community should have is . . .
3. Each one in the group takes one of these roles:
   Speaker: Give your message in one minute.
   Listener: Tell the speaker what you heard.
   Observer: Tell what you noticed about the speaker and listener.
4. Rotate roles so that each person has the opportunity to take all the roles.

BREAK

Enjoy refreshments and each other's company.

WRAP-UP

1. Look ahead to the "During the Week" follow-up activities.
2. Look ahead to the scripture passage and the theme of the next session.
3. Participate in a Closing Prayer.

DURING THE WEEK

Note: Each week some activities will be suggested as a follow-up to the session. These activities are designed for your personal growth rather than to be used in the group, so are optional and to be used at your discretion. You will find it helpful to keep a notebook or journal to focus your observations.

1. In three conversations you have this week, practice your role as *listener:* attending, understanding, responding. Keep a log of comments about all three conversations. Did you notice any change in your usual behavior? Summarize your observations.
2. What is your personal "definition" of spirituality? Share this with someone else. Then, reflect on your experience of talking about spirituality. Which of the feelings listed below did you experience while sharing?

—excited	—uncertain	—confused	—irritated
—relaxed	—pleased	—insecure	—alert
—uncomfortable	—curious	—interested	—bored
—nervous	—helpful	—worried	—stupid

Do you see any pattern? Notice that your feelings could have come from either the topic, the *content,* or from the conversation, the *process* of sharing out loud with another person a part of you that's somewhat personal and private. Since your feelings will affect how you approach this class, give yourself time to develop a comfortable attitude.

2. Call To Know Our God

Scripture Passage

Genesis, chapters 1–11: **God loves all creation into existence and lovingly enters human experience.**

PRAYER

Introduction: A Note on the Text

Leader: The book of Genesis is the very first book of the Bible, although it took the form in which we know it fairly late in the history of the Chosen People. The hand of three authors is evident, and there is some repetition since the final editor was inspired to bring forward the actions of God, not only through the actual events at the core of the narrative, but also through the perspective and retelling of the different peoples who preserved the stories over several centuries. For example, chapter 1 gives us a solemn and stylized account of how God created the world, while chapter 2 gives us a more intimate and homey account. The first twelve chapters use tales of generalized human experience to bring home to us the cosmic significance of our human experience. God is shown as taking a direct role in human events.

We have chosen for our prayer the chapter 2 account of creation because the author makes it easy for us to enter into the experience of God, who "with love beyond all telling" personally and intimately creates and tailors a situation such that the individual can continue the work of creation which has begun.

Call to Prayer

Leader: Let us gather ourselves to that inner place where God continues to be at work. (Music, song or a gathering gesture may be used.)

Reading

Reader: A reading from the book of Genesis (2:4b–23).

At the time when the LORD God made the earth and the heavens—while as yet there was no field shrub on earth and no grass of the field had sprouted, for the LORD God had sent no rain upon the earth and there was no man to till the soil, but a stream was welling up out of the earth and was watering all the surface of the ground—the LORD God formed man out of the clay of the ground and blew into his nostrils the breath of life, and so man became a living being.

Then the LORD God planted a garden in Eden, in the east, and he placed there the man whom he had formed. Out of the ground the LORD God made various trees grow that were delightful to look at and good for food, with the tree of life in the middle of the garden and the tree of the knowledge of good and bad.

A river rises in Eden to water the garden. . . .

The LORD God then took the man and settled him in the garden of Eden, to cultivate and care for it. . . .

The LORD God said: "It is not good for the man to be alone. I will make a suitable partner for him. So the LORD God formed out of the ground various wild animals and various birds of the air, and he brought them to the man to see what he would call them; whatever the man called each of them would be its name. The man gave names to all the cattle, all the birds of the air, and all the wild animals; but none proved to be the suitable partner for the man.

So the LORD God cast a deep sleep on the man, and while he was asleep, he took out one of his ribs and closed up its place with flesh. The LORD God then built up into a woman the rib that he had taken from the man. When he brought her to the man, the man said:

"This one, at last, is bone of my bones
and flesh of my flesh;

This one shall be called 'woman,'
for out of 'her man' this one
has been taken.

Individual Reflection

Leader: Who is God for me? Close your eyes for a moment and become conscious of the pace of your heartbeat. Allow your mind to summon up a name for God (Lord, Yahweh, Jesus, Spirit, etc.) Repeat the name interiorly with each heartbeat. (All pause for silent reflection.)

Prayer

All: O my God, you are truly **my** God. Just as you showed your deep concern for this first human being by providing not only for physical needs, but also a person to share his inner journey, so you have cared for me. Open my eyes to know you more clearly and to follow you more nearly. Amen.

LESSON

Various Notions of God

There is no need to prove to the readers of this book that God exists. You would not pick up a book on spirituality if you were not already committed to serving God in your neighbor and wished to deepen that commitment. But is it reasonable to ask, "Just what God do you believe in?"

Not that there are many Gods, but that our understanding of God is unique to each one of us. It varies according to our age, vocation in life, culture, stages of moral and faith development, etc. Therefore it is imperative that as we begin our journey, we explore our personal interiorization of God and how we came to it. All of this will be done in the light of sacred scripture, which is "good for instruction" (2 Tim 3:16). One of the most profound instructions on how human beings can picture God is found in the book of Genesis, which was "written" (actually collected from more than ten centuries of Israelite tradition) and edited in the 5th century B.C. according to three major "schools" of spirituality.

The earliest tradition was that of an author who referred to God as "Yahweh." Our prayer passage today was from this "Yahwist" who

Many people encounter the God of revelation for the first time in the book of Genesis. What can this book teach us about the various concepts of God that have not changed very much over the past three thousand years? First of all, as we hinted at above, we can learn a great deal about the God of the Hebrews from the names they gave to God, for to truly know an individual is to know that person's name.

Biblical Names for God

In the Old Testament we do not find just one name for God, but rather a variety, according to when the particular book was written. As we mentioned in chapter 1, God inspired many persons over a period of about eight hundred years to write down their understanding of who God was for them; gradually these texts were acknowledged as inspired and were collected in the form we call the Bible. Consequently, a particular word can have more than one meaning. "El," for example, can be applied to the one God worshipped by the Hebrew people or to the many "gods" worshipped by their neighbors. This name denotes a sense of superior power and emphasizes God's total "otherness." In one passage, it points to a God who is both male and female: "Then God said, "Let us make man in our image, after our likeness. . . . God created man in his image; in the divine image he created him; male and female he created them" (Gen 1:26–27).

The most popular name for God in the Old Testament is "Yahweh," which is a very personal name, for it is the name revealed through the covenant of Abraham, and signifies a personal relationship between God and the people. Later, in the book of Exodus, God spoke to Moses from the burning bush, giving the name as "I am who am" or "I am the one who brings things into being." (See Ex 3:4–14.) Other names were also given to God, such as "Shaddai," which was also used by the patriarchs to invoke God. "Adonai" conveyed the idea of lordship or the power to rule.

Personal Images of God

What is the name of your God? Do you find yourself using the title "Lord" in your prayer and in your conversations? You might find yourself saying, "Lord, no!" or "Oh, Lord!" or "Lord have mercy!" As a Christian, you might call out to "Father," "Abba," "Jesus," "Come, holy Spirit!" or to all of these persons of the blessed Trinity. The way we address God in prayer tells us something about our relationship with God.

saw God in a close-up view, breathing life directly into the nostr
the human form. Another tradition is built around a view of G
less directly involved, though no less caring. This author referr
God as "Elohim" and tended to write in a more stately and rev
manner. The tradition which related to God through orderly r
such as what we associate with liturgy is titled "Priestly." The
familiar opening chapter of Genesis where God's work of creat
described as being done in "days," gradually bringing order (
chaos, is a good example of this spirituality.

The word "genesis" suggests a beginning or origin. Our ow:
of God had an origin. When did God first become real to you? I
Adam and Eve who, according to the Genesis story, knew God
their creation, we had to go through a long process of sortin
various images of God from childhood to adulthood. Like the H
Bible, we have several mind's-eye pictures of God, but like t:
thors, one or the other is probably more comfortable for us.

For some of us, our first remembrance of God was associate
a church—"That's where God lives." Older children might ha
some experience of God in their play, especially if they were for
enough to walk and talk with God as they roamed through the
or strolled along the banks of a river or lake. Children who lived
urban ghetto might have known a God who protected then
thugs, criminals, or drug dealers in their neighborhood.

Unfortunately, some of us never outgrew our childhood not
God and this can have a stifling effect on our spirituality. For
ple, if you believe in a God who loves "good" people and punis:
"evildoers," you just might spend the rest of your life trying to p
God that you are good and worthy. Some people will get invo
ministry for this very reason, although most do so uncons
Such an attitude can affect our attitudes toward other people b
ing us to be authoritarian, judgmental and controlling, much l
God we believe in.

While some people maintain childish (not child-like) not
God, others go to the opposite extreme and have notions of G
are too adult. Their understanding of God is philosophical—
the "great architect," all-knowing, all-powerful, etc. This no
God is often arrived at after many years of intellectual purs
though it is amazing how many ordinary people, when asked
their concept of God, give a similar response. The God of philos
can do very little to help a person grow in the spiritual life un
philosopher receives a "new heart" from the God we discover t
revelation.

The same can be said about our mental image of God. For an African artist, God is black, whereas Western artists are largely responsible for picturing God as an old man with a long white beard sitting on a throne in heaven. Pictures that portray biblical personalities with white faces, blue eyes, and blond hair may be fine for Europeans, but they do little for people in Asia or Africa. Even literature helps us form an image of God. A good example is "Creation" by the black poet, James Weldon Johnson.

> Then God walked around,
> And God looked around
> On all that He had made
> He looked at His sun,
> And He looked at His little stars;
> He looked on His world
> With all its living things,
> And God said: "I'm lonely still."
>
> Then God sat down
> On the side of a hill where He could think;
> By a deep, wide river He sat down;
> With His head in His hands,
> God thought and thought,
> Till He thought: "I'll make me a man!"
> Up from the bed of the river
> God scooped the clay;
> And by the bank of the river
> He kneeled Him down;
> And there the great God Almighty
> Who lit the sun and fixed it in the sky,
> Who flung the stars to the most far corner of the night,
> Who rounded the earth in the middle of His hand,
> This great God,
> Like a mammy bending over her baby,
> Kneeled down in the dust
> Toiling over a lump of clay
> Till He shaped it in his own image;
>
> Then into it He blew the breath of life,
> And man became a living soul.
> Amen. Amen.

At one point in the poem, God is pictured as sitting down to think; at another point, God is pictured as a black mother affectionately bending over her little child. As do the writers of scripture (who were probably male, since it was men who received an education in that culture), Johnson refers to God as male: "He," "Him." The name for this "picturing" process is **anthropomorphism,** whereby we give to God human-like qualities. Since **we** are made in **God's** image, we find it easy to turn the process of creation around and describe **God** in **our** image. This is very common in scripture, as in the book of Genesis where God is described as walking and talking with Adam and Eve.

While anthropomorphisms help us to recognize the personal love of God, we must constantly remind ourselves that God doesn't have human limitations. God isn't "He" or "She," but God **is** personal. Some scriptural passages emphasize what we would call masculine images, such as ". . . his arms are made strong by the power of the Mighty One of Jacob, because of the Shepherd, the Rock of Israel," (Gen 49:24). Other passages reveal what we would consider a more feminine side, such as, "Can a mother forget her infant, be without tenderness for the child of her womb? Even should she forget, I will never forget you" (Is 49:15). The important thing is that the human writer was inspired to convey the picture of a God who cares for us, "with love beyond all telling."

God still walks and talks with us today, especially through the Word of sacred scripture. It is imperative that we as seekers really listen to the text and reflect on the Word if we expect to grow in deeper union with God and in love for the people we serve. The many images of God which scripture presents to us expand our understanding of who God is.

Reflecting On the Word of God

Why is reflection important? Is there any better way to learn than by reflecting on experience? Doesn't reflection help us to develop an adult intellectual and affective attitude? Doesn't it facilitate that necessary integration of life with belief? In short, reflection helps us to rise above the mundane and the superficial, and to become authentically human. There can be very little growth in spirituality without reflection. That's why this book is set up with questions for reflection, both by yourself and with the others in your study group. In order to help you gain the most from such reflection, perhaps an example will assist.

Take your Bible and turn to Genesis 3:1–13. Read over this passage and think about it for a few moments. Notice that God directs four poignant questions to Adam and Eve after their "fall"—the same questions God might address to us after we sin.

The first question is: "Where are you?" The author gives us a picture of how things were before and after "the fall." He seems to indicate that before, Adam and Eve and God were very friendly towards one another. They used to walk and talk together in the garden in the cool of the day. But after they sinned, they hid from God because they were afraid and ashamed. Although we know that God is all-knowing, the author doesn't take this point of view. Rather, in keeping with the anthropomorphic style, we get the idea that God missed walking and talking with these friends. Thus God is forced to call out, "Where are you?"

The second question: "Who told you that you were naked?" Here we sense the deep shame experienced by Adam and Eve after their sin. It is expressed in terms of nakedness because of the abhorrence on the part of the people of ancient Israel of appearing before God naked. Don't we feel "naked" when we have sinned seriously? Don't we feel exposed and full of shame? No one has to tell us that we did something wrong; we know it and we feel it.

The third question: "Have you eaten of the tree of which I commanded you not to eat?" Disobedience. Every sin is a matter of disobeying God's law or God's word. We think we know better than God. It's as though a little voice comes from within or without and says to us, "God really didn't mean that." We always seem to be able to rationalize and justify. We always want to put the blame on someone else when we are caught, as did Adam and Eve. Like the first couple, we want to be like God, knowing good and evil. And when we sin, we surely come to know good and evil. Our eyes are opened and we see how our pride has caused us to choose, sometimes fundamentally, evil over good, death over life. It appeared good, it sounded good, it felt good, but we were deceived, we were tricked. Chalk one up for the snake!

The fourth question: "What is this that you have done?" Call it what you want—sin, missing the mark, whatever. We know that something has happened to us. We are naked and alone, afraid and ashamed. We begin to experience the three-fold effects of sin:

1. Tension and turmoil **within.** We are not at peace with ourselves. We feel broken and defeated.

2. Broken relationships **with others.** Adam blamed God for giving him a tempter. He forgot how happy he was the day God gave Eve to him as a partner. Here we see the social consequences of sin.
3. Broken relationship **with God.** After their sin, Adam and Eve no longer walk and talk with God in the garden. They go into hiding instead. But God finds them and puts them, along with the serpent, on trial, punishing them accordingly. In fear and in shame, Adam and Eve depart from the garden and the gates are locked after them.

Is this the end of the story of sin? Certainly not for a Christian. As we draw out the meaning of this powerful little story, we can't help recalling that in the course of time, "the Word became flesh" (Jn 1:14) and "pitched his tent among us." Not only did Jesus live with us and for us, but he died for us and rose again so that the "sin of the world" would be taken away. Just as Jesus took away the fear and the shame and the guilt of the woman caught in adultery, so he takes away our fear and shame and guilt when we put our faith in his merciful love, confess our sins, and resolve to go and sin no more. He leaves us with peace, within, with our neighbors, and with God—and just enough sorrow to be penitent, but joyful in hope.

In this method of reflection, we have: (1) read the passage; (2) identified main ideas; (3) pondered on how the ideas are connected to our lives; and (4) put the ideas in the context of other scriptural passages and of our knowledge of the faith, and of our liturgical experience of the sacrament of penance. Although our source of reflection during the first part of the book will be Old Testament passages, our personal reflections invariably lead us—as Christians—to Jesus in the New Testament, and to our experience as church. We can see that the scripture story is much more than a well-constructed tale, for it has implications for how we go about our lives. Scripture **forms** our spiritual outlook and our actions. It will be important to take time to practice this method on your own by using the passages suggested at the beginning of each chapter. If you have not yet obtained your own copy of the Bible, do so this week.

DISCUSSION

In the first chapter, we gave some thought and time to deepening the activity of listening **from** a merely social skill **to** the level of spirituality. Today we want to practice that skill as we sharpen the sense of our "spiritual streak" by taking time to examine more closely our own personal idea of God. Just as scripture gives us many viewpoints as to what God is like, so each person has a unique approach to God.

1. Take a moment to think about God. Write down three words which most closely describe or name God. If you think of more than that, go back and trim your list to three.
2. Find a partner. Each one **shares** his or her idea of God, mentioning the personal experiences which have contributed to forming his or her current understanding of God or way of relating to God.

BREAK

Enjoy refreshments and each other's company.

WRAP-UP

1. Look ahead to the "During the Week" follow-up activities. (optional)
2. Look ahead to the scripture passage and the theme of the next session. Decide on a time during the upcoming week when you will read the chapter.
3. Participate in the Closing Prayer.

DURING THE WEEK

1. Read Genesis 1:4–2:4 and compare this writer's idea of God to the version we used during our prayer.
2. Practice the skill of biblical reflection described in this chapter. Read Genesis 3:1–24. God is revealed to Adam and Eve in word and action. What does God **say** and **do** that reveals who God is and what "God-ness" is?

3. Call To Journey in Faith

Scripture Passage

Genesis, chapters 12–26: **Abraham is called to be our Father in Faith.**

PRAYER

Introduction: A Note on the Text

Leader: The book of Genesis has several distinct parts. In chapter 2 we drew from the first section of the book, which stressed the power of the Creator who invites human beings to participate in the continuance of that creation. The characters are easily recognizable for they are drawn from the inspired author's observation of people very like those we encounter in our everyday experience. The second section of the book traces the story of the man who actually "founded" the Israelite nation, Abraham.

The passages used for prayer are two incidents from Abraham's life which dramatize the degree to which Abraham was asked to demonstrate his faith in God. First, he and his family were totally uprooted and asked to move into a strange land. Then, God asked that the son born of the promise late in life be returned to God by the hand of his father. Since faith asks us to "plant our feet firmly in thin air," we 20th-century Americans, so accustomed to controlling our life choices, need to ponder this scripture story and what it reveals about God's promises and their demands on us.

Call to Prayer

Leader: Let us attend to the presence of the divine within ourselves. Think of yourself as a child of the Promise. (Music, song, or a gathering gesture may be used.)

Reading

Reader: A reading from the book of Genesis (12:1; 21:1–8; 22:1–12).

The LORD said to Abram: "Go forth from the land of your kinsfolk and from your father's house to a land that I will show you. . . .

The LORD took note of Sarah as he had said he would; he did for her as he had promised. Sarah became pregnant and bore Abraham a son in his old age, at the set time that God had stated. Abraham gave the name Isaac to this son of his whom Sarah bore him. When his son Isaac was eight days old, Abraham circumcised him, as God had commanded . . . Sarah then said, "God has given me cause to laugh and all who hear of it will laugh with me. Who would have told Abraham," she added, "that Sarah would nurse children! Yet I have borne him a son in his old age." Isaac grew, and on the day of the child's weaning, Abraham held a great feast. . . .

Some time after these events, God put Abraham to the test. He called to him, "Abraham!" "Ready!" he replied. Then God said: "Take your son Isaac, your only one, whom you love, and go to the land of Moriah. There you shall offer him up as a holocaust on a height that I will point out to you." Early the next morning Abraham saddled his donkey, took with him his son Isaac . . . and set out for the place of which God had told him. . . . As the two walked on together, Isaac spoke to his father Abraham. "Father!" he said. "Yes, son," he replied. Isaac continued, "Here are the fire and the wood, but where is the sheep for the holocaust?" "Son," Abraham answered, "God himself will provide the sheep for the holocaust." Then the two continued going forward. When they came to the place of which God had told him, Abraham built an altar there and arranged the wood on it. Next he tied up his son Isaac, and put him on top of the wood on the altar.

Then he reached out and took the knife to slaughter his son. But the LORD's messenger called to him from heaven, "Abraham, Abraham!" "Yes, Lord," he answered. "Do not lay your hand on the boy," said the messenger. "Do not do the least thing to him. I know now how devoted you are to God, since you did not withhold from me your own beloved son."

Individual Reflection

Leader: Even though many incidents in his life had "proved" that God had a reason for what was asked, Abraham flinched; what possible purpose could God have for such a seemingly senseless sacrifice? Take a moment to think of some times in your own life where you were called to do something with no clear understanding of the outcome or of the steps which were required. (All pause for silent reflection.)

Prayer

Leader: Although as children we may have memorized our prayers with little understanding of their meaning, reminded of the story of Abraham's faith, let us say together the familiar "Act of Faith."

All: O my God, I firmly believe that you are one God in three divine Persons, the Father, Son and holy Spirit. I believe that your divine Son became human and died for our sins, and that he will come to judge the living and the dead. I believe these and all the truths which the holy Catholic Church teaches, because you have revealed them, who can neither deceive nor be deceived. Amen.

LESSON

Ancient Persons As Models for Today

Many people in this world acknowledge themselves to be agnostics. They believe in God, but claim that it is impossible to have any kind of personal relationship with that God. Therefore they refer to their God as a "higher power," "great architect," etc. The God arrived at through the process of philosophical reasoning sometimes falls into this category. There is a tremendous difference between belief in this kind of God, and faith in a God who knows us personally and can be known by us in a limited but real way. It takes faith to know a God who calls.

Upon returning from her religious education classes one day, a pretty, bright-eyed teenager was asked by her older brother, "What did you learn today?" "We learned about Abraham," she replied. Then after a short pause she complained, "Who wants to know about Abraham and all that stuff?"

That question is not unique to adolescents, for there are many Christian adults who know little about Abraham and why he is called "Father in Faith" by Christians, Jews and Moslems. Even after reading his story in the book of Genesis, how many people can identify with this old man who came from an unknown land, had a very unusual relationship with his wife and her slave, contemplated human sacrifice and who finally died at the age of 175 years? At first glance, Abraham is a most unlikely person to emulate; but when we begin to strip away the accidental layers of time and custom, we discover a very human individual who must struggle with his response to a call from God. Today we might refer to this struggle as "faith development" and, in truth, Abraham developed beautifully, thus deserving the title, "Father in Faith."

Who was he and what did he do that could possibly help us on our journey in faith? What role did Sarah, his wife, play in his faith development? What about his children, his neighbors and that strange, mystical priest, Melchizedek? All of these people played an important part in the growth of Abraham's faith.

The Call of Abram

The first step in Abraham's journey of faith took place when he, then known as Abram, was called by God to leave his native land and his father's house and to travel to a land called Canaan. God would show the way and would eventually make of him a great nation and a source of blessing to all the communities of the earth.

How did Abram hear this call? Did it come about because of the death of his father? Was there a natural spirit of wanderlust in his makeup that did not find free expression until his father died? What prompted him to give up an apparently prosperous, comfortable life in Ur and follow an unknown God to an unknown land? The answer lies in the word, "unknown." Not always to our comfort, faith always implies a leap into the unknown.

We will never know all the circumstances that surrounded Abram's call, and perhaps the less we know the better. For indeed, all calls from God are mysterious and complex, but unmistakable. Some people hear an "inner voice" while others claim to hear an audible

voice telling them to do something. Many people will describe their
call as, "all the pieces of a puzzle coming together," or perhaps the call
is given through the instrumentality of a third person. In Abram's
case, the call required a geographical change, which was not uncommon in a nomadic society, but may have seemed like a pointless ven-
ture for someone as well-established as Abram seems to have already
become. Yet he responded apparently without hesitation. This blind
faith of his was tested for the first time when, after settling in the land
of promise, a severe famine forced him to again pull up stakes, this
time to move to Egypt.

Abram's Temptation

One wonders what Abram's thoughts were at this time. Here he
was an old man, without children, forced out of his new settlement
because of famine and about to enter Egypt where his life might be in
grave danger because of all the covetous eyes on his beautiful wife,
Sarai. Does he continue on his journey trusting that God will make a
way for him? No; his thoughts and his faith turn from dependence on
God to faith in his own ingenuity. And here we have the first sign of
weakness in this otherwise strong and faithful man. He told the Egyptians that Sarai was his sister, whereupon Pharaoh, seeing her beauty,
took her to himself. God, of course, was not pleased with this situation
and punished the Egyptian who then confronted Abram with his de-
ception and sent him on his way. Even when Abram's faith failed him,
God was ever-faithful to his promise, partly because it's part of being
God to be faithful, and partly perhaps to prepare Abram for the covenant which was to come in the future.

How often in our own lives have we put more faith in ourselves
rather than in God, only to discover that God was able to turn a
painful and even sinful situation into an opportunity for stronger and
deeper faith? The incident in Egypt was a "happy fault" for Abram
and Sarai, for it taught them to depend on the power of God. The very
fact that, upon returning to his promised land, Abram gave his
nephew, Lot, first choice in selecting land for his cattle, seems to
indicate that he had learned his lesson.

And witness the faith of Abram when he was willing to give a
tenth of everything he had to the priest, Melchizedek, in thanksgiving
for victory over his enemies. Most pastors would agree that people
who tithe are generally people of great faith. An example of such faith
is the elderly lady who lived on a fixed income and who insisted on
giving 10% of her check to the church. When her pastor told her that

she needed the money more than the parish did, she reminded him that Jesus did not tell the widow to keep her "mite." "God has always taken care of me," she told the priest. "Please let me do what I can for his church." It takes faith to think and speak like that.

God's Covenants with Abram

Martin Luther once said that people shouldn't bargain with God. He was correct. But that does not prevent God from making a covenant with people. When we bargain with God we usually say, "God, if you do such and such for me, I will make a pilgrimage, burn candles, say so many rosaries, go to mass so often, etc. Or perhaps we begin a novena for a special intention and at the end of nine days or weeks we wait for God to fulfill the divine part of our human bargain.

A covenant is not the same as a bargain. The call to covenant comes from God. The initiative comes from God. In the case of Abram, God saw that this octogenarian was getting restless, being bounced around like a rubber ball from one land to another and still without an heir to begin the long line of descendants that was promised. So God reaffirmed the divine promise and Abram believed. This time God sealed the covenant with an ancient ceremonial rite of splitting animals in half (Gen 15:1-21). In covenant, it is God who "cuts the deal."

After this mystical experience, Abram's faith was bolstered for a while, but it was still not perfect. Because the couple so greatly desired a child as proof of God's favor, Sarai proposed that Abram produce a child through her slave girl, Hagar (Gen 16:1-6). While we can understand this action on the basis of local custom, still it shows a lack of complete trust in God. In Egypt Abram relied on his own ingenuity. Now he relies on his wife's ingenuity and no good comes from it.

God tried again with another covenant when Abram was 99 years old (Gen 17:1-14). Once again the promise of land and descendants was reaffirmed. This time there was a dual ratification of the covenant; with Abram it was the change of his name to Abraham, and with his descendants it was another "cutting," not of animals but the rite of circumcision of male children. Circumcision was simply the sign which showed that Abraham and his descendants had a God who would be with them. Reduced to its simplest form, the covenant from God merely said, "I will be your God." No ifs, ands, or buts.

A covenant with God is no laughing matter, but Abraham (Gen 17:17) and Sarah (Gen 18:12) laughed when they heard that they would have a son in their old age. It is possible that the name Isaac, which in Hebrew is closely related to the word "laugh," came from this incident. Whatever the case, Isaac was born when Abraham was 100 years old and everybody, especially Sarah, had a good laugh over it.

But the joy went out of Abraham's life on the day God told him to offer his only son, Isaac, as a holocaust. The story is not only familiar to us, but it is so vivid in our memories because of the graphic detail of the narrator (Gen 22:1–18). We can almost smell the scent of the wood and the smoke of the fire which Abraham carried with him. We can faintly hear the anguished questioning of Isaac when he asked about the sacrificial animal. We can see the bright gleam of the knife blade as Abraham prepared to sacrifice his beloved son. And no matter how many times the story is told, we breathe a sigh of relief when the Lord's messenger tells Abraham, "Do not lay your hand on the boy."

Abraham's journey of faith reached its destination with his willingness to sacrifice his only son, the child of the promise. Thus begins the fulfillment of the promise in terms of land and posterity. Isaac married Rebekah, Abraham married again and had more children and they all "lived happily ever after." Abraham died at a very advanced age. (We are told 175, although this, like the other ages given by the author, could be symbolic.) He was buried next to Sarah by their sons, Isaac and Ishmael.

So we see that Abraham's journey of faith had many ups and downs. Like us, he had to learn by experience what it meant to "fly by radar," to set aside our own ingenious solutions which often prove to be a fog which clouds the issue, and concentrate instead on the instrument readings of God's inner directions.

ACTIVITY: SHARING OUR FAITH STORY

Take a few moments to write brief responses to the following questions:

1. One time in the past when I heard a call from God was when. . . .
   (Note: Your recollections could center around one of the following.)
   a) person
   b) event
   c) experience
2. I felt this to be a call because. . . .
3. I received help at that time from. . . .
   (Note: Be sure to include *who* helped you and *what* was helpful.)

4. The things that made the "call" difficult for me personally were:
   (**Note:** Be as specific as possible.)

   After allowing about ten minutes, share your response with a partner.

BREAK

Enjoy refreshments and each other's company.

WRAP-UP

1. Look ahead to the "During the Week" follow-up activities.
2. Look ahead to the scripture passage and the theme of the next session.
3. Participate in a Closing Prayer.

DURING THE WEEK

Once again, practice the skill of biblical reflection. Read chapters 12–26 of the book of Genesis, looking for the human situations through which Abraham and Sarah came to know God. Note down the obstacles they faced. Which obstacle would you have found the most difficult? Why?

4. Call To Be a People

Scripture Passage

Genesis, chapters 27–35; and chapter 46: **God continues the covenant with humankind through Abraham's grandson, Jacob, who carries on the tradition of ordering the activities of family, work and relationships according to the call of God.**

PRAYER

Introduction: A Note on the Text

In our study of spirituality, we are being guided by the scriptures because we understand them to be inspired, more than simply stories. We believe that God intends us to see ourselves as the characters. This week we read further in the book of Genesis with what is called the "patriarchal narratives," or the stories of the early family tree of the Israelites. As we have seen, Abraham and Sara had a son, Isaac, who married Rebecca. The child of this union, Jacob, becomes the main character in the third section of the book (chapters 25–36). Then, the story of Joseph, one of Jacob's twelve sons, becomes the subject of the final section (chapters 37–50).

Jacob's story is that of an enterprising and successful man, but a somewhat questionable model, since he seems to be a shrewd conniver intent on grasping as much as life will allow him. The passage chosen for our prayer, the famous story of "Jacob's ladder," portrays Jacob in one of his better moments. The biblical image of the ladder is probably similar to a Mesopotamian "ziggurat," or a huge pyramid-style mass constructed to symbolize the union of earth's realities with heaven's promises. In this story, the surety of heaven's promises is reinforced in two ways. First, it is actually the Lord who comes to speak the blessing. Second, even though the words are by now familiar, this time they are spoken to someone who is unlikely, even hopeless. Yet God comes. We too often feel unworthy. We think of ourselves as unlikely or hopeless candidates for a deeper spiritual life because we are too caught up in earthly affairs to attend to those of heaven. In this reading, the symbol of the ladder gives us confidence that our work and our family are God's way of bringing "love beyond all telling" to the human community.

Call to Prayer

Leader: Let us place our left palm open on our laps, imagining that we hold within it all our earthly surroundings and the people we hold dear. (Pause). Now let us place our right palm open in our laps, imagining that we hold within it all our spiritual longings. (Pause. Music or song may be used.)

Reading

Leader: A reading from the book of Genesis (28:10–20).

Jacob departed from Beer-sheba and proceeded toward Haran. When he came upon a certain shrine, as the sun had already set, he stopped there for the night. Taking one of the stones at the shrine, he put it under his head and lay down to sleep at that spot. Then he had a dream: a stairway rested on the ground, with its top reaching to the heavens; and God's messengers were going up and down on it. And there was the LORD standing beside him and saying:

"I, the LORD, am the God of your forefather Abraham and the God of Isaac; the land on which you are lying I will give to you and your descendants. These shall be as plentiful as the dust of the earth, and through them you shall spread out east and west, north and south. In you and your descendants all the nations of the earth shall find blessing. Know that I am with you; I will protect you wherever you go, and bring you back to this land. I will never leave you until I have done what I promised you."

When Jacob awoke from his sleep, he exclaimed, "Truly, the LORD is in this spot, although I did not know it!" In solemn wonder he cried out: "How awesome is this shrine! This is nothing else but an abode of God, and that is the gateway to heaven!" Early the next morning Jacob took the stone that he had put under his head, set it up as a memorial stone, and poured oil on top of it. He called that site Bethel, whereas the former name of the town had been Luz.

Jacob then made this vow: "If God remains with me, to protect me on this journey I am making and to give me enough bread to eat and clothing to wear, and I come back safe to my father's house, the LORD shall be my God. This stone that I have set up as a memorial stone shall be God's abode. Of everything you give me, I will faithfully return a tenth part to you."

Individual Reflection

Leader: Who are my people? At certain times of life we feel a closeness to people, a sense that they are not there by chance, but by God's design. Somehow I realize that my life here has a meaning beyond its simple dailiness. In my own life, how has God given me "bread to eat, and clothes to wear, and safe return home"? (All pause for silent reflection.)

Prayer

All: God of my family, God of my people, I look to you for help. Open my eyes so I may see the angels who come and go in my own life. Inspire in me such a willingness to serve you that the witness of my life may become a memorial stone for others. Amen.

LESSON

God Calls A People

By the time we meet Jacob, we are in the third generation of God's covenant love. It is clear that God's intention is not simply to touch the lives of individuals by themselves, but to work with a people, a community, a society. As the family grows, new influences come in. The community in which individuals live plays a big role in forming their attitudes and in dictating how they live. How does God use these formation communities?

Actually, the book of Genesis itself is the product of a formation community. It is a mosaic of the work of three authors whose names are unknown to us but who are named by scripture scholars according to their style: the Yahwist, the Elohist, and the Priestly authors. It was not until centuries after they wrote out the oral stories which had circulated in their communities about the lives of Abraham, Isaac, Jacob, and Joseph that an editor wove their separate versions into the form we have today. The editor wanted to preserve the specific flavor of each of these rich strands of his Israelite tradition. This makes the book somewhat repetitious, but generally speaking, the story of Jacob reads fairly easily, almost like a modern soap opera or novella.

Jacob's Life and Character

Jacob was Abraham's grandson, the child of Isaac and Rebekah. After Abraham had followed God's command to migrate from Mesopotamia to Canaan (the modern-day countries of Iraq and Israel), he had sent back home to find a wife for his son. Consequently, Jacob was the second generation born in Canaan, but born of homeland stock. He was a twin, and very different from his brother Esau, growing up to be much more comfortable in a domestic setting with his mother, Rebekah, than out hunting like his father's favorite, Esau. From his mother he seems to have inherited the character trait of cunning and even developed it into outright duplicity, as we learn from the stories about how he acquired Esau's birthright and blessing.

Yet this trait stood him in good stead when Isaac echoed Abraham's command and sent him back to the fatherland to acquire a wife. Not only did Jacob need to deal with his wily uncle, Laban, but his double marriage to Laban's daughters, Leah and Rachel, resulted in overlapping relationships that would test anyone's character. Add to this the concubinage relationships with their maidservants, Zilpah and Bilhal, as well as the twelve sons and at least one daughter, and we find a family situation that challenges the contemporary imagination! Even though the social customs of that time dictated how these relationships would be handled, the biblical texts make it clear that jealousy and conniving complicated his life. We can also see from the description of how he handled the flocks so as to increase his wealth, that he was an able manager who used his skill in breeding sheep to become wealthy in his own right.

Jacob's Spiritual Formation

How does Jacob, so tied up with these many family and business concerns, develop spiritually? How does he orient his life beyond its day-to-day demands? The authors make it clear that it is his deepest religious hopes which give direction and meaning to his life. Many of the same motifs through which they explain his grandfather Abraham's relationship with God in chapter 12 are repeated to tell Jacob's story in chapter 28. Just as God spoke to Abraham, he also speaks to Jacob. The land is promised to Abraham's descendants and, already begun to be realized in Jacob, this promise is repeated for his descendants, together with the covenant of protection. Just as Abraham had built an altar to the Lord as a sign of his commitment to the covenant, so also does Jacob.

In recent years, the work of developmental psychologists has attuned us to the significance of certain of life's transitions as key moments for our readiness to receive God's message. The ancient authors seem to have had an intuitive grasp of such moments, for many relate interventions of God in Jacob's life at the key transitional points we recognize today. As Jacob moves from youth to young adulthood, he encounters God in the dream of the stairway to the heavens (Gen 28:10–22). During his "mid-life crisis," he receives word to return to his father's land (31:3), then wrestles with God's messenger and receives a new name, Israel (32:23–31). In the twilight of his life, after weathering the death of his beloved wife, Rachel, the crises of his adult children, the loss of his son, Joseph, famine, and separation from his youngest son, Benjamin, God speaks to him once more as he travels to Egypt (46:2–4). These moments of revelation seem always to come when he is on a journey.

Our Formation Community

How does this story speak to us today? We too are on a journey through life. Like Jacob, we too have other people whose lives are closely intertwined with ours, people who make up our community. We can even say that they are a *formation* community because, to a large extent, we are continually formed by the people in our everyday surroundings.

Such formation can be either positive or negative. Your spouse may have commented to you after a family visit, "You're just like your mother, always looking at the bad side of things!" And in your own quiet moments of truth, you acknowledge that growing up in an environment where you were constantly nagged about your messy room rather than commended on your regular piano practicing, has indeed influenced your own attitude. You find yourself quick to criticize and slow to compliment.

On the other hand, the formation your community exerts can also be positive. The concern expressed by your boss over a tough assignment you're facing can strengthen your natural tendency to give it the best you've got. Even if the boss takes you for granted, such a casual supervisory attitude could strengthen your sense of independent judgment and self-worth.

This subtle influence isn't accidental, but rather is part of God's providential plan for each of us. Not only are we created as unique individuals with special gifts, but we are also placed in an environment which will somehow make it possible for us to use those gifts to bring about the fulfillment of God's design. During the Second Vatican Council, the Catholic bishops of the world declared: "For when, by the work of their hands or with the aid of technology, men and women develop the earth so that it can bear fruit and become a dwelling worthy of the whole human family, and when they consciously take part in the life of social groups, they carry out the design of God" (*The Church in the Modern World,* #57).

Our Human Development

How do we find our place in this divine design? The critical community is the family. It is here that we find our vocation, our calling. Our makeup in terms of our physical and mental endowments is genetically traceable to our parents. The home they provide is the environment where these natural gifts unfold. It is our parents who notice our talents and try to provide ways to develop them. They listen as our childish babblings become more coherent statements of our world's realities. They talk to us about what matters to them and help us sense the larger picture. They help us notice who we are and who we might become.

Our families are situated in a larger community, so during our growing-up-years, we find ourselves spending more of our time there, testing out the values of our home against those of the people we meet and come to regard as important. Little by little we gain a sense of who we are called to be. We chart a course based on the "radar" of responses returned by our associates to our inner sense of self. Depending on the resources and opportunities which are available to us, we find a use for our talents. But to really make the most of life, we need another reference point—a goal, a dream, a vision.

Our Guiding Vision

Anthropologists, whose study centers on human beings, call this larger than life dream or vision a "myth." As Christians, we recognize that the "myth" or vision which stabilizes us and directs us outward is actually God's revelation given to us gradually over the centuries. God gave Jacob a direct vision of a "ladder" linking earth and heaven. God gives us the Bible, where Jacob's visions are linked to many others. We are the People of God, and it is to this people that God has entrusted the vision of the world as it should be—the kingdom of God. It is to this people that God continues to reveal that vision as we discover our vocation, our participation in bringing about the reign of God.

Like Jacob, there are many events that mark off our lives which seem to have little to do with its ultimate outcome, yet in special moments of the journey we see clearly what is being accomplished. Like Jacob, God uses our community—both family and work—to bring about a world where God's values reign. Like Jacob, we are both formed by our community and also come to the point where we are the ones who influence others as we establish and foster families and communities where *our* deepest religious hopes can find realization.

DISCUSSION

Take a few minutes to complete the following statements:

1. A person who has greatly influenced me is . . . because. . . .
2. Something our family did when we were kids that has really stayed with me is. . . .
3. What I enjoy most about my work is. . . .
   Form groups of four persons. Talk over your responses with others in your group. How do they compare? Is there a sense of vocation? Of a formation community?

BREAK

Enjoy refreshments and each other's company.

WRAP-UP

1. Look ahead to the "During the Week" follow-up activities. (optional)
2. Look ahead to the scripture passage and the theme of the next session. Decide on a time during the upcoming week when you will read the chapter.
3. Participate in the Closing Prayer.

DURING THE WEEK

1. Read Genesis, chapters 25–35, to trace the influence of each of these aspects on Jacob's inner self:
   a) his family
   b) his work
   c) his deepest religious hopes
2. Reflect on these same aspects as they are shaping your own vocation:
   a) my family
   b) my work
   c) my deepest religious hopes
3. Reflect on the following paragraphs from the Vatican II document, *The Church in the Modern World*, #35.

> Just as human activity proceeds from human beings, so it is ordered toward them. For when a person works, he or she not only alters things and society, but himself or herself as well. This involves learning much, cultivating available resources, and going outside and beyond oneself.
>
> Rightly understood, this kind of growth is of greater value than any external riches which can be garnered. A person is more precious for what he or she is than for what he or she has. Similarly, all that men and women do to obtain greater justice, wider brotherhood, and a more humane ordering of social relationships has greater worth than technical advances. For these advances supply the material for human progress, but of themselves alone they can never actually bring it about. Hence, the norm of human activity is this: that in accord with the divine plan and will, it should harmonize with the genuine good of the human race, and allow men and women as individuals and as members of society to pursue their total vocation and fulfill it.

5. Call to Covenant

Scripture Passage

Exodus, chapters 1–20: **God calls Moses to lead the people out of slavery in Egypt, to guide them through the desert, and to give them the land by which they can be God's own people by covenant.**

PRAYER

Introduction: A Note on the Text

Leader: The book of Exodus may be considered the linchpin of the Bible, for it links the theological and patriarchal narratives of Genesis to the historical narratives which follow. The reader can sense two "layers": (1) the ancient 14th-century activities of the Israelites which were handed on through the oral tradition; and (2) the hand of 8th-century editors who arranged the texts into a form which would help the Jews of a later time to understand who they were as God's people. We today still find ourselves gripped by the accounts of the dramatic interventions of God rescuing the people from slavery in Egypt and bringing them into the promised land.

The passage chosen for our prayer describes the instructions for the Passover meal. It is typical of much of Exodus in that it reads as "law." The specific directions for observing the celebration are presented as God speaking directly to the people through Moses and Aaron. The role of families coming together to form the community is stressed. The ancient layer of tradition is evident in the actions which are prescribed to help people of the current time to relive the experiences of their forbears. We sense the roots of our own liturgical spirituality.

48

Call to Prayer:

Leader: Let us gather our inner selves so that we may listen to God's call to covenant. (A song or music may be used.)

Reading:

Reader: A reading from the book of Exodus (12:1–14).

The LORD said to Moses and Aaron in the land of Egypt, "This month shall stand at the head of your calendar; you shall reckon it the first month of the year. Tell the whole community of Israel: On the tenth of this month every one of your families must procure for itself a lamb, one apiece for each household. If a family is too small for a whole lamb, it shall join the nearest household in procuring one and shall share in the lamb in proportion to the number of persons who partake of it. The lamb must be a year-old male and without blemish. You may take it from either the sheep or the goats. You shall keep it until the fourteenth day of this month, and then, with the whole assembly of Israel present, it shall be slaughtered during the evening twilight. They shall take some of its blood and apply it to the two doorposts and the lintel of every house in which they partake of the lamb. That same night they shall eat its roasted flesh with unleavened bread and bitter herbs. It shall not be eaten raw or boiled, but roasted whole, with its head and shanks and inner organs. None of it must be kept beyond the next morning; whatever is left over in the morning shall be burned up.

"This is how you are to eat it: with your loins girt, sandals on your feet and your staff in hand, you shall eat like those who are in flight. It is the Passover of the LORD. For on this same night I will go through Egypt, striking down every first-born of the land, both man and beast, and executing judgment on all the gods of Egypt—I, the LORD! But the blood will mark the houses where you are. Seeing the blood, I will pass over you; thus, when I strike the land of Egypt, no destructive blow will come upon you.

"This day shall be a memorial feast for you, which all your generations shall celebrate with pilgrimage to the LORD, as a perpetual institution."

Individual Reflection

Leader: What is my relationship with God? When I listen to specific commands which tell the Israelites how to remember the good things the Lord has done, what similar commands come to mind for me? How am I called to worship God in my own life? What ways has God used to show us the same care and concern shown to the Israelites? (All pause for silent reflection.)

Prayer

All: Lord God, we thank you for calling us to be among the people you have chosen. You are our God and we are your people. Stir up our hearts so that our celebrations of worship may reawaken our memories of your loving care and lead us to reverence your commands. Amen.

LESSON

The Time of Deliverance

When we consider our call to a covenant relationship with God, an image that often comes to mind is that of Moses standing on the mountain holding the tablets of the Ten Commandments above the heads of the people. God's presence is powerful. The figure of Moses, eyes flashing, arms raised up to show the tablets, body poised against the craggy mountain, rivets our attention. We feel moved to place ourselves among the crowd, shoulder to shoulder with others who feel the power of the moment.

Who are these others? Why is this moment so compelling? The scripture narratives tell us that Jacob's son Joseph was sold into slavery by his brothers. Joseph's rise to power put him in a position to rescue his family from famine as well as providing a reason for them to migrate to Egypt. Here they stayed for centuries, their fortunes changing with the rise and fall of dynasties and the migration of tribes. When Moses was born around 1300 B.C., the fortunes of the Israelites were at a low ebb, because they were living as an oppressed labor force for the Egyptians.

The adoption of Moses into an upper-class Egyptian family provided him with the nurturance of his Hebrew mother and the education of an Egyptian aristocrat. This bicultural upbringing created tensions for him, so much so that, in anger Moses killed an Egyptian who was punishing one of his relatives. Now an outcast, his flight from punishment for this deed led him to the land of Midian where he married Zipporah, the daughter of Jethro, a priest. The people among whom he found himself seem to have been following the religion of Abraham and Jacob, for Zipporah circumcised their son to ensure that Moses would be "a spouse of blood" to her (Ex 4:24–26). So, even though far removed from the time of the patriarchs, Moses was formed in their traditions through the influence of his wife and father-in-law.

The Mystery of Moses' Call

It was while living in Midian that Moses received the call that would change his life and imprint the covenant upon God's people. The story of Moses' vision of the burning bush can be read over and over, for it brings us as well as Moses face-to-face with God (Ex 3:4–4:17). Like Moses, we start out willingly enough in answering the Lord: "Here I am." We too have found ourselves at times on "holy ground." When we are named as one of a family which has known God's favor, many of us can recognize God's action in our parents, grandparents, and beyond. Yet when the Lord makes clear what we are expected to do to bring about God's plan: "Come now! I will send you . . . ," we get a little nervous. Even when we continue to wait, to listen, to ponder, we find ourselves wanting to understand more, yet grateful we are not overwhelmed by the mystery.

The mystery . . . who is it? We hear the name YHWH, or Yahweh. A great deal of speculation has surrounded the meaning of this name. We know it comes from the basic verb, "I am" which is built into so much of our communication in its many forms: I'm here . . . ; I'm going to . . . ; I'm involved in . . . ; I'll work on it. . . . All of this helps us understand that God is revealed in *action,* as doing for the people. To be in relation with such a God is to *do,* to *act* on behalf of, and to be on the receiving end of such action.

However it was that Moses actually experienced God on that occasion, it was to forever change his life. The next step was clear, but the chain of events was such that Moses' life became a rhythm of human weakness rescued by divine intervention. God acted in Moses' life and this action was for the sake of the people. God bound Moses by covenant and used him as the instrument to form a people of covenant.

Moses is a unique figure in the Bible, a true hero in the "larger than life" manner in which he is portrayed. Over and over we read that

"God said to Moses," and that Moses then had the task of bringing the people to understand and accept these directions. To enable him to carry out his formidable task, God graced Moses with other special visions and signs: the staff (Ex 7:8–13), the plagues (Ex 7:14–11:10), the crossing of the sea (Ex 14:10–31), the quail and manna (Ex 16:4–15), water from the rock (Ex 17:1–7), the presentation of the commandments (Ex 19:16–20:21; 24:12–18; 34:1–35) the meeting tent (Ex 33:7–23). As these stories were passed on from generation to generation, a new layer of the tradition was formed. The people recognized that God was truly among them, acting on their behalf. This realization was so strong that the people never wanted to forget what God had done for them.

Forced out of Egypt by a mighty series of events, their years as nomads, moving from place to place, gave them a new focus. Their grumbling and murmuring took place against a backdrop of God's outpouring of signs—quail, manna, water from the rock—which sustained them; a new social structure which reorganized their interactions; new ceremonies which formed their worship; and, most dramatic of all, a new law which bound them. What we know as the Ten Commandments is the kernel of several "Books" which the Israelites accepted from God as guidance for their lives.

Celebration As Memorial

Unlike their neighbors, who experienced confusion about who their gods were and what these gods demanded of humans, the Israelites could count on a law which came from Yahweh. *Their* God had rescued and sustained them, and now told them how to be a pleasing people who responded by living their lives according to the Law. A whole series of festivals arose as regular reminders of God's care.

We don't know exactly when the Israelites began to celebrate the Passover meal but we are clear about why they did so—to bring home to themselves in every generation their call to be God's people in a particular way. As they performed the actions and spoke the words, they realized anew their spiritual heritage. Over the centuries the order (seder) of the service has varied, but its purpose has remained the same—to pass on the tradition through a ritual meal.

The foods which are used all have a special meaning, as the words of the seder explain. The King of the Universe is praised by partaking of the fruit of the vine. The bread is unleavened to remind those present of the need for haste, the lack of time to wait for bread to rise.

A bitter herb is dipped in salt water, symbolic of tears and sorrow. Horseradish reminds everyone of the bitter hard work of cementing the bricks of Egyptian building projects. The main dish is lamb or goat meat, symbolic of the killing of the animal whose blood was smeared above the door to warn the angel to pass over the Israelite home, sparing the first-born.

Liturgical Spirituality

It was during such a Passover meal that Jesus instituted the eucharist, using the same symbolic foods but giving them a new meaning. Just as God spoke to the people through Moses and Aaron, commanding them to celebrate the passion, Jesus spoke to us through the apostles—"Do this in memory of me" (Lk 22:19). Thus the early Christians borrowed many of the Jewish customs as they developed their weekly liturgical celebration to remember Jesus' dying and rising. As Christians, we too are reminded of our call to covenant by our regular attendance at liturgy. Each of our actions in this special setting has a meaning for our lives. Here we, like the Jewish people of old, stand shoulder to shoulder facing our God who comes among us to form us as a people.

How does belonging to a people affect our spirituality? We might call this a liturgical spirituality, because it is when we come together in an assembly to "break the bread and tell the stories" that we are bonded not only to our God but to one another. It is as we listen to God's word and share in the sacraments that we come to know ourselves as Christ himself still present in the world. As Catholics, we are formed spiritually through the annual rhythm of seasons and feasts which help us relive Jesus' life.

Liturgy is a place of action. As we listen, and take to heart the prayers and readings, we gain the insight and strength to live Christ's life in ours. YHWH—a God of *action*—reaches into our lives to transform us. We act out our beliefs: asking forgiveness and praising God's mercy; reliving the events of salvation through hearing the word of God; witnessing the coming of the Lord among us in eucharist; allowing ourselves to be transformed by receiving the Lord into our bodies. Finally, we pledge ourselves to take this message into our daily lives.

It is possible, on rare occasions, to live a deeply spiritual life and never "go to church" or "go to mass." Each of us can point to examples of such people. When we attend a liturgy which fails to engage us, it is easy to take the position that we can be close to God without such formal services. On the other hand, when we celebrate liturgy in a meaningful way, we realize the power of the symbols to capture our attention and imagination, allowing the Spirit to flow within us. Clearly it is of benefit to do whatever we can do.

DISCUSSION

Divide into groups of three to respond to these questions.

1. How does your participation in the liturgy affect your spirituality?
2. What parts of the liturgy do you find especially meaningful?
3. How does living according to God's law give a direction to your spiritual journey?

BREAK

Enjoy refreshments and each other's company.

WRAP-UP

1. Look ahead to the "During the Week" follow-up activities. (optional)
2. Look ahead to the scripture passage and the theme of the next session. Decide on a time during the upcoming week when you will read the chapter.
3. Participate in the Closing Prayer.

DURING THE WEEK

1. A version of the seder meal appears in the Appendix. Your group may want to arrange to have an actual meal together. If not, simply read over the prayers of the seder, trying to experience the feelings of the Israelites.
2. For the Israelites, there was a strong and direct connection between what God did for them and the Law (Torah). Study the following passages:

   a) Deuteronomy 4:32–38—What had happened to them that they saw as making them special?

   b) Deuteronomy 4:39–40—What was the required response? .

3. Can you identify a pattern in your life of God's power rescuing you from your human weakness?

6. Call To Discern God's Will

Scripture Passage

Judges, chapters 4–8; 1 Samuel, chapters 1–3: **The stories of the judges Deborah, Gideon, and Samuel illustrate how God used leaders with listening hearts to help the people discern what God expected them to do.**

PRAYER

Introduction: A Note on the Text

Leader: Exodus is easily the key event for understanding the revelation of God in the Hebrew scriptures. In the historical prologue in Genesis, the patriarchs are all seen in light of how the promise was fulfilled when God brought the people into the land of Canaan. Then, after the Exodus, the leadership was passed from Moses to Joshua, whose exploits of conquest are detailed in the book which bears his name. Then came the period of the Judges, when the people had to live side-by-side with the people of Canaan and looked to leaders they called judges. Tradition lists twelve judges, among them the familiar ones, Gideon and Samson. In addition, the book of Judges names Deborah as a judge (4:4), while the first book of Samuel refers to Samuel as the last of the judges (8:1–9).

Just as we today find it easy to go along with the customs of our secular culture, so too did the Israelites. The 8th-century editor who brought together the stories of how God raised up leaders to keep the people true to the covenant, had a definite opinion about what was going on. When the people disobeyed God, disasters came upon them. When they heeded the judges and fought against the forces of the society around them, they experienced rescue and salvation. But how could they know the difference? How could they "judge"? How could

56

they experience God's "love beyond all telling"? Our passage for prayer, the call of Samuel, focuses on the chief ingredient for such discernment—a listening heart.

Call to Prayer

Leader: Let us direct our attention to the love of the Lord which comes into our lives with constant invitation. (Song, music, or a gathering gesture may be used.)

Reading

Reader: A reading from the first book of Samuel (3:1–11).

During the time young Samuel was minister to the LORD under Eli, a revelation of the LORD was uncommon and vision infrequent. One day Eli was asleep in his usual place. His eyes had lately grown so weak that he could not see. The lamp of God was not yet extinguished, and Samuel was sleeping in the temple of the LORD where the ark of God was. The LORD called to Samuel, who answered, "Here I am." He ran to Eli and said, "Here I am. You called me." "I did not call you," Eli said. "Go back to sleep." So he went back to sleep. Again the LORD called Samuel, who rose and went to Eli. "Here I am," he said. "You called me." But he answered, "I did not call you, my son. Go back to sleep."

At that time Samuel was not familiar with the LORD, because the LORD had not revealed anything to him as yet. The LORD called Samuel again, for the third time. Getting up and going to Eli, he said, "Here I am. You called me." Then Eli understood that the LORD was calling the youth. So he said to Samuel, "Go to sleep, and if you are called, reply, 'Speak, LORD, for your servant is listening.' " When Samuel went to sleep in his place, the LORD came and revealed his presence, calling out as before, "Samuel, Samuel!" Samuel answered, "Speak, for your servant is listening." The LORD said to Samuel: "I am about to do something in Israel that will cause the ears of everyone who hears it to ring."

Individual Reflection

Leader: Often we are like Samuel, going to others in search of spiritual wisdom or advice. At other times we find ourselves in the place of Eli, helping someone listen to the voice of God. When I make decisions, do I take time to think about God's viewpoint? To what extent does this reflection influence my decision or my advice? (All pause for silent reflection.)

Prayer

All: Lord our God, give us light to know your paths. Open our inner ear so that we may hear your call. Give us the strength to respond, "Here I am," and to carry out your will in our daily lives. Amen.

LESSON

Deborah "Judges" What God Wants for the People

God has given us the example of many people who have had to find their way in adverse circumstances. How did they discern? Let's consider the example of Deborah, which is described in Judges 4:1–5:31. Like Genesis, this book is a mosaic of several authors. Written in the 6th-century B.C., it describes events which occurred in the 13th to 11th centuries when the Israelites, after forty years of nomadic travel through the wilderness, entered the promised land and gradually secured Canaan for themselves. "Judges" is so named because it tells of the exploits of twelve of the leaders during these tumultuous years. The authors had for their raw material the sagas which had been retold and retouched over the centuries, so their heroes assume a stature which is larger than life.

Among them, strangely enough, we find a woman, Deborah. Deborah is described as a prophetess who served her people by acting as a mediator for their disputes. At that time the people were suffering greatly from the guerrilla parties of the army of the Canaanite king, Jabin, whose soldiers had the advantage of iron chariots. Acting as Judge, Deborah summoned the Israelite general, Barak, and told him that he was to lead the attack against their oppressors. Naturally he was reluctant to go. He thought that since the message came through Deborah, she should go too. She was willing, but not at all shy to inform him that she would get the glory. Nor did she have any doubts that God would deliver the victory, as indeed God did!

Somehow, Deborah heard God's voice prompting her, as her own song gives testimony: "Awake, awake, Deborah! . . . Strength! arise, Barak, make despoilers your spoil" (Jgs 5:12). The violent exploits of war to which she encourages Barak and for which she gains the unexpected support of the Kenite woman, Jael, are far from our own experience. Yet it was in those times, when her listening heart was made a brave heart, that God won a forty-year measure of peace for the Israelite people.

The author's description is brief, yet it raises provocative questions for our modern minds. Why was a woman judging Israel? What had she done to gain the degree of recognition necessary to have a place designated as "Deborah's palm tree" (4:4) as her "office" where the people came to her for judgment? How did she get the authority to summon Barak and order him to lead an army in the name of the Lord? So great is her influence that Barak is willing to have her—a woman—get the credit if she will only come with his force! How did Deborah gain the assurance to command, "Be off, for this is the day on which the LORD has delivered Sisera into your power"? What inspiration prompted her to express in such beautiful poetry the power of God? Since the biblical account doesn't tell us these things, we must allow our imaginations to reconstruct Deborah's life and inner thoughts in order to answer these questions and to enter into the spirit of discernment which she experienced.

In the fifth chapter of the book of Judges, the ancient hymn, the Canticle of Deborah, gives us some clues (Jgs 5:7–16):

> When I, Deborah, rose,
>   when I rose, a mother in Israel,
> New gods were their choice;
>   then the war was at their gates. . . .
> My heart is with the leaders of Israel . . .
> Sing of them to the strains of the harpers at the wells,
>   where men recount the just deeds of the LORD,
>   his just deeds that brought freedom to Israel.
> Awake, awake, Deborah! . . .
> Among the clans of Reuben
>   great were the searchings of heart.
> Why do you stay beside your hearths
>   listening to the lowing of the herds?

All of the people had heard the "just deeds of the LORD" sung at the wells, but it seems that the memory of these deeds touched a powerful chord in Deborah's keenly responsive nature. She found the new gods abhorrent and was so strongly moved that she brought the role of "mother in Israel" to a new prominence. Because the "searchings of heart" were great among all the people, her challenge was heeded.

Pressures Which Affect Our Decisions

As we grow from childhood through adolescence into adulthood, we are called upon to make decisions. Some of the decisions we made were more significant than others because they had major consequences for others as well as for ourselves. Other decisions were about small matters but became significant as part of a pattern—either a good habit or a bad habit.

You would be very unusual if you felt totally satisfied with your record of decisions. As you think about the various options you've had in life, you are undoubtedly able to identify many pressures that tended to make you feel at the time as though you really had no choice. Such pressures can come either from **within ourselves** or from **outside sources.**

To focus on the pressures which come from within, recall the Johari window we studied in chapter 1. Remember the "unknown" area of our personality? Many of our motivations are hidden in these blind spots. However, taking time to recall a series of decisions is helpful in bringing some of them to the surface. We are able to discover patterns in our habitual decision-making styles. Deep-seated fears and insecurities of which we are not fully aware may have created the inner pressure of a defensive stance which has forced some decisions.

Three basic drives which we all experience within ourselves at different times are money, power, and sex, which trigger many of our decisions, even though we might be ashamed to admit it. These drives are also associated with many of the outer pressures we experience, since our society describes success in terms of acquiring possessions, achieving status, and accomplishing marriage and family goals. Because everyone wants to be considered successful, such exterior pressures can easily become major motivators.

On the more ideal side, among the many other motivations which we experience, many of us would list our religious beliefs. These are often hidden, but they can exert a strong influence. For example, some women who explained their decision at the time they considered an abortion have described a deep inner conviction that they simply could not destroy the life growing within them. Another instance would be that of a man or woman who experiences such a strong infatuation with another person that they cannot resist having an affair, although they admit to a fierce inner conflict of knowingly damaging their spousal relationship.

"God's Will"

In the face of such pressures, how can we make better decisions, choices more in keeping with God's will? First of all, we need to understand what is meant by "God's Will." The following passage from the Vatican II document, *The Church in the Modern World*, helps clarify the meaning of this phrase:

> The Spirit . . . frees all . . . so that by putting aside love of self and bringing all earthly resources into the service of human life, they can devote themselves to that future when humanity itself will become an offering accepted by God. (#38)
>
> For after we have obeyed the Lord, and in his Spirit nurtured on earth the values of human dignity, brotherhood, and freedom, and indeed all the good fruits of our nature and enterprise, we will find them again, but freed of stain, burnished and transfigured. This will be so when Christ hands over to the Father a kingdom eternal and universal. . . . On this earth that kingdom is already present in mystery. When the Lord returns, it will be brought into full flower. (#39)

In this context, "God's will" means our active participation in preparing the world for the full flowering of the kingdom. All our actions which "nurture the values of human dignity, brotherhood, and freedom" are actions which are "God's will." Rather than a blueprint or computer program, God gives us the opportunity to freely put our talents to work. God's will is not a multiple-choice test with only one correct answer. God, being God, is not limited by our choices. Rather, the dynamic workings of the Spirit prompt us to understand and do what is required.

Consequently, those of us who feel called to a deeper spirituality must cultivate a sensitivity to those things which foster God's kingdom. We must not only choose good over evil, but we must look for the greater good. We must become adept at recognizing our motivations and fine-tuning them to this framework. Christian spirituality calls this the "discernment of spirits."

Discernment

The meaning of the word discernment becomes clearer if we study its Latin roots: *dis* means to separate or to take apart, while *cernere* means to sift, to separate, to decide, judge, or cut. As we apply this to spiritual discernment, we see that it requires a careful and attentive use of our normal human powers of perception and discrimination.

The activity of discernment requires the ability to use both our senses and our intelligence to perceive a situation as clearly as we can. In addition, we must also discriminate both the motivations which influence the choice we are contemplating and also the consequences which will follow. This activity is called discernment of spirits because we attempt to recognize the "spirit" of our actions. We take into account that God's will is the flowering of the kingdom, but that weeds are allowed to grow in the garden. We discern not only the good spirits —what will encourage the flowering—but also the bad spirits—what will encourage the weeds and thus prevent the flowering.

How do I discern? A basic requirement is a listening heart—that is, a sense of inner quiet and peace which recognizes that God's spirit is within me, guiding me and trusting me to make a good choice. While morality demands a firm commitment to choose good over evil, spirituality adds an extra dimension to this desire. Spirituality requires us to cultivate an ethical sense that consistently applies certain criteria to our choices. Some of these are:

1. Will this make me more selfish or more a person for others?
2. Will this choice contribute to the well-being of my community— my family, neighborhood, and workplace—and so foster the flowering of the kingdom?
3. How does this choice fit in with the church's teaching and tradition?

At times, we will need to make more significant life decisions, so will need to spend more time in weighing the pros and cons. These additional criteria should be considered at such times:

1. How will this choice enable me to use the talents and abilities that God has given me?
2. How does this grow out of the direction of my life at this point—the commitments I have already made?
3. What does N. (a person you regard as wise and holy) think?
4. What might I be overlooking? Are there other options?

Far-reaching decisions invite us to spend more time in prayer. Almost more important than logical and factual information are the inner movements we experience during prayer. What feelings develop inside me as I consider this decision? Am I enthusiastic, energetic, and eager, or bored, depressed, and uneasy? What do I resist? What am I willing to change or undergo?

It is important to actually decide, rather than to simply let events carry you along. Afterwards, test your decision. Do you experience the fruits of the Spirit: love, joy, peace, patient endurance, kindness, generosity, faith, mildness, chastity? (Gal 5:22–23). If not, you are called to reassess the situation, to learn from your mistakes, to once again open yourself to the movement of the Spirit.

REFLECTION AND DISCUSSION

Our lives in contemporary America don't have the drama or color of Deborah and Barak's battle, but our decisions do have impact. Take some time to try to reconstruct several decision-making episodes in your life. Such decisions could include:

—a purchase
—the use of your time for a particular project
—the friends with whom you would associate
—marriage
—having a child
—pursuing a career or a job change
—going to college
—taking up a hobby
—becoming active in church
—becoming active in a club or association

1. Recall the circumstances of three or four such decisions. Write your responses on a sheet of paper:

   My age at the time: **Decision:**
   What influenced me:

2. Now take a look at the decisions you made. What influenced you? A certain person or group of people? The attractiveness of one particular option that made it really stand out? A gut-level feeling that you should "go for it"? A vivid image of a future which would hinge on your choice?

3. Next, look over these choices.

—Have you made many decisions, or do you feel you've drifted into them?
—Is there a pattern to what influences your choices?
—Have there been any radical shifts in your beliefs or goals so that your decisions take a new direction?
—To what extent have your deepest religious hopes influenced these decisions?
—What feelings do you have as you review these decisions?

4. Select a partner and talk over your responses to some of these questions.

BREAK

Enjoy refreshments and each other's company.

WRAP-UP

1. Look ahead to the "During the Week" follow-up activities. (optional)
2. Look ahead to the scripture passage and the theme of the next session. Decide on a time during the upcoming week when you will read the chapter.
3. Participate in the Closing Prayer.

DURING THE WEEK

1. Spend some more time on the reflection about your pattern of decisions.
2. Read the story of another Israelite judge who was called to discern God's will as he exercised the leadership which his times required: Gideon, Judges 6:1–8:28. Ask these questions:
   a) What background information do we have that helps us understand why Gideon discerned that he was called to leadership in the Israelite community?

b) What difficult decisions needed to be made?
c) What methods did Gideon use to discern God's will? Do these seem practical or unusual?
d) Reading between the lines, what human struggles do you think Gideon had to go through to discern wisely?
e) Of the criteria for discernment listed in this chapter, do any of them seem useful to Gideon?

7. Call to Fidelity

Scripture Passage

The Book of Ruth: **Ruth, a Moabite woman, chooses to go with her Israelite mother-in-law, Naomi, back to the land of Judah where she marries Boaz.**

PRAYER

Introduction: A Note on the Text

Leader: The book of Ruth is found in our Bibles between Judges and 1 Samuel because, although it did not take its final written form until centuries later, the events it describes date from the time when the Israelites had established themselves in the promised land. The spare and uncluttered form of the short story is unusual for biblical writings, but is well-suited to invite us to imagine the details of this very human struggle to find a place in life. We are able to enter a world where, because of the covenant, the manner of human relationships is governed by a sense of relationship to God.

The passage chosen for our prayer is that of the famous scene where Ruth makes her choice to be part of God's people. Although she grew up in Moab, a country southeast of Israel, Ruth married into the immigrant family of the Israelite, Elimelech. Her mother-in-law, Naomi, appears to have become her mentor during her childless marriage to their son. In a way unusual for the scriptures, we get a sense of the feminine viewpoint, of how women made decisions in a world where their identity was determined by their relationships with men.

Call to Prayer

Leader: Let us call ourselves to inner quiet as we focus on God's call to fidelity. (Music, song, or a gathering gesture may be used.)

Reading

Reader: A reading from the book of Ruth (1:1–18).

Once in the time of the judges there was a famine in the land; so a man from Bethlehem of Judah departed with his wife and two sons to reside on the plateau of Moab. The man was named Elimelech, his wife Naomi, and his sons Mahlon and Chilion; they were Ephrathites from Bethlehem of Judah. Some time after their arrival on the Moabite plateau, Elimelech, the husband of Naomi, died, and she was left with her two sons, who married Moabite women, one named Orpah, the other Ruth. When they had lived there about ten years, both Mahlon and Chilion died also, and the woman was left with neither her two sons nor her husband. She then made ready to go back from the plateau of Moab because word reached her there that the LORD had visited his people and given them food.

She and her two daughters-in-law left the place where they had been living. Then as they were on the road back to the land of Judah, Naomi said to her two daughters-in-law, "Go back, each of you, to your mother's house! May the LORD be kind to you as you were to the departed and to me! May the LORD grant each of you a husband and a home in which you will find rest." She kissed them good-by, but they wept with loud sobs, and told her they would return with her to her people. "Go back, my daughters!" said Naomi. "Why should you come with me? Have I other sons in my womb who may become your husbands? Go back, my daughters! Go, for I am too old to marry again. And even if I could offer any hopes, or if tonight I had a husband or had borne sons, would you then wait and deprive yourselves of husbands until those sons grew up? No, my daughters! my lot is too bitter for you, because the LORD, has extended his hand against me." Again they sobbed aloud and wept; and Orpah kissed her mother-in-law good-by, but Ruth stayed with her.

"See now!" she said, "your sister-in-law has gone back to her people and her god. Go back after your sister-in-law!"

But Ruth said, "Do not ask me to abandon or forsake you! for wherever you go I will go, wherever you lodge I will lodge, your people shall be my people, and your God my God. Wherever you die I will die, and there be buried. May the LORD do so and so to me, and more besides, if aught but death separates me from you!" Naomi then ceased to urge her, for she saw she was determined to go with her.

Individual Reflection

Leader: When life takes a different turn from what I expected, what is my reaction? Whose advice has been most helpful to me in my life? Have there been any significant choice points for me? Who has challenged me? When have I sensed a deeper meaning to events?

Prayer

All: God our Creator, you continue to act in our lives. You continue to send people and events to challenge us and to help us know your ways. Give us eyes to see clearly and faith to walk firmly as we echo today the words of Ruth: "Wherever you go, I will go. Your people will be my people, and you will be my God too."

LESSON

Hard Times for the Israelites

Each week as we have reflected on another facet of our spiritual growth, we have looked to the story of someone whose life was remembered and retold in a way that helps us understand how God acts among humans. By now we can see a thread of continuity. With Abraham and Jacob, God's special intervention could have been seen as the favor given to a family. However, as we find a remembrance of God within the families which descended in Egypt, and even in Midian, where Moses met his wife Zipporah, we sense the larger implications. God's plans will not be swallowed up by changes in the political fortunes of human beings. So we come to the awesome events of the Exodus, when Yahweh makes it definitively clear: "You will be my people and I will be your God."

The constant theme of the time of the judges is the backsliding of the people followed by the intervention of God. The pattern is clear: God is faithful, and constantly sends leaders who call the people to turn away from local gods and to be faithful to the One God. While the book of Ruth is set at the time of the Judges, it takes a different tack. Rather than dramatic events of war and rescue, the setting is peaceful. We get a sense of ordinary people trying to work out their lives with a view toward being faithful to their God. The focus is on the people and their assessment of their lives in terms of God's designs. We come to understand that God acts not only in dramatic intervention, but through providence—God's faithful reliance on human beings. It is the faithful choices of the people, actively engaged in life's events, which bring about the Creator's designs.

But how much choice did Naomi and Ruth have? The very first verse tells us that Elimelech and Naomi felt forced by the economic conditions of famine to move to Moab. Though Moab was less than a hundred miles from Bethlehem, and similar work in agriculture and grazing was readily available, the transition was undoubtedly difficult. The various tribes which populated the area maintained their own culture and gods and customs by a fierce clannish attitude toward outsiders. Any hopes of returning home would have disappeared by the time they arranged marriages with girls from the formerly de-tested Moabites so the family would be better accepted in their new community. Elimelech's death was a further cruel blow to Naomi. Even after she had the satisfaction of seeing her sons adapt to life in Moab, Naomi's life was further shattered when they too were snatched so inexplicably by death. Her faith was sorely tested and she reacted in a cynical manner, telling her friends not to call her "Naomi," which means fullness or plenitude, but "Mara," "for the Almighty has made it very bitter for me" (1:20).

The Meaning of Fidelity

Naomi may have cried out against God, but nonetheless she continued to rely on what her religion had taught her to expect—that God would remain faithful, that her people would once again receive her. Hadn't God visited the people to once again give them food? Could she not expect that they would give her the place which the covenant bond assured her? But what of these daughters-in-law? The covenant law only found a place for them beside a man. Better that they should stay with their own people, faithful to their gods. The choice seemed clear, if not easy.

The moment of parting was one of high emotion, tears all around. Naomi seems still to be trying to convince herself that all is for the best. Her genuine affection for these two women is clear from her grief, from her blessing for them, and from their response. Two will go on one way, and one go alone. But why is the result unexpected?

Naomi's path is as planned. She accepts her bitter fate: "The LORD has brought me back destitute" (1:21). Orpah's decision is grounded in her upbringing; she accepts her mother-in-law's advice as sensible and consonant with her experience of life. To be faithful is to seek a place in life among her own people, with her god.

It is Ruth who does the unexpected. Though she is remembered for being faithful, she is in fact unfaithful to her upbringing. Somehow she makes a leap of faith, allowing herself to be gripped and swept into the action of a God and people who have entered her life with an invitation that cannot be refused. The call of the unknown country is stronger than the familiar surroundings. To be true to herself, she must go with Naomi and make Naomi's God and people to be her own God and people. Fidelity has an inner dimension that routes her unswervingly. The unexpected choice is the only choice for her.

The remaining three chapters of this small book lead us to understand the rightness of the choice. God's fidelity is seen in the continued willingness of the Creator to allow human beings to carry on the work of the world. The fidelity of God's people is expressed through their choices to act according to God's designs. For the Israelite people, God's designs were clear through their law. It is their choices, guided by their laws and customs, which become the story of Ruth.

Naomi plays a leading role, although behind the scenes. She gives the information and suggestions which Ruth follows so that she meets Boaz, gains his favor and proposal. Satisfied, Naomi shrewdly observes, "The man will not rest, but will settle the matter today" (3:18). Sure enough, wise in the ways of his world, Boaz makes the arrangements to marry Ruth and purchase Naomi's property. Naomi in her old age becomes the nurse of her grandson Obed. Ruth, the foreigner, becomes the great-grandmother of David, the greatest king of Israel.

Fidelity

Like much of the scriptures, the book of Ruth is a story which was handed on from the early days of Israelite history and was reworked by editors many centuries later. This later view places events in a new perspective, wider and wiser. It is not simply the event itself, but its deeper significance that becomes apparent. Beautiful as this love story is at the human level, it is more the deeper spiritual dimension of people who are acting in response not simply to "What's best for my family?" but to, "How do our customs and laws help me bring about what's best for my family?" Yet fidelity isn't measured only by the perspective of laws and customs, but by an inner sense of God's designs, such as the foreigner Ruth had noticed and appreciated at the root of the social arrangements she had learned from Naomi.

What of ourselves? What is apparent to us as we look back over our lives and try to view them objectively? Although we might be afraid to discover our weakness—our lack of fidelity—we might also be able to sense a continuity and flow below the seemingly jumbled events of life over which we have so little control. We might be able to discover some pattern in our journey.

One method which may help us get in touch with a pattern is the "Spiritual Steppingtones" of Ira Progoff. He describes these as the dozen or so main events of our interior life. We remember them because they are significant in our ongoing search for meaning. All of us experience sudden insights at times, but we tend to lose them or allow them to pass us by because we get on with the business of life, or because we recognize that our ideas would be considered odd by our family or friends. The purpose of the steppingstones activity is to recall and recover such moments of intuition when reality became sharp and clear. Then we can step back and explore the continuity, the fidelity, of our inner journey.

EXTENDED REFLECTION

Note: Rather than discussing individual responses to questions, this time segment should be devoted to the quiet activity of having someone lead the group through the steps of identifying spiritual steppingstones. Each one should have a blank sheet and a pen or pencil.

Step 1: Establishing the Atmosphere

The purpose of this step is to free our minds of conscious control and to encourage spontaneous surfacing of subconscious memories. Just as God came to Jacob when his guard was down, in a dream while sleeping, we allow ourselves to relax our normal defenses in order to be aware of our "hidden self." Each one sits quietly, breathing deeply and slowly while the leader reads a centering meditation. (See Progoff, pp. 95–103 for samples, or use a music recording.) Close your eyes and gradually let go of any outer distractions, concentrating all energies on inner movement.

Step 2: Observing Inner Movements

Listen for any interior words or music which might rise to the surface. Allow your inner eye to see any items or symbols. Notice any sensations your body feels. Attend to any ideas, inspirations, or emotions. Allow total freedom of movement, not judging, repressing, or embellishing what occurs to you. Try to stay in an alert, yet withdrawn state.

Step 3: Recording Your Impressions

Allow yourself to feel the movement of your life as a river moving at the depth of your being. When you come to an event of significance, note it on your sheet. Don't be concerned about any particular order, but rather the quality of the experience, the questions you felt, your feelings at that time.

Move back and forth from step 2 to step 3 until you have identified about a dozen events. You may need to pause and return to step 1 at times.

Step 4: Tracing the Pattern

This will be done during the week.

BREAK

Enjoy refreshments and each other's company.

WRAP-UP

1. Look ahead to the "During the Week" follow-up activities. Although optional, this exercise is highly recommended for the full benefit of the steppingstones experience.
2. Look ahead to the scripture passage and the theme of the next session. Decide on a time during the upcoming week when you will read the chapter.
3. Participate in the Closing Prayer.

DURING THE WEEK

Take some time to reflect on the spiritual steppingstones which you identified during the session. Find a quiet place where you will not be disturbed for an hour or so. Take a few moments to allow yourself to become quiet, to come to inner stillness. In this quietness, read back to yourself (out loud) your spiritual steppingstones. As you read, try to sense a thread of movement in your life. Let the remembrances stir you—observe your reactions (crying, smiling, etc.) as you reread what you wrote during the class session. Write these reactions as an appendix to the earlier writing.

Reread your list again aloud slowly, in privacy. Some people find it helpful to read aloud into a tape recorder and play the comments back. Add any further comments which occur to you.

After some moments of quiet, respond to this question:

How has God been faithful in my life?

List events which, looking back, strike you as coming from God, whether in the form of joy or of difficulty:
youth . . .

List actions which, whether easy or difficult for you, showed your attempt to respond to God:
youth . . .

"starting out" years . . .

"starting out" years . . .

recent years . . .

recent years . . .

8. Call to Leadership

Scripture Passage

1 Samuel, chapters 11–31; 2 Samuel: **God gives the people a king, first Saul, then David, allowing sin and slaughter as they struggle to understand this new form of leadership.**

PRAYER

Introduction: A Note on the Text

Leader: This section of the Bible makes an extremely captivating story, and indeed has become the script for more than one cinematic production. Not only do we learn the epic history of God's people at the time of their molding into a powerful kingdom, but we gain tremendous insight into the psychology of power. These books were probably written at the height of Israel's strength, during the reign of King Solomon (960–930 B.C.), relatively close to the actual events which are described (ca. 1060–960 B.C.). We learn of the choice of Saul to be king, of the youthful David's military exploits, his friendship with Saul's son, Jonathan, and his marriage to Saul's daughter, Michal. We learn of Saul's vacillation, paranoia, and eventual death on the field of battle.

After David becomes king, we see him mature as a leader through the experiences of lust for Bathsheba, the murder of her husband, Uriah, and repentance after the accusations of the prophet Nathan. He is faced with the constant challenge of uniting the independent clans as a fighting force, as well as deciding how the Law would be interpreted in these new circumstances. He undergoes wrenching personal sorrow as he tries to bring up his children in the turbulent times, and lives to see his beloved son, Absalom, raise up a force to take away his kingdom from him and to be slain in his treachery.

Our passage for today's prayer portrays David as a man with a well-developed ego. He was not afraid to be himself as he charted new rituals of leadership, despite what others, even his wife, Michal, might say. In order to lead others to God, no matter how few or how many, we too must not be afraid to be our best selves in spite of criticism. In short, we must take the risk of being a leader.

Call to Prayer

Leader: Let us put our concerns of today aside for the moment as we turn our attention to the Lord in the moment of joyful exuberance when the Ark of the Covenant was brought to Jerusalem. (Song, music, or a gathering gesture may be used.)

Reading

Reader: A reading from the second book of Samuel (6:12–23).

When it was reported to King David that the LORD had blessed the family of Obed-edom and all that belonged to him, David went to bring up the ark of God from the house of Obed-edom into the City of David amid festivities. As soon as the bearers of the ark of the LORD had advanced six steps, he sacrificed an ox and a fatling. Then David, girt with a linen apron, came dancing before the LORD with abandon, as he and all the Israelites were bringing up the ark of the LORD with shouts of joy and the sound of the horn. As the ark of the LORD was entering the City of David, Saul's daughter Michal looked down through the window and saw King David leaping and dancing before the LORD, and she despised him in her heart. The ark of the LORD was brought in and set in its place within the tent David had pitched for it. Then David offered holocausts and peace offerings before the LORD. When he finished making these offerings, he blessed the people in the name of the LORD of hosts. He then distributed among all the people, to each man and each woman in the entire multitude of Israel, a loaf of bread, a cut of roast meat, and a raisin cake. With this, all the people left for their homes.

When David returned to bless his own family, Saul's daughter Michal came out to meet him and said, "How the king of Israel has honored himself today, exposing himself to the view of the slave girls of his followers, as a commoner might do!" But David replied to Michal: "I was dancing before the LORD. As the LORD lives, who preferred me to your father and his whole family when he appointed me commander of the LORD's people, Israel, not only will I make merry before the LORD, but I will demean myself even more. I will be lowly in your esteem, but in the esteem of the slave girls you spoke of I will be honored." And so Saul's daughter Michal was childless to the day of her death.

Individual Reflection

Leader: Perhaps it is because we have seen so many leaders—political, religious, sports, and entertainment—fall from grace that many of us hesitate to take on leadership roles. Are we afraid of failure? of criticism? of having no time left for ourselves? As for David, it's obvious that he was a man of prayer. Here he prays with his whole body! We know he sang and played the harp, as many of the psalms are attributed to him. David praised God, thanked God, even fell flat on his face and begged for mercy. Could it be that his prayer life was the secret of his success as a leader?

Prayer

All: O God, God of David, incarnate as Son of David, hear the prayers of your follower. With faithless timidity, I hesitate to serve you as a leader. Give me strength, for you are all powerful. Give me fortitude and courage, for you are Spirit. Sustain the leaders you have chosen, and raise up new leaders in the church and in the world, so that all will recognize you as their one, true Leader. Amen.

LESSON

David, The Great Leader of His People

Talk about charm—David had it from the first moment we met him in the Bible. "He was ruddy, a youth handsome to behold and making a splendid appearance . . . a skillful harpist . . . a stalwart soldier besides being an able speaker, and handsome. Moreover, the LORD is with him" (1 Sm 16:12–18).

It took more than good looks, however, to become a successful leader. It was not David's appearance that defeated Goliath, but his marksmanship with a sling and stone that killed the giant. It was not David's masculine beauty, portrayed so elegantly in Michelangelo's statue, that brought victory after victory for the young military leader, but rather it was his genius at warfare. Clearly, God blessed David with many talents.

Before David became a true servant of the Lord, he was a dedicated servant of Saul. With good reason he was fearful of the jealous king. Had it not been for his genuine friendship with Jonathan, David certainly would have lost his life at an early age. Later, when he did flee from Saul, his leadership abilities once again surfaced as he led a band of 400 outlaws in a life of extortion and violence. It was a period in David's life when he was interested in serving only himself.

It is sometimes said that "the office makes the man," and in David's case this was true. Upon becoming King of Judah at age 30 and King of all Israel seven years later, David offered leadership and ministry to God and his people in an astute and often violent way. In his day violence toward one's enemies was one way of serving the God who was "on his side." While tradition holds him to be an ideal ruler, and many incidents at this period of his life bear this out, he was morally weak, as we know from the Bathsheba affair and subsequent cover-up. This incident was the beginning of many family and political misfortunes in his life, none of which detracted from his efforts to do what he thought Yahweh wanted him to do, to lead as he thought Yahweh wanted him to lead.

The Psalms As Liturgical Leadership

Some scripture scholars say that it is impossible to know with certainty which, if any, of the psalms were written by David, but who can resist putting scholarship aside for the vicarious experience of imagining David praying Psalm 51, The Miserere, after being confronted with his sins by the prophet Nathan. It would not be out of character for God's servant, as he is referred to in some of the psalms, to throw himself at the feet of Yahweh and plead for mercy. The virtue of humility, that *sine qua non* condition for ministerial leadership, began to grow in David's life when he came face-to-face with his sinfulness. A heart contrite and humbled God did not spurn.

The strong traditional link between the psalms and David evidently grew up because of their widespread use in Israelite worship, which became centered in Jerusalem when David brought the Ark there. Later, when his son Solomon built the Temple and liturgical ministries multiplied, the psalms became official prayers. These poems, so obviously composed out of a life lived passionately, support us who can identify our own experiences of joy and pain in the verses.

Indeed, those of us who draw back from influencing others because of our fears of inadequacy or rejection can take heart from many of the psalms. Each Sunday, the liturgy gives us the occasion to remind ourselves that we rely on the Lord for our strength, as these examples indicate:

"O LORD, how many are my adversaries! . . .
But you, O LORD, are my shield:
   my glory, you lift up my head!" (Ps. 3:2, 4)
"What is man that you should be mindful of him, . . .
You have given him rule over the works of your hands,
   putting all things under his feet . . ." (Ps 8:5, 7)
"How wonderfully has he made me cherish
   the holy ones who are in his land! . . .
O LORD, my allotted portion and my cup,
   you it is who hold fast my lot.
For me the measuring lines have fallen on pleasant sites . . ."
   (Ps. 16:3, 5–6)

True to God's promise, David's throne was passed on, not just to his son, Solomon, but a throne without end. The Hebrew scriptures stop short of the greatest descendant, Jesus. It is only in him, the complete revelation of God, that we are able to find a perfect leader. Where David was violent, Jesus is the Prince of Peace. Where David was an adulterer, Jesus is the pure, sinless, spotless lamb of God. Where David was a ministerial leader in a very limited and primitive way, Jesus is the Good Shepherd and Servant of God who is the prime example for all Christian leaders and ministers.

The Art of Ministerial Leadership

Much has been written lately about the various types of leadership exercised within the context of a contemporary Roman Catholic parish. Most of these writings and workshops on the same topics are addressed to pastors, future pastors and pastoral associates (usually religious sisters and brothers and deacons). But what about the laity who have been assuming ministerial duties in the church within the past few decades? Do not they deserve the same kind of nurturing in their new responsibilities?

Let us focus on leadership qualities for all ministers, from priest to parking-lot attendants. Would you believe that there is a parish where they have a "Ministry of Parking"? It stretches the term, but why not? To minister is to serve, and what could be of greater service on Sunday morning than to ease our entry into worship?

Ministry in the church today is a grassroots movement, and it is wonderful to behold. This has upset some of the ecclesiastical officials who are presently trying to define, delineate, and distinguish "official" ministry from "unofficial" ministry. In the meantime, ministry is happening and people are being served. But how long will it last? Movements have a way of dying out—usually because the issue has been resolved (eg., the anti-Vietnam War movement) or because of a lack of charismatic leadership (eg., the Civil Rights movement after the death of Dr. Martin Luther King, Jr.). In the case of the "Ministerial Movement" the issue is no problem—people will always need service. But without the proper leadership at the local, diocesan, and national levels, the "Ministerial Movement" may have a very short lifespan.

What is ministry? Is it the same as leadership? Why do we call ministerial leadership an art? What are the spiritual qualities of ministerial leadership, and how can they be surfaced and reproduced?

In trying to define ministry we run into two extremes. On the one hand, everything is ministry and everyone is minister. The man who works in the church parking lot on Sunday morning is indeed helping people; but does that make him a minister? Does the fact that he is baptized have anything to do with ministry? What about his motivation or his faith dimension? What, if anything, makes him a minister?

On the other hand, many Catholics (both clergy and laity) hold that the only ministers are ordained males. Some don't even like the term "minister" because it is "too Protestant." Who, then, is a minister? What is ministry?

First, we must look at the word itself. And we discover the common prefix "mini" meaning "small" or "less." The mini-ster is the one who looks up, while the magi-ster (magistrate) is the one who looks down, as from a judge's bench. St. Paul described minister accurately when he wrote "let all parties think humbly of others as superior to themselves, each of you looking to others' interest rather than his own" (Phil 2:3-4). Ministry therefore is related to service (*diakonia*) and only remotely to power. David learned this lesson the hard way by abusing his power. Nathan confronted him with the story of the rich man who took and slaughtered the pet lamb of a poor servant. "You are the man!" exclaimed Nathan. Power had displaced leadership, and David recognized this and repented. Later, Jesus warned:

You know that those who are recognized as rulers over the Gentiles lord it over them, and their great ones make their authority over them. But it shall not be so among you. Rather, whoever wishes to be great among you will be your servant; whoever wishes to be first among you will be the slave of all. For the Son of Man did not come to be served but to serve and to give his life as a ransom for many (Mk 10:42–45).

During the time of the covenant there was a two-way appreciation of ministry in that God ministered to the people, Israel; and Israel ministered to God. But Israel's idea of ministry was imperfect. It was flawed. The Law called for rituals of sacrifice to heal relationships broken when rights were violated. At times such ritual replaced efforts to maintain right relationships. A minister of ritual was regarded as a replacement for the service of one individual to another. Again, it was when Jesus, Son of David, came that the true meaning of ministry became clear.

It was Jesus who responded perfectly to the love of his Father and in his teaching ministry invited others to do the same. During his public life, Jesus exercised many other ministries (healing, preaching, caring, organizing and celebrating) and his followers have continued to practice them down to the present day. Whether "official" or "unofficial," all ministries are rooted and centered in Jesus. In him, the ministerial priesthood of the clergy and the common priesthood of the faithful both find their source.

Leadership

Having described and defined ministry in a way that is workable and applicable to all Christians, let us now move on to the concept of leadership and relate it to ministry as an art. Just how are these concepts related? The answer to this question depends on one's perception of leadership. Is one born a leader or is one trained to be a leader, or is it a combination of both nature and nurture?

There are those who say, "Leaders are made, not born." They divide leadership into types or levels, depending on the amount of influence they exert. Secondary or tertiary leaders tend to be issue-oriented, passive, reactive individuals with authority over small institutions or a limited number of followers. Sometimes they become primary leaders, who have proper authority over collectives of influential people. There are techniques, skills and procedures to follow if one is to become a leader in this formal sense. But many of these same people will never become the kinds of leaders people remember unless they possess something more.

What is it that makes people stand out in our minds as exceptional leaders? Most people would list qualities such as energy, enthusiasm, healthy anger, sense of humor, and a strong and healthy ego. Leaders usually have a good ability to listen and to develop relationships. They are not afraid to take risks. They know how to develop people and resources. Most of these qualities are natural talents rather than skills that are learned. These aspects of leadership are more of an art than a science.

To the list above we should also add the ineffable quality of "charisma" or simple "charm," which has a way of captivating people. We saw that David was an excellent example of a person who had this quality. How does one obtain this charm which is such an essential ingredient of mature Christian leadership? The same way that Pope John XXIII and Mother Teresa became "charming"—by responding to the Spirit with love for God and neighbor, and by being willing to change for the better.

Mature Christian leadership, then, is both a science and an art. The techniques and skills have to be learned and practiced, but then, like an artist, put in the background while creatively developing the unique God-given talents and virtues which make up a mature, Christian personality. Just as not every artist becomes great, so every Christian leader does not become a canonized saint. The important thing is to work at it so that God can use the instrumentality of ministerial leadership to bring about the kingdom on earth.

Sooner or later, most people involved in the life of their parish will be asked to serve in a leadership capacity. Some will accept the responsibility and others will refuse with the excuse, "I'm a follower, not a leader." In biblical terms, a leader is one who first and foremost is a servant of God. In this sense we are all called upon to be leaders. No matter how large or small may be our spheres, from boardroom to altar to kitchen, God can use us to influence others. We need only say "yes," give it our best shot and rely on God's power.

DISCUSSION

Spend a few moments thinking about these questions. Jot down a brief response.

1. Who are the best leaders you know? (from current headlines, from history, or people you know personally)
2. What makes them good leaders?

Divide into groups of four and share your responses.

BREAK

Enjoy refreshments and each other's company.

WRAP-UP

1. Look ahead to the "During the Week" follow-up activities. (optional)
2. Look ahead to the scripture passage and the theme of the next session. Decide on a time during the upcoming week when you will read the chapter.
3. Participate in the Closing Prayer.

DURING THE WEEK

1. Read 2 Samuel 5:1–5, and try to answer the following questions:
   a) Why did the tribe of Israel choose David for king?
   b) What action of David did they cite to show his leadership ability?
   c) In what two ways was David's leadership publicly recognized?
2. 2 Samuel 11:1 through 12:25
   a) What parts of the story show David's misuse of his power as an official leader?
   b) When Nathan presents the case for David's judgment, what does David's decision tell us about him?
   c) When Nathan confronts him, what does David's reaction tell us about his personality?

9. Call to Prayer

Scripture Passage

The book of Amos: **Amos gives us an example of an ordinary workman who learned to pray. Because he prayed, his vision of the world was drastically altered, and from him we learn how to pray prophetically.**

PRAYER

Introduction: A Note on the Text

Leader: In the biblical sense, prophecy is the phenomenon of mediating the divine mind and will. Thus, a prophet is called "God's mouthpiece," although there are times when he proclaims God's message more by what he does than by what he says (Jer 18:1–10). Two types of prophets are found in the Bible: (1) the itinerant prophets, such as Elijah and Elisha, who are described in the book of Kings, and (2) the classical prophets, those whom we know through their writings, such as Isaiah, Jeremiah, Amos and Hosea.

As we read the scriptures, prophets frequently come across as arrogant and self-righteous. Even when we attempt to see them as human beings, we wonder at their boldness in announcing, "Thus says the Lord." How did they gain the confidence to put themselves forward as holy, as God's spokespersons? We must assume they had a very close relationship with the Lord. Such a relationship can only be found in prayer, when the human person develops a listening heart.

In our reading for today, we learn where such a relationship leads. Bethel was the site of a shrine made holy as the place of Abraham's altar, Jacob's ladder, and the Ark of the Covenant. The priest in charge of this shrine, Amaziah, was appointed by the king, Jeroboam.

83

When Amos, a common workingman, heard in prayer God's call to prophesy, he was attacked by Amaziah because his words went against the country's policies.

Call to Prayer

Leader: Let us open our hearts to the "Word of the Lord," so that prayerfully we may speak to ourselves and others, words we need to hear. (Music, song, or a gathering gesture may be used.)

Reading

Reader: A reading from the book of Amos (7:10–16).

Amaziah, the priest of Bethel, sent word to Jeroboam, king of Israel: "Amos has conspired against you here within Israel; the country cannot endure all his words. For this is what Amos says:
Jeroboam shall die by the sword,
and Israel shall surely be exiled from its land."
To Amos, Amaziah said: "Off with you, visionary, flee to the land of Judah! There earn your bread by prophesying, but never again prophesy in Bethel; for it is the king's sanctuary and a royal temple." Amos answered Amaziah, "I was no prophet, nor have I belonged to a company of prophets: I was a shepherd and a dresser of sycamores. The LORD took me from following the flock, and said to me, Go, prophesy to my people Israel. Now hear the word of the LORD!"

Individual Reflection

Leader: Amos' reaction was single-minded and unafraid. How do I react when I'm an outsider to socially acceptable norms? Do I have the courage of my convictions, based on a sure knowledge that "The Lord took me . . ."? Do I spend time in prayer, allowing God to lead me? Empty your mind of other concerns and repeat softly, "Lead me on, O Lord, lead me on." (All pause for silent reflection.)

Prayer

All: O God of all the prophets, consider my open mind and heart. Speak to me a word of love to sustain me on my way to you. With the help of your grace, may I speak your loving words to others so that we may all come closer to you. Amen.

Amos: A Man of Prayer in Troubled Times

Usually we think of people who have been officially designated as "holy" as being in a class apart, somehow above us. Since he was a biblical prophet, we would be likely to see Amos this way. Yet a close reading of his book gives glimpses of someone who was very much like us in many ways. He describes himself as a "shepherd and dresser of sycamores" (7:14), so it's not surprising to find many agricultural allusions. Oxen are domesticated for plowing (6:12), and time is marked by growing seasons (7:1). He brings a spiritual outlook to his work, seeing God as the ultimate controller of human enterprises: "I also withheld the rain from you/when the harvest was still three months away" (4:7); "I struck you with blight and searing wind;/your many gardens and vineyards,/your fig trees and olive trees the locust devoured" (4:9).

We get a picture of a well-ordered society with many workers: farmers, sellers of grain, plowmen, reapers, vintners, priests and prophets. Cities were laid out with streets and squares and were protected by a wall. The gate was an important point of gathering. A wealthy class may be supposed by reference to summer and winter houses (3:15). The government was monarchical, with princes and judges; taxes were collected even in those days, for we read of the "king's mowing" (7:1), "levies of grain" (5:11), fines and pledges (2:8). Religion and government were closely connected.

We know that Amos lived around 750 B.C., a time when Israel had been experiencing a period of prosperity which was then threatened by Assyria's efforts to subjugate its neighbors into satellite nations. Political maneuvering, civil unrest and violence became part of life in Israel. We find references to "breached walls" (4:3), corpses (6:10), the pillaging of an enemy (3:11), the decimation of a force which marches out (6:9), horses and camps (4:10), and a general "reign of violence" (6:3) and threat of exile (6:7).

Amos was from Tekoa, south of Jerusalem and apparently along a trade route, so he had opportunity to converse with travelers as they passed by. He had absorbed the Israelite culture with its hatred for the traditional enemies of the countries roundabout, such as the Philistines and Moabites, as well as its tradition of visiting the shrines of ancestors at Bethel. It is evident that the covenant values were of central concern to Amos, because he rails against his countrymen for their lack of concern for one another and their willingness to take advantage of the poor and the weak. He criticizes those who use their positions of power for self-advantage, cheating and accepting bribes.

While they go through the motions of prescribed feasts, sacrifices and tithes, they give these a false ring by their failure to live just lives.

In the midst of this world, Amos was a man of prayer, even a mystic of sorts. God instructed him by means of visions as to the fate of Israel.

> "This is what the LORD GOD showed me: a basket of ripe fruit. "What do you see, Amos?" he asked. I answered, "A basket of ripe fruit." Then the LORD said to me:
> "The time is ripe to have done with my people Israel" (8:1).

During these moments of intimacy with God, Amos pleaded on behalf of his people: "Cease, O LORD GOD!/How can Jacob stand?/He is so small!" (7:5) Yet that same intimacy gave him the strength to proclaim to these people, "Now hear the word of the Lord!"

Holiness through Prayer

The example of Amos shows us that God can choose an ordinary person and make him or her holy through a life of prayer. Jeremiah was another prophet who was willing to endure conflict because of his convictions. Yet, he resisted his call: "Ah, LORD GOD," I said, "I know not how to speak; I am too young" (Jer 1:6). Like Jeremiah, we often come up with excuses when God calls us and chooses us for a certain mission. We are either too young or too old, too tired or too busy, underqualified or overqualified. "Why me?" we ask.

Nowhere is this more true than when God invites us to a greater closeness through prayer. Our excuses are legion, and like Legion they represent hundreds of devilish ways to avoid the union with our God, for which we were created. Perhaps we have tried praying and it "didn't work." This could mean that our prayers were not answered as we expected, or possibly that we didn't "feel anything." Maybe we read books "about" prayer and found them so overwhelming and confusing that we gave up on the idea. This is quite understandable. Today there are books on prayer for every personality type, every stage of faith development; for adults, children, males, females and right-brain and left-brain people. In bookstores, the sections on prayer and spirituality are constantly expanding. The age of specialization and the knowledge explosion have a definite impact on matters spiritual, perhaps prompting one to ask "What are the basic fundamentals of prayer?" The following five points might be helpful:

1. Decide to pray. Like hell, heaven is paved with good intentions, especially when it comes to prayer. Prayer is the result of choosing to spend time with God. The first step is to whet our appetite for communion with God. Divine grace might eventually turn this appetite into a gnawing hunger. In prayer God always rewards our good intentions.

2. Pray actively. All intentions should lead to some action, before, during and after prayer. Before prayer, prepare by calling upon the Spirit of God for help, by finding the right time and place for maximum attention, by dismissing all "junk" from your mind and heart (and by fasting, from your body), and by placing yourself in God's loving presence. During prayer, it might be helpful to respond to scripture, chosen at random or from a selected text. Allow God to speak to you through the word and, after reflecting on the passages that speak to you personally, respond to God in your own way and with your own words.

3. Pray affectively. Prayer is not a "head trip." Responding to God's loving word calls forth from our deepest being feelings of awe, admiration, thankfulness, and dependence on God for what we need, especially mercy and forgiveness.

4. Pray faithfully. You might begin with twenty minutes of quality time each day. See where the Lord leads you. (A spiritual director is most helpful at this time.) Some people find themselves making a "Holy Hour" each day. Others practice a "Prayer of Presence" with little remembrances of God all during the day. The saints did both of the above and lots more, but they all started by being faithful to the "little things" of prayer and by God's grace were led to greater joys.

5. Pray prophetically. Like the prophets of old we too must become God's spokespersons. Today we might call this evangelization —proclaiming God's word to a world hungry for Good News. This, of course, presumes that we ourselves are evangelized, for we cannot give what we do not have. To pray prophetically means that we do not pray alone (we have help from the Spirit, the angels, friends, etc.), and our prayerfulness impacts not only our own spiritual life, but the lives of all with whom we come in contact. For the prophets this sometimes meant death. For us it will at least involve suffering, misunderstanding and sometimes rejection. It is the price of being a prophet.

PRAYER ACTIVITY

Since many people *want* to pray, but don't know how to go about it in a serious, prolonged way, spend the usual discussion time by having someone serve as leader, providing directions while others follow along in silence.

Twenty Minutes in Prayer

ENTRY (5 minutes)
Sit in a relaxed position. As you breathe you may begin by saying the words "Abba" or "Jesus" or just sitting in the knowledge and awareness of the tenderness of God's love . . . just as if you were slipping into a warm tub of water. Allow God's love to penetrate your mind, your heart, your body, your being.

RESPONSE (5 minutes)
What is your response to this great love of our Father? How does it make you feel? What do you want to say? Perhaps you prefer to remain silent and just bask in the divine presence as your response. Is your response adoration, praise, thanks, or ?????

SCRIPTURE (5 minutes)
Pick out at random a text from scripture, or choose one with special meaning to you or one which fits the liturgical season. Reflect: What does this mean to you at this time in relation to your experience of God's love, Jesus' message? How does it fit into your present life? God's love is a gift—you have not earned it, you cannot merit it. How does the Good News relate to it? (The leader reads aloud a verse from today's prayer.)

PETITION (5 minutes)
Time for petition, for resolution, for remembering the needs of those who have asked for your prayers, those for whom you may be responsible, your own needs, the needs of the world.

CLOSE with an act of praise or thanks and briefly, again, be aware of God's tender acceptance of you shown in the abiding love expressed in every breath of the environment that caresses you. Continue your day, knowing that you have nothing to fear because your Friend loves you and knows your needs.

BREAK

Enjoy refreshments and each other's company.

WRAP-UP

1. Look ahead to the "During the Week" follow-up activities. (optional)
2. Look ahead to the scripture passage and the theme of the next session. Decide on a time during the upcoming week when you will read the chapter.
3. Participate in the Closing Prayer.

DURING THE WEEK

Look over the week ahead. Identify the best time for you to pray each day. Start with at least twenty minutes, or more if it takes longer to unwind. Use the following scripture passages as texts, or others of your own choice.

Psalm 23	Isaiah 49:1–6
Psalm 139	Isaiah 52:13–15
Jeremiah 3:1–25	Isaiah 53:1–12

Follow the five rules of prayer, plus any other methods that have been helpful to you through the years. Be flexible. Be loved. Be at peace.

10. Call to Justice and Proclamation

Scripture Passage

Jeremiah, chapters 15–20: **A profile of Jeremiah's career: he listens closely to the Lord's complaints, vents complaints of his own, and issues predictions of doom through words and symbols.**

PRAYER

Introduction: A Note on the Text

Leader: Prophetic writings make up a large portion of the Hebrew scriptures. God's revelation comes to us in this form because, after a time of growth and prosperity, the Israelites found themselves caught up in world class struggles. How did politics fit with their special role as God's people? Different people had differing answers to this question and many voices were raised. Conflict was common, both with the surrounding nations and within the Israelite leadership. As we saw in the case of Amos, anyone who was called to speak out could expect personal conflict. This was even more true of Jeremiah.

Our passage for prayer is the heart-rending prayer of Jeremiah, who struggles to rid himself of the burden of his call. His recounting of the spiritual power of feeling his lips touched with the hand of the Lord (1:9) leaves no doubt of his dedication. Chapters 2–19 are filled with incidents of the energy he poured into his task. But at the point of his prayer here, he is wary of conflict and pleads that God will deal directly with his enemies. The passage puts us in mind of the psalmist's lament, and of our own in the face of misunderstanding. The final verses recover that sense of balance that we strive toward as we wend our way through this "vale of tears."

Call to Prayer

Leader: Let us quietly draw our energies within, recalling the strong call of God who moves and guides us. (Music, song, or a gathering gesture may be used.)

Reading

Reader: A reading from the book of Jeremiah (20:7–13).

You duped me, O LORD, and I let myself be duped;
    you were too strong for me, and you triumphed.
All the day I am an object of laughter;
    everyone mocks me.
Whenever I speak, I must cry out,
    violence and outrage in my message;
The word of the LORD has brought me
    derision and reproach all the day.
I say to myself, I will not mention him.
    I will speak in his name no more.
But then it becomes like fire burning in my heart,
    imprisoned in my bones; I grow weary holding it in,
I cannot endure it.
    Yes, I hear the whisperings of many:
    "Terror on every side! Denounce! let us denounce him!"
All those who were my friends
    are on the watch for any misstep of mine.
"Perhaps he will be trapped; then we can prevail,
    and take our vengeance on him."
But the LORD is with me, like a mighty champion;
    my persecutors will stumble, they will not triumph.
In their failure they will be put to utter shame,
    to lasting, unforgettable confusion.
O LORD of hosts, you who test the just,
    who probe mind and heart,
Let me witness the vengeance you take on them,
    for to you I have entrusted my cause.
Sing to the LORD,
    praise the LORD,

For he has rescued the life of the poor
from the power of the wicked!

Individual Reflection

Leader: As I have tried to discern and do God's will, when have I found myself in trouble or in conflict with others? Take a few moments to recall any situations where you have had to take a stand for something you believed in. (All pause for silent reflection.)

Prayer

All: Lord our God, you probe our minds and hearts and call us to your service. At times your call becomes too much for us, when others turn against us because we are true to your call. Make your name burn in our hearts and be with us in moments of testing. Amen.

LESSON

Jeremiah Endures Considerable Conflict During the Years of his Ministry

The scriptures have many incidents which make it clear that God's people did not always live up to the ideal. To be faithful to the covenant, God needed to keep the people in a right relationship with themselves, with their God and their neighbors. At times the people drifted into life-styles which gave priority to themselves rather than to God. Such times required a special summons to return to a covenant relationship. At such times, certain people developed a keen sense of justice, of the disparity between God's design and the ways of their people. Even though it meant considerable conflict, they spoke out clearly for the sake of justice. The life of the prophet Jeremiah is a good example of a human being who never lost sight of the vision of the kind of world to which God invited the people by covenant. His inspired words have come down to us in one of the longest books of the Bible (52 chapters).

Jeremiah's formation occurred in a religious household, for his father was a priest. The moment of his call (Jer 1:4–10) was one of transformation, that set him on a long course of 45 years of public life and prophesying. He lived at a time when his people were caught up in a moment of world history which saw the clash of the mighty superpowers, Assyria, Egypt and Babylonia. It was a time when many religious leaders in Israel laid claim to the gift of prophecy as they attempted to influence their kings to capitalize on this moment of strife to bring Israel to a position of power.

Early in his life we find Jeremiah at home in powerful court circles since his beliefs supported the reforms which King Josiah was implementing. At this time, his conflicts were with the idolatry and injustices of his people, so he confronted them with impassioned reminders of the Exodus covenant. Later, when the political scene changed, unlike the false prophets who changed their preaching to fit the fortunes of war, Jeremiah scorned the switch of allegiance to new rulers and new gods. Though a coalition of religious leaders might have been able to influence the course of events, Jeremiah would not compromise.

> I have heard the prophets who prophesy lies in my name say,
> "I had a dream! I had a dream!" How long will this continue?
> Is my name in the hearts of the prophets who prophesy lies
> and their own deceitful fancies? (23:25–26).

Sensitive to the ways and memories of his people, he used persuasive parables and actions to get across his points:

> This message came to me from the LORD: Do not marry any
> woman; you shall not have sons and daughters in this place,
> for . . . sword and famine will make an end of them (16:1–2: 4).

> Indeed, like clay in the hand of the potter, so are you in my
> hand, house of Israel (18:6).

> And you shall break the flask, in the sight of the men who
> went with you, and say to them: Thus says the LORD of hosts:
> Thus I will smash this people and this city, as one smashes a
> clay pot so that it cannot be repaired (19:10–11).

All through the book, we find strong cries of personal pain from a man struggling to be faithful to the call in spite of the constant conflict in which he finds himself. At times his conflict seems not to be with the people, or with the kings, but with his God. Only an unwavering spiritual sense could sustain him over the many years of his mission. Somehow he found energy to continue a ministry of discernment and preaching through years of terrible times for his people. When he was called in 627 B.C., the kingdom of Judah was still strong; by 582 B.C.

the Babylonian invaders had demolished Jerusalem, not once but twice.

An Analysis of Conflict from a Spiritual Perspective

The activity of discernment comes about when we bring our Christian values to bear on our decisions, whether of the day-to-day variety, or of those which have far-ranging significance. Frequently such decisions involve us in conflict situations, because it's unusual that all of the significant persons in our community, whether family or associates, agree with our decision. We find people coming down on one side or the other, and not at all shy about voicing their opinions. Somehow, no matter how much we pray or try to grow spiritually, everything seems to go out the window when we find ourselves in a conflict situation. We end up feeling vulnerable, emotionally drained, and inadequate. Do we simply "offer it up for the poor souls in purgatory"? How can conflicts be integrated into a spiritual journey?

In her book, *The Transformation of Man,* Rosemary Haughton devotes her introductory chapter to an in-depth analysis of a quarrel between two children and the way it is handled by their mother. She points out that, for a spiritual observer, there is a great deal more to such ordinary "fights" than is apparent on the surface. Each of us goes along from day to day, following our own little agenda with its personal goals and frustrations blending into a kind of "emotional soup." We're usually not conscious of this until someone confronts us with a situation in which two different temperaments clash. Often a violent emotion leaps to the surface to defend against the threat to the self, and the sudden contrast forces us to see ourselves in a new light.

Haughton describes this a "flashpoint of self-discovery." How this key moment is handled can lead to different results. Two possible methods result in formation, while the third leads to transformation.

First, if the two children fight it out until the stronger one wins, they'll get over it, but the feelings aren't resolved, only hidden where they continue to churn around. It may happen that the winner becomes the scapegoat for what is really "bugging" the loser. Because they are gradually acquiring interaction skills which are socially acceptable, on the surface they appear to be getting along.

A second solution occurs when, irritated that the peace of the household is being disturbed, the children's mother may intervene. She may listen to both sides, scold, require apologies, or even punish. Peace (as the absence of conflict) is restored. This type of intervention puts the children's feelings off onto an authority figure, but usually makes them feel it was "fair." The mother feels she has done her duty by instilling good behavior patterns. Both of these possible methods of dealing with conflict provide formation towards responsible action in community.

Finally, a third possible method would occur when a mother who is more sensitive recognizes the potential for growth in this seemingly negative release of emotional energy. She is able to help the two children lower the barriers that divide them because her extra sensitivity somehow conveys to them a sense that she appreciates the feelings that give rise to the disagreement. Her words and actions center on their feelings, which enable the children to be together peacefully once more, but in a manner which repents of having hurt the other. The acknowledgment of the hurt feelings releases an inner power which resolves them and somehow transforms both children. Once again at a deeper level, the family is a peaceful community, at least for the time being.

Haughton recognizes the need for *both* formation and transformation. She emphasizes: "The occurrence of the point of transformation can be called the salvation event, and in my example this occurrence clearly depends on the mother's success in reaching the 'spiritual' reality of the two children and communicating with it. This communication, then, is her giving of love, her personal decision of self-surrender" (p. 32). She also acknowledges: "Her success in reaching each child, in achieving a communication that will enable the children to reach each other, will depend on the kind of formation *they* (already) had" (p. 33).

Justice As Grounds for Facing Conflict

How does this example of a children's quarrel help us think about a more spiritual approach to dealing with conflict? As adults, we need to focus on the mother, about whom Haughton comments: "Unless her own formation has taught her to think of herself as primarily at the service of her children, spiritually as well as physically, she will not have the kind of 'feel' for the situation that makes possible the lowering of barriers, so that the communication of love can take place" (p. 32). From this we see that our first step is to "get our head on straight"—to think of ourselves as servants.

Take a few moments to consider a situation in which you find yourself in conflict. What is your role in the group? Are these people and projects you care about? In what respect do you see yourself as a servant to others in the group? Is there a spiritual aspect to the relationship? What is there about the situation which demands your involvement in conflict?

Your ability to take a spiritual view of a conflict situation will depend a great deal on your responses to these questions. Your role may be that of a boss over persons who are in conflict, or you yourself may be one of the parties to the conflict. A variety of psychological motivations may further complicate the situation: determination to push through a project to its completion; friction of ambitious associates; agreement on the goal, but not on the means to achieve it; a vacuum of leadership.

The key question is: What in this situation demands that I get involved, even if it means conflict? Usually it is because we are convinced that we are right. From a spiritual perspective, to be "right" means that we are seeking justice. Let's take a closer look at the notion of justice as its scriptural meaning is described in *Economic Justice for All*, the 1986 Pastoral Letter of the United States Bishops:

> Justice has many nuances. Fundamentally, it suggests a sense of what is right or of what should happen. For example, paths are just when they bring you to your destination (Gn 24:48, Ps 23:3), and laws are just when they create harmony within the community, as Isaiah says: "Justice will bring about peace; right will produce calm and security" (Is 32:17). God is "just" by acting as God should, coming to the people's aid and summoning them to conversion when they stray. People are summoned to be "just," that is, to be in a proper relation to God, by observing God's laws which form them into a faithful community. Biblical justice is more comprehensive than subsequent philosophical definitions. It is not concerned with a strict definition of rights and duties, but with the rightness of the human condition before God and within society. Nor is justice opposed to love; rather, it is both a manifestation of love and a condition for love to grow. Because God loves Israel, he rescues them from oppression and summons them to be a people that "does justice" and loves kindness. The quest for justice arises from loving gratitude for the saving acts of God and manifests itself in wholehearted love of God and neighbor. (39)

Notice that "fair" isn't the same as "just." We Americans find our tempers rise quickly when things aren't "fair" to us, or even to someone we regard as "the underdog." We're not so quick to grasp God's viewpoint of justice. In the face of an unfair situation, some people have a natural tendency to flare up and speak up. Others want to smooth things over and avoid conflict at all costs. Both of these attitudes have a great deal to do with our upbringing, our observation as to how significant people in our lives solved conflict situations. Not too many people have had the advantage of a Rosemary Haughton analysis to help their formation/transformation! But each of us can learn from the prophet that the first step is to discern what is just from God's standpoint, while the second step is proclamation, speaking up on behalf of those who are truly oppressed.

DISCUSSION

A. Take a few minutes to complete these sentences. Do it quickly, jotting down the first thoughts that occur to you.
   1. When someone criticizes a decision I've made to my face in front of others, I usually . . .
   2. When I get angry, I . . .
   3. When I think about confronting an unpleasant situation, I . . .
   4. When I try to negotiate, I . . .
   5. I am most likely to assert myself in situations that . . .
B. Discuss your responses with a partner. What is your basic style in dealing with conflict? How can you improve on your style?

BREAK

Enjoy refreshments and each other's company.

WRAP-UP

1. Look ahead to the "During the Week" follow-up activities. (optional)
2. Look ahead to the scripture passage and the theme of the next session. Decide on a time during the upcoming week when you will read the chapter.
3. Participate in the Closing Prayer.

DURING THE WEEK

1. Read the following passages from the book of Jeremiah, noting down indications of conflict or his reaction to conflict:

   Jer 1:4–10   The Call of Jeremiah
   Jer 26:1–19   The Temple Sermon
   Jer 15:10–21   Jeremiah's Complaint
   Jer 18:18–23   Jeremiah's Prayer
   Jer 20:7–18   Jeremiah's Crisis
   Jer 31:1–26   Good News of the Return

2. Describe an incident from your own life where you felt you must take a stand even though it meant conflict. How did you get through it? As you look back, how do you view the outcome?

11. Call to Repentance

Scripture Passage

The book of Jonah: **Long considered a "whale of a tale," this is one fish story where the one who didn't get away was Jonah. Note:** Before beginning the prayer, look over the reading, which is printed to indicate specific parts for different characters. Assign these roles and allow a few moments for the readers to familiarize themselves with the text.

PRAYER

Introduction: A Note on the Text

Leader: Although Jonah is considered one of the twelve minor prophets, the book is actually more of a satire on prophets, a short narrative which pokes fun at them while making a point. We can situate many of the prophets (Jeremiah, for example) in a particular time of Israel's history by matching historical references to words of reform. With Jonah, however, the tension arises not from history but rather from the human condition. The book uses a series of purposely exaggerated divine interventions to make the point that God is God and that Jonah (and other humans who flee from God) simply are not able to understand the way things really are. Jonah is a comic-tragic hero. He is comic because he plays a straight role against the outrageous events of being transported by a fish, being upstaged by a powerful pagan king, and finally done in by the wilting of a leafy tree. Yet, he is tragic as well in that he misses the point.

We will use the whole of this brief book for our prayer, using the form of a dramatic reading to help ourselves enter into the movement of God's call and Jonah's response.

99

Call to Prayer

Leader: Let us quiet our minds and hearts in order to be open to the inner meaning of the word of God to us today. (Music, song, or a gathering gesture may be used.)

Reading

Reader: A reading from the book of Jonah (1:1–4:10).

Narrator: This is the word of the LORD that came to Jonah, son of Amittai:

Lord: Set out for the great city of Nineveh, and preach against it; their wickedness has come up before me.

Narrator: But Jonah made ready to flee to Tarshish away from the LORD. He went down to Joppa, found a ship going to Tarshish, paid the fare, and went aboard to journey with them to Tarshish, away from the LORD.

The LORD, however, hurled a violent wind upon the sea, and in the furious tempest that arose the ship was on the point of breaking up. Then the mariners became frightened and each one cried to his god. To lighten the ship for themselves, they threw its cargo into the sea. Meanwhile, Jonah had gone down into the hold of the ship, and lay there fast asleep. The captain came to him and said:

Reader 1: "What are you doing asleep? Rise up, call upon your God! Perhaps God will be mindful of us so that we may not perish."

Narrator: Then they said to one another:

All: "Come, let us cast lots to find out on whose account we have met with this misfortune."

Narrator: So they cast lots, and thus singled out Jonah.

All: "Tell us, what is your business? Where do you come from? What is your country, and to what people do you belong?"

Jonah: "I am a Hebrew." "I worship the LORD, the God of heaven, who made the sea and the dry land."

Narrator: Now the men were seized with great fear. . . . They knew that he was fleeing from the LORD, because he had told them.

All: "What shall we do with you that the sea may quiet down for us?"

Narrator: For the sea was growing more and more turbulent. Jonah said to them:

Jonah: "Pick me up and throw me into the sea, that it may quiet down for you; since I know it is because of me that this violent storm has come upon you."

Narrator: Still the men rowed hard to regain the land, but they could not, for the sea grew ever more turbulent. Then they cried to the LORD:

All: "We beseech you, O LORD, let us not perish for taking this man's life; do not charge us with shedding innocent blood, for you LORD, have done as you saw fit."

Narrator: Then they took Jonah and threw him into the sea, and the sea's raging abated. [Slight pause.]

Struck with great fear of the LORD, the men offered sacrifice and made vows to him.

But the LORD sent a large fish, that swallowed Jonah; and he remained in the belly of the fish three days and three nights.

From the belly of the fish Jonah said this prayer to the LORD, his God:

Jonah: Out of my distress I called to the LORD,
   and he answered me;
From the midst of the nether world I cried for help,
   and you heard my voice.
For you cast me into the deep, into the heart of the sea,
   and the flood enveloped me;
All your breakers and your billows
   passed over me.
Then I said, "I am banished from your sight!
   yet would I again look upon your holy temple."
The waters swirled about me, threatening my life;
   the abyss enveloped me;
   seaweed clung about my head.

> Down I went to the roots of the mountains;
> the bars of the nether world
> were closing behind me forever,
> But you brought my life up from the pit,
> O LORD, my God.
> When my soul fainted within me,
> I remembered the LORD.
> My prayer reached you
> in your holy temple.
> Those who worship vain idols
> forsake their source of mercy.
> But I, with resounding praise,
> will sacrifice to you;
> What I have vowed I will pay:
> deliverance is from the LORD.

Narrator: Then the LORD commanded the fish to spew Jonah upon the shore. [Pause.]

The word of the LORD came to Jonah a second time:

Lord: "Set out for the great city of Nineveh, and announce to it the message that I will tell you."

Narrator: So Jonah made ready and went to Nineveh, according to the LORD's bidding. Now Nineveh was an enormously large city; it took three days to go through it. Jonah began his journey through the city, and had gone but a single day's walk announcing:

Jonah: Forty days more and Nineveh shall be destroyed,

Narrator: When the people of Nineveh believed God; they proclaimed a fast and all of them, great and small, put on sackcloth.

When the news reached the king of Nineveh, he rose from his throne, laid aside his robe, covered himself with sackcloth, and sat in the ashes. Then he had this proclaimed throughout Nineveh, by decree of the king and his nobles:

King: "Neither man nor beast, neither cattle nor sheep, shall taste anything; they shall not eat, nor shall they drink water. Man and beast shall be covered with sackcloth and call loudly to God; every man shall turn from his evil way, and from the violence he has in hand. Who knows, God may relent and forgive, and withhold his blazing wrath, so that we shall not perish."

Narrator: When God saw by their actions how they turned from their evil way, he repented of the evil that he had threatened to do to them; he did not carry it out.

But this was greatly displeasing to Jonah, and he became angry.

Jonah: "I beseech you, LORD, is not this what I said while I was still in my own country? This is why I fled at first to Tarshish. I knew that you are a gracious and merciful God, slow to anger, rich in clemency, loathe to punish. And now, LORD, please take my life from me, for it is better for me to die than to live."

Narrator: But the LORD asked:

Lord: "Have you reason to be angry?"

Narrator: Jonah then left the city for a place to the east of it, where he built himself a hut and waited under it in the shade, to see what would happen to the city. And when the LORD God provided a gourd plant, that grew up over Jonah's head, giving shade that relieved him of any discomfort, Jonah was very happy over the plant. But the next morning at dawn God sent a worm which attacked the plant, so that it withered. And when the sun arose, God sent a burning east wind; and the sun beat upon Jonah's head until he became faint. Then he asked for death, saying:

Jonah: "I would be better off dead than alive."

Narrator: But God said to Jonah:

Lord: "Have you reason to be angry over the plant?"

Narrator: Jonah answered:

Jonah: "I have reason to be angry. Angry enough to die!"

Narrator: Then the LORD said:

Lord: "You are concerned over the plant which cost you no labor and which you did not raise; it came up in one night and in one night it perished. And should I not be concerned over Nineveh, the great city, in which there are more than a

hundred and twenty thousand persons who
cannot distinguish their right hand from their
left, not to mention the many cattle?"

Individual Reflection

Leader: As our lives move along, we develop a game plan and
resist persons and events which force us to reconsider, to adapt. Like
Jonah, I find myself angry with God because things don't turn out the
way they "should." What events in my life have caused me to "make
ready to flee away from the Lord"? To what extent has my personal
agenda prevented me from coming to a better sense of God's designs?
Let me honestly answer God's question to me: "Have you reason to be
angry?"

Prayer

All: God our Creator, you alone understand the course of the
universe and direct all things to ultimate glory. I praise you for your
infinite wisdom and care. As I enter more deeply into your mystery
through prayer and study, help me to grasp more fully what it is that
you ask of me and to have the courage to set aside all that separates me
from you. Amen.

LESSON

The Points of the Plot

What can we make of this book? The story has usually been told
around the fish as the most fantastic feature, but we also notice the
plant which grows and whithers within twenty-four hours. Centuries
later, it doesn't seem significant, but had we been among the Jews who
were first to hear the tale, we would have regarded the fact that the
Ninevites repented as equally unimaginable. It would also strike us as
ironic that the pagan sailors pray while the pious Jew neglects to call
upon God. All these implausible features make it evident that the
author is needling us.

When we go back and take a closer look, we see that God and
Jonah are the main characters in a two act play. In Act 1, Scene 1,
God's command that Jonah preach to the Ninevites is immediately
followed by Jonah quietly making his escape, only to be followed by

God stirring up such a storm that Jonah is forced to admit that he is the cause of probable shipwreck for his companions. At this point, Jonah looks like the stereotypical prophet, for the sea does indeed calm, and the pagans are indeed converted.

Scene 2 brings another round between God and Jonah. Now God takes the initiative, sending a large fish to rescue his intended prophet. Finally, it seems that Jonah does repent, for at least we find him praying. To this effort God responds by putting the discomfited Jonah right back where he started.

Act 2 starts out just as Act 1 did, with God commanding Jonah to go to Nineveh. This time it seems that Jonah has profited from the crisis and is converted, for he does as God directs. And, wonder of wonders! Once on the streets of Nineveh, not only does Jonah's simple announcement convince the people, but their own ruler reinforces the message both by his own actions and also by issuing an edict requiring compliance with God's request. Through the author's anthropological style, we learn that God "repents" and does not punish the Ninevites.

It seems as though the drama should end on this happy note; however, like life, the book goes on to a final scene which gives us further insight into Jonah's character. Is he happy because his gutsy obedience has resulted in a successful mission? No—he is angry. In his heart of hearts he is so prejudiced against the wicked oppressors of his countrymen that he actually wanted them to be punished. He knew all along it was a waste of time to expect that a gracious God would wreak vengeance. He has wasted his time and energy. If God wants to be that kind of God, once again he would like to go overboard, but this time he doesn't want a fish to rescue him. He simply wants to get away and find a real god instead of a wimp.

Yet, gentle God simply asks him to reconsider. So Jonah gives God another chance; he builds a hut and waits to see if God will do as stated in his prophetic announcement and destroy the hated enemy. Once again God provides rescue for Jonah, this time by means of a tree whose leafy branches provide shelter. Jonah becomes so distracted by the beauty of the plant that he fails to get the larger picture; he literally can't see the forest for the tree. Presently, God recalls that Jonah came around better by suffering than by safety, so he causes the tree to wither, then adds insult to injury by sending hot, searing winds. Once again, God does not rail at this recalcitrant prophet, but simply raises questions. The ending isn't satisfying. As the story stops, we don't know Jonah's answer, but we know quite a bit about Jonah.

We saw Jonah play the coward, running away from the difficult task. Yet he was extremely resourceful, having not only a getaway plan but also money at hand to carry it off. Once his mind was made up, he didn't look back. So settled was he in his decision that he even fell asleep in the midst of a storm! He had developed a strong religious philosophy with the expectation that God would behave in a certain way, so he prayed accordingly. Jonah's point of view was clearly self-centered since he put his own expectations and comfort ahead of broader-based humanitarian concerns. He showed a stubborn streak, not willing to listen to God, not willing to follow a train of thought in an unexpected direction.

What is the underlying point of the plot? God wants human beings to repent, to recognize that our ways of doing things stand under divine scrutiny and that it is possible that we are wrong and need to change our ways. Did Jonah repent? He did do as God asked. He hung in there with his questions, even while nursing his wounded pride. Was he converted at heart? We simply don't know. The author allows us to come up with our own ending, because the point of the story is to examine our own willingness to repent.

Giving Up the Merely Human Viewpoint

What do we mean by repentance? It's a change, **from** one set of attitudes **to** another. Repentance occurs when we come to a moment of truth, when we recognize that because our point of view is limited, our perception is either inaccurate or incomplete. We could recall Marius Pontmercy of Victor Hugo's novel, *Les Miserables,* who judged Jean Valjean to be a deceitful criminal worthy of scorn. Once he learned that it was this same man who had heroically rescued him from death, he completely reversed his opinion and brought about reconciliation and reunion.

Spiritual repentance takes place at another plane. We recognize that there is more to life than meets the eye. On a human level we usually don't have all the information possible, so we simply move ahead according to our best assessment of the facts at hand. Like Marius, once we know more, we change our opinion. On a spiritual level, we acknowledge a higher power, a God who continues to create, to infuse people with energy toward good. Spiritual repentance occurs when we allow God's universal perspective to replace our particular viewpoint. We relinquish previously held beliefs in favor of new directions. It is a painful moment. Even though we know deep down that God is God and we are human, it **hurts.** Our intellectual insight prompts emotional reactions of confusion and shame. We want to change.

Some people experience a great moment of conversion, often associated with a time of crisis. We think of the classic case of Augustine who, after hearing the words, "Take and read," took up Paul's letter to the Romans (13:13–14) and completely changed his life. We think of persons who join Alcoholics Anonymous and, allowing a higher power to move them, never take another drink. Such stories make it clear that conversion is irrevocable; there is no looking back. Once converted, the person never loses sight of the fact that God is God and we are human. Repentance is the first step toward conversion, when we not only change our viewpoint, but go on to change our lives.

Even though we are inwardly convinced of this reality, we also recognize that we must live our lives within human limitations, so are not surprised when we (and others) don't always respond as we "should." Much of our formation comes from social and cultural sources, rather than from revealed sources, so we often misinterpret the "right" thing to do. Jonah saw no point in seeking the conversion of the Ninevites since he had been taught and had come to believe that his God resided in Israel and acted only for the Israelites.

It's easy for us to pick on Jonah, but what of us? We take our surroundings for granted. It's natural to gravitate toward people who have the same viewpoint as we do, so we can't easily be objective about life's situations. We are acculturated, formed by society to fit in. We have a constant need to question our values, to compare our twentieth-century American perspective to the eternal perspective of God's revealed truth. Repentance and spiritual growth will be given to us as we willingly submit our human values to God's scrutiny.

REFLECTION AND DISCUSSION

1. Take a few moments to complete several of these open-ended sentences, being as honest as possible as to how the particular condition indicated by brackets dictates certain attitudes:
   a) [sex] Because I'm a man, I . . . —or—Because I'm a woman, I . . .
   b) [nationality] Because I'm an American, I . . .
   c) [race/ethnicity] Because I'm Black/Irish/Mexican, I . . .
   d) [job/role] Because I'm a housewife/salesperson/manager (etc.), I . . .

e) [status] Because I'm a committee chair/eucharistic minister
   (etc.), I . . .
2. Discuss your responses with a partner. To what extent do our acculturated attitudes fit in with God's intentions for our world?
   Where am I in need of conversion?

BREAK

Enjoy refreshments and each other's company.

WRAP-UP

1. Look ahead to the "During the Week" follow-up activities.
   (optional)
2. Look ahead to the scripture passage and the theme of the next
   session. Decide on a time during the upcoming week when you will
   read chapter 12.
3. Participate in the Closing Prayer.

DURING THE WEEK

1. Since only you can change yourself, write your own homily to yourself. Refer to the list of socially acceptable viewpoints in the Re-
   flection/Discussion section. Choose one which is a problem for you.
   Prepare a five-minute talk, using the following outline:
   a) A story drawn from life experience which shows how culturally
      formed and socially acceptable attitudes have the potential to
      affect other people in a hurting manner. (2 minutes)
   b) A scripture passage which shows that we need to change this
      socially conditioned attitude to fit God's viewpoint. (2 minutes)
   c) A summary of your message about our need for conversion. (1
      minute)
2. The role of the prophets was to call the people to repentance. As we
   saw in Chapter 10, the prophet Jeremiah felt his own need for
   repentance. Examine the following passages from the book of Jeremiah, asking yourself:
   a) What is Jeremiah's human viewpoint?

b) Imagine God's viewpoint on this subject. In what way does Jeremiah need to experience repentance to come to God's viewpoint?

c) Do I need this type of conversion?
   PASSAGES: Jeremiah 12:1–5; Jeremiah 15:10–21; Jeremiah 18:19–23

3. Pray the prayer of Jeremiah 17:14.

12. Call to Abandonment

Scripture Passage

Job 29–42: **A three-way debate: Job states his case, his friend Elihu angrily challenges him, and finally, God speaks. Note:** Before beginning the prayer, it would be helpful to look ahead to the reading and assign four parts: Narrator, Job, Elihu, and God.

PRAYER

Introduction: A Note on the Text

Leader: The book of Job is one of the Wisdom books of the Hebrew scriptures. It was written at a time in their history (7th–5th century B.C.) when they had suffered much—war, invasion, deportation and finally, exile. Composed in poetic dialogue, it is the story of an extremely wealthy and morally blameless man, Job, who loses nearly everything he has except a wavering faith in God. When his wise friends insist that his suffering is the result of his sin (a common theological belief at the time), and urge him to repent, Job answers them that he is innocent. They can only conclude that their friend is a hypocrite and a blasphemer.

Finally, at the end of the story, God and Job have it out. God tells Job that it is useless to try to understand divine ways, for when we do that we make ourselves greater than God. Job then realizes his mistake and repents, after which his fortunes are restored.

Although the book of Job gives us a mature look at the problem of evil and suffering, the lesson is still incomplete. It was necessary for God to send Jesus to help us understand the fuller meaning of suffering.

Call to Prayer

Leader: Let us reflect on the dialogue between Job and his God. (Pause. Music, song, or a gathering gesture may be used.)

Reading

Reader: A reading from the book of Job (29:1–3; 16–17; 20–21; 25).

Narrator:	Job took up his theme anew and said:
Job:	Oh, that I were as in the months past!
	as in the days when God watched over me,
	While he kept his lamp shining above my head,
	and by his light I walked through darkness . . .
	I was a father to the needy;
	the rights of the stranger I studied,
	And I broke the jaws of the wicked man;
	from his teeth I forced the prey.
	My glory is fresh within me,
	and my bow is renewed in my hand!
	For me they listened and waited;
	they were silent for my counsel . . .
	Mourners took comfort from my cheerful glance.
	I chose out their way and presided;
	I took a king's place in the armed forces . . .
Narrator:	Then the three men ceased to answer Job, because he was righteous in his own eyes. But the anger of Elihu . . . was kindled. He was angry with Job for considering himself rather than God to be in the right. He was angry also with the three friends because they had not found a good answer and had not condemned Job. . . . his wrath was inflamed. So Elihu, son of Barachel the Buzite, spoke out and said:
Elihu:	I am young and you are very old;
	therefore I held back and was afraid
	to declare to you my knowledge. . . .
	But it is a spirit in man,
	the breath of the Almighty, that gives him understanding . . .

Hearken to this, O Job!
Stand and consider the wondrous works of God!

God: Then the LORD addressed Job out of the storm
and said:
Who is this that obscures divine plans
with words of ignorance?
Gird up your loins now, like a man;
I will question you, and you tell me the answers!
Where were you when I founded the earth?
Tell me, if you have understanding.
Who determined its size; do you know?
Who stretched out the measuring line for it?
Into what were its pedestals sunk,
and who laid the cornerstone . . .
And who shut within doors the sea,
when it burst forth from the womb? . . .
Have you ever in your lifetime commanded the
morning
and shown the dawn its place?
For taking hold of the ends of the earth,
till the wicked are shaken from its surface? . . .

Narrator: Then Job answered the LORD and said:

Job: Behold, I am of little account; what can I answer
you?
I put my hand over my mouth.
Though I have spoken once, I will not do so again;
though twice, I will do so no more.
I know that you can do all things,
and that no purpose of yours can be hindered.
I have dealt with great things that I do not
understand;
things too wonderful for me, which I cannot
know.
I had heard of you by word of mouth,
but now my eye has seen you.
Therefore I disown what I have said,
and repent in dust and ashes.

Narrator: And it came to pass after the LORD had spoken
these words to Job, that . . . the LORD restored the prosperity of Job, after he had
prayed for his friends; the LORD even gave to
Job twice as much as he had before.

Individual Reflection

Leader: Each human being must discover for himself or herself a theology of suffering, and through the ages the book of Job has been an excellent starting point. Having reflected last week on repentance, let us now move to the next step of turning everything over to God. As we try to make Job's sentiments our own, let us repeat softly to ourselves, over and over, "My Lord and my God, I abandon myself into your hands."

Prayer

All: O Lord, my God,
Forever and always, your ways are not mine,
    and my ways are not yours.
Especially is this true, O Lord, when it comes
    to my suffering, disappointments, pain, and, yes, my sinfulness.
Give me, I pray, not only the patience of Job,
    but also his faith in you, his hope that we will see you
    and his loving longing for you. Amen.

LESSON

The Wisdom Writers Tackle the Problem of Evil

Our consideration of the prophets brought us face-to-face with our need to get a handle on the right relationships with God, ourselves, and our world. The very concept of repentance implies that God's view is the universal one, and we humans cannot be peaceful until we bring ourselves into harmony with God. But is it possible to know God's view? Our Catholic faith assures us that it is, and that the Bible helps us to do so, for the bishops of the Second Vatican Council declared:

> Therefore, since everything asserted by the inspired authors or sacred writers must be said to be asserted by the Holy Spirit, it follows that the books of Scripture must be acknowledged as teaching firmly, faithfully, and without error that truth which God wanted to put into the sacred writings for the sake of our salvation." (*Dogmatic Constitution on Divine Revelation,* #11)

The story of Job is our story. Each one of us must sooner or later come to terms with the problem of suffering in our lives. "Why did this happen to me or to someone I love?" Since most of us are not as innocent as Job, the next question is: "Is God punishing me for my sins?" Sometimes this question is followed by: "If God is so good, how can God permit such an evil thing to happen?" And finally, for many people, as if it is a logical consequence to the above statement: "Therefore, God does not exist."

We all know people who have gone through this process. It is easy enough to criticize them for their lack of logic or even for their lack of faith, but rarely does that do any good because of the emotional intensity of the problem of suffering. What can we say to a little girl whose mother is dying of cancer? She and her uncle, a priest, were sitting outside the Intensive Care Unit of the hospital. The child was trying to muster enough courage to go in and see her mother perhaps for the last time. And then came the big question, the one that has been asked for thousands of years, "Why?" "Why Mom?"

The priest, whose tears had mingled with those of his niece for what seemed to be hours, all of a sudden became defensive. The wisdom of his "Boss" was being questioned. And, in so many words, he reminded the girl that her mother was human, and human beings are vulnerable, prone to accidents and sickness, and they die sooner or later. In a sense, God has nothing to do with it—that's just the way the Creator made us. Would she want it any differently? Would she rather be a robot or an animal? To his amazement, she answered, "Yes." At this point she did not want to be human. It wasn't so much that she wanted to be an animal or a robot, but rather she wanted to be divine. She wanted to live forever.

The priest had led many funeral services, so he was acutely aware that his faith had an answer to this deep human longing. By his death and resurrection, eternal life was exactly what Jesus promised us. The priest was about to share his insight with her when he admitted to himself that he had said too much already, too many words, too many wrong words, and so he decided to let his tears do the talking.

God too seems to have decided to wait until the human race gained more maturity before providing us with the fullness of revelation in Jesus. Like the little girl who wasn't ready for this answer, God's people needed to "grow up" in their faith. In our study over the last eleven weeks, we have tried to learn more about the truths that the Hebrew scriptures present. These scriptures are divided into three parts: the Law, the Prophets, and the Writings. The book of Job stands first in the category of the Writings, or Wisdom books, although it has much in common with the prophets of the Exile, Ezekiel and Jeremiah, and much of it is in poetic form, like another Wisdom book, the Psalms. The Wisdom books take what we might regard as the "conventional wisdom" and recast it in the light of the faith of the Israelites as it had developed over the years between Abraham and the Exile.

Unlike the author of the book of Jonah, the writer of the book of Job does not leave us hanging. His literary technique was to use the dramatic confrontation of persons with sharply diverging views to bring forward several solutions to the intractable problem of evil. In the final dialogue between God and Job, the inspired author tips his hand about his preferred solution. Job "solves" the problem of all the suffering which has been given to him in spite of his averred innocence by simply abandoning his own limited views of the situation and acknowledging that it's up to God to call the shots.

Anyone who is seeking to follow a spiritual path recognizes that this truly tough question has been around for a long time before Job and has continued to plague us even after many people have read and pondered the Job response. Scholars have actually coined the term **theodicy** to describe the problem of God's relation to the innocent person who suffers evil. Jewish theologians who have tried to explain the Holocaust have been led back to Job's solution simply because no other seems to be adequate.

Contemporary Approaches to Dealing with Human Limits

Whether we take the philosophical approach or the theological approach to the problem of suffering, we will always come up short. The human mind and soul are just not capable of comprehending such a mystery. But that doesn't mean that we shouldn't try. Actually, many people have tried and have found enough answers, enough truth, to help them rise above their sufferings. By studying the behavior of human beings through psychology and sociology, then considering our findings in the light of revelation, we can learn a great deal about productive spiritual ways of living with suffering. The interesting thing about the two approaches which are described below is that they either begin or end with Job's solution: surrender or abandonment.

In 1969, Dr. Kubler-Ross wrote about five basic stages that most people go through as they face impending death. These stages apply

equally to people who try to deal with hurt, suffering and wounded-
ness of any kind:

1. A tendency to *deny* we have been hurt—simply to refuse to see the
   problem at all.
2. The stage of *anger*—blaming everyone else and taking consolation
   in anger and resentment.
3. The stage of *bargaining*—playing "Let's Make a Deal" with God,
   saints, doctors, etc.
4. The stage of *depression*—turning the anger into ourselves and
   blaming ourselves for letting others hurt us.
5. The stage of *acceptance*—deciding that since we cannot overcome
   the situation, we simply "die" to it, giving it over to God.

In order to move through these stages, we need to be converted—
to move from our viewpoint to God's viewpoint. It is a process of
"letting go":

1. Let go of denial. Instead, acknowledge what is happening as honestly as possible.
2. Let go of anger; instead, seek help from others so I can forgive
   myself, accept myself and then forgive and accept the other.
3. Let go of bargaining. Who are we to bargain with God? Doesn't
   that indicate a lack of faith?
4. Let go of depression; instead, do something to make amends if
   necessary.
5. Abandon yourself to God. Let God be God.

The above process ends with abandonment. Some people, in their
great suffering, begin with it. Look at the millions of people throughout the world who have dealt with the pain of alcoholism, drug addic-
tion, neurosis, and compulsions of any kind and who have found relief
when they surrendered their lives to God. The first three steps of the
famous twelve steps of Alcoholics Anonymous deal with surrender or
abandonment. Of course it is quite possible that these twelve steps
pick up where the above five stages leave off—the two processes are
not mutually exclusive.

For those who are not familiar with the Twelve Steps, they are
printed here for your inspiration:

1. We admitted that we were powerless over alcohol—that our lives
   had become unmanageable.

2. We came to believe that a Power greater than ourselves could restore us to sanity.
3. We made a decision to turn our will and our lives over to the care of God as we understand Him.
4. We made a searching and fearless moral inventory of ourselves.
5. We admitted to God, to ourselves and to another human being the exact nature of our wrongs.
6. We were entirely ready to have God remove all these defects of character.
7. We humbly asked God to remove our shortcomings.
8. We made a list of all persons we had harmed, and became willing to make amends to such people whenever possible except when to do so would injure them or others.
10. We continued to take personal inventory and when we were wrong, promptly admitted it.
11. We sought through prayer and meditation to improve our conscious contact with God as we understood Him, praying only for the knowledge of His will for us and the power to carry that out.
12. Having had a spiritual awakening as a result of these steps, we tried to carry this message to alcoholics, and to practice these principles in all our affairs.

Alcoholics Anonymous, as we can see, is a very spiritual program. For many it is a religion, for they find in AA what they never found in denominational churches. Its founders, however, never meant it to be a substitute for "organized religion," but rather a supplement to it. In our study of how the scriptures guide us spiritually, we have already seen the strong correlation between God's revelation in the Word with our own life experiences. As we move into the Christian scriptures, we can expect greater enlightenment, for the teaching and example of Jesus provide unparalleled hope and inspiration. For Catholics especially, the grace of the sacraments brings us into contact with the dying, rising Christ, and it is here that we are able to penetrate the mystery of suffering and death.

DISCUSSION

In order to make a personal commitment to the Lord, each one of us has to come to terms with suffering in our lives. We have to abandon our tendency to play God and judge what's "fair," and instead to realize that our viewpoint is pretty limited. Yet we need to find a position we can live with in faith.

A. Take a few moments to jot down what you might say in any **one** of these situations:
   1. What do you say to a man whose wife has just died of cancer, leaving him with three small children?

      or
   2. What do you say to your best friend who has just had a child with Down's syndrome?

      or
   3. What do you say to someone you know who is in a similar unresolvable situation?
B. Share your responses in a group of three persons.

BREAK

Enjoy refreshments and each other's company.

WRAP-UP

1. Look ahead to the "During the Week" follow-up activities. These are optional, but because our ingrained responses to hurts and sufferings are so crucial to our spiritual growth, the first activity is highly recommended.
2. Look ahead to the scripture passage and the theme of the next section. You may be taking a longer break before starting up your sessions again, so it would be well to make sure the date of starting again is clear to all. Someone may be designated to send out a reminder so each one can set aside a time for reading the Introduction to Part II and chapter 13.
3. Participate in the Closing Prayer.

DURING THE WEEK

1. Before beginning this exercise, we would do well to reflect on the way we ourselves deal with suffering and hurt. Take a few minutes

to think about the times in your life when you were deeply hurt, or when you knew you had deliberately hurt someone else.

Now proceed with your own self-examination. Place a check in the column that best describes how you have usually dealt with such a situation. This will not be shared with anyone, so be as honest as possible.

	usually	often	once or twice	never
1. I put myself down as a no-good	___	___	___	___
2. I brood over what happened and concentrate on my hurt, my needs, my opinion	___	___	___	___
3. I blame someone or something else	___	___	___	___
4. I make excuses to justify myself that I am right	___	___	___	___
5. I make light of what happened and say it is not important	___	___	___	___
6. I simply say it wasn't my fault	___	___	___	___
7. I "cop out" and stop trying to deal with the problem, putting my mind on other things	___	___	___	___
8. I pretend it doesn't hurt and ignore my feelings	___	___	___	___
9. I say the "right things" and hide what I really feel from others	___	___	___	___

Go back to the listing of Kubler-Ross's stages and read through them once again. Look over your responses above to see if any pattern emerges. Do you sense a need for change? Do you feel ready to change? What do you need to bring to prayer? You may try to pray by using the sentiments expressed by Father Charles de Foucald:

Father, I abandon myself into your hands; do with me what you will. Whatever you may do, I thank you: I am ready for all, I accept all. Let only your will be done in me, and in all your creatures—I wish no more than this, O Lord. Into your hands I commend my soul: I offer it to you with all the love of my heart, for I love you, Lord, and so need to give myself, to surrender myself into your hands without reserve, and with boundless confidence, for you are my Father.

2. Simply visit someone who is suffering. Let the Holy Spirit guide you as to what to say, or what not to say; to do, or what not to do. Then come home and reflect on your presence to that suffering person. What do you think? How do you feel? How are you going to pray?

PART II

Spiritual Formation through the Life of Grace in the Church

We are now at the halfway point of our course. During the first half, we considered different aspects of the spiritual life through the eyes of persons called by God to live a covenant relationship. Our scripture readings, our prayer, our models, were all taken from the Old Testament, the Hebrew scriptures. It was in this tradition that Jesus' spiritual formation took place.

With the coming of Jesus, however, we find a different emphasis. The presence of Jesus is the direct revelation of God within a human being, a presence so powerful that it cannot be restricted to Jesus alone, but radiates into each person who recognizes and accepts him. A new people of God is formed—the church—the body of all those who continue to make his presence visible in the world.

How has our participation in this new people of God contributed to our spiritual formation? In this new order of things—the new covenant—our attention is no longer directed toward a few outstanding heroes, but rather toward the one "hero," Jesus, because each and every person can become part of the body of Christ. **We are Jesus!**

Once again, our search begins with the scriptures, but at this point we move from the Hebrew scriptures (Old Testament) to the Christian scriptures (New Testament). These writings were inspired by God among the followers of Jesus who lived in the second half of the first century. As we pick up our New Testament today, we find four types of writings to guide our search: epistles, gospels, the "Acts" of the early church, and the stirring visions of the book of Revelation.

As different communities of Christians formed in the major cities of the Roman empire, their leaders, especially Paul, communicated with the other "churches" by means of **epistles,** or letters. Four of Jesus' followers, who we have come to call evangelists (Matthew, Mark, Luke and John), undertook to compose a record of Jesus' life and teachings in the form of the **gospels.** Luke recorded the exciting events of the early church's dramatic expansion in **Acts,** while John of Patmos described his visions in the book of **Revelation.** Sessions 13–24 will draw from all of these to help us share their same spirit in our twentieth-century spirituality.

13. Call To Begin a Life of Grace

Scripture Passage

Luke, chapters 1—2: **The astonishing events of God's personal entry into human history**

PRAYER

Introduction: A Note on the Text

Leader: When Luke put his considerable talents to work in writing his gospel around the year A.D. 80, he had at hand the gospel of Mark, which had been circulated among the Christian communities for about a decade. He also made use of other narratives describing the events and impact of Jesus' life. Central to Luke's organization of his material is the theme of a journey—Jesus' actual travels in the land of Palestine, and also the journey of the Spirit-led Jesus returning to the Father.

The gospel begins with a series of stories which serve as a sort of prologue to Luke's insightful presentation of Jesus as our savior, a person of compassion and prayer, of strength and of joy. Our author does not hesitate to draw from the Hebrew scriptures' most beautiful imagery and provocative claims to make the point that Jesus makes present among us humans a new possibility for union with God. Chapters 1–2 are called the "Infancy Narratives" because they relate the significance of events surrounding Jesus' birth. They introduce us to Jesus' family, Mary and Joseph, Elizabeth, Zechariah, and John; as well as to those who seek the face of the Lord in the Temple, Simeon, Anna, the teachers. We notice that to be close to Jesus is to expect an encounter with the divine.

Call to Prayer

Leader: Let us once again gather our inner energies, bringing them before the Lord in quiet expectation. (Music, song, or a gathering gesture may be used.)

Reading

Reader: A reading from the gospel of Luke (1:26–38).

In the sixth month, the angel Gabriel was sent from God to a town of Galilee called Nazareth, to a virgin betrothed to a man named Joseph, of the house of David, and the virgin's name was Mary. And coming to her, he said, "Hail, favored one! The Lord is with you." But she was greatly troubled at what was said and pondered what sort of greeting this might be. Then the angel said to her, "Do not be afraid, Mary, for you have found favor with God.

Behold, you will conceive in your womb and bear a son, and you shall name him Jesus. He will be great and will be called Son of the Most High, and the Lord God will give him the throne of David his father, and he will rule over the house of Jacob forever, and of his kingdom there will be no end." But Mary said to the angel, "How can this be, since I have no relations with a man?" And the angel said to her in reply, "The holy Spirit will come upon you, and the power of the Most High will overshadow you. Therefore the child to be born will be called holy, the Son of God. And behold, Elizabeth, your relative, has also conceived a son in her old age, and this is the sixth month for her who was called barren; for nothing will be impossible for God." Mary said, "Behold, I am the handmaid of the Lord. May it be done to me according to your word." Then the angel departed from her.

Individual Reflection

Leader: In this mystical experience, Mary is overwhelmed by the power of God. What similar moments of spiritual "high" have I experienced when I felt myself to be a "favored one" of God? What are the occasions in my life when I have been able to say, "I am the handmaid of the Lord"? Allow your breathing to pace itself to the phrase, "Spirit within me . . ." "Spirit within me . . ." (All pause for silent reflection.)

Prayer

All: Spirit of God, enter my being and take possession of my soul. Make me mindful of your constant presence which but awaits my attention and response. Remind me that I have no need for fear because I have your favor. Strengthen me to echo in my life the response of Mary: "I am your servant." Amen.

LESSON

What Is God's Intention for Humanity?

As the central figure in our reading from Luke's gospel, Mary is also the central figure to help us answer this question. It is significant that so many artists have frequently chosen for their subject the various gospel scenes which include the mother of Jesus, for these scenes help us understand ourselves in "the world according to God." How many "Annunciations" have occurred in human history?

Galilee was the hinterlands of the Roman Empire, of the province of Syria, and even considered such by the Jews themselves. Still, we learn that God does not overlook what others consider marginal but rather regards each human being as valuable, even seeking us out in ordinary, out-of-the-way places. The presence of the angel Gabriel alerts us to the fact that this was an extraordinary visitation of the divine among the human. Many of us would also say that we have felt the presence of angels in our own lives, certainly in the sense of recognizing God's hand in certain events.

Catholic devotion has taken to its heart the special place of Mary by repeating over and over the salutation of Gabriel. The scriptural translation, "Hail, favored one!" is rendered, "Hail Mary, full of grace." This same "favor" or "grace" is given by God to each of us. Just as the author of Genesis reiterated over and over, "and God saw that it was good," God intends that each of us would be seen as good.

Certainly God called Mary to an unparalleled role. But just as certainly, God calls us to whatever role is needed to complete the divine plan in our time, our place. We are not surprised that Mary replies, "I am the handmaid of the Lord. May it be done to me according to your word" (1:38). We **are** surprised when **we** are able to say it. But once again we see God's intention—that human beings will respond wholeheartedly, will recognize that the Most High makes all things possible and that our role is one of cooperation with grace.

By observing the situations where Mary appears in other scriptural passages, we gain additional perspectives as to God's intentions for us. When Mary visits her cousin Elizabeth (Lk 1:39–56), we sense the strength of family, of community, of concern for the other. The beautiful words of the Magnificat again remind us that God is the power, so we praise the One who works in us. Our yearly celebration of Christmas has intensified our appreciation of God's preference for the poor ones of society.

From Mary and Joseph's careful observance of the Law when they presented Jesus in the temple (2:22–40) and when they observed the Passover (2:41–42), we learn the importance of participating in the community's religious traditions. We see at times a conflict between human expectations and God's mode of operation, as when Jesus ignores his mother in favor of the crowds (Lk 8:19–21). At several points in his chronicle, Luke points out Mary's need to take time to reflect, to puzzle out the happenings (Lk 1:19; 50–51). We notice that God takes things a little at a time with us humans.

To round out our understanding of Mary as the model for God's intentions for humanity, we must include passages from other New Testament books. We learn of the need for fortitude in the face of persecution through the flight into Egypt (Mt 2:13) and the scene at the foot of the cross (Jn 19:25–27). We come to see ourselves as active participants in the ministry by observing Mary's key role at Cana (Jn 2:1–11). We come to understand, like the disciples after the ascension, the need to persevere in prayer in order to discern the path along which we are being led (Acts 1:12–14).

Through our reflections on Mary, we see that God has specific intentions for human beings. We don't appear at random on the face of the earth. God chose Mary to bring the Word into the world as a human person like ourselves. Jesus is unique in that he has, so to speak, a foot in the world of the divine and a foot in the world of the human. Mary, being close to him, is the "favored one"—"full of grace." Is such a description possible for the others of us who form the human race? If so, how?

What Does It Mean to Be Human?

Spiritual writers use the expression, "grace builds on nature." In other words, God gifts us with human nature and then goes beyond that to give us grace. So in order to explore grace, we must first look at human nature. This is a topic that could be pursued in many ways, depending on how it is approached, for human beings are surely complex creatures. In the ranking of God's creation, we come in Number 1. (At least as far as earth's creatures are concerned; it would take us far afield here to explore the scriptural references to those premier creatures, angels.)

One way to gain insight about ourselves would be to take a look at the various disciplines which have developed as we have studied ourselves over the centuries. Most ancient would be the field of medicine, for our **physical** nature is basic. It is through our bodies that we are able to communicate with our world. Indeed, the very appearance of our bodies goes a long way toward determining our path in life: male or female; culturally attractive or repulsive; skin color and bone structure—all these affect how and where we will find our place in the world.

Closely linked to the physical is the **emotional/psychological** aspect of our being. Our **intellectual** makeup has the potential for organizing and directing all these powers. Each person is indebted to his or her parents for the genes which dictate the starting point of each of these gifts. But we know that nature teams with nurture. In order to explain why individuals who seem to be evenly matched in natural gifts differ so greatly, psychologists and sociologists point out the great impact of our early formation. While each of us has a natural capacity for **moral, aesthetic,** and **spiritual** growth, it requires the absence of severe trauma and the presence of caring discipline to develop these tendencies.

While all human beings have these generic abilities, each person has specific gifts which make him or her unique. Some talents are easily recognizable on a physical level as outstanding, such as personal beauty or athletic ability. Other persons, such as artists and musicians, exhibit the capacity to blend physical and spiritual talents. Still others are remarkable for spiritual talents such as a keen moral sense or a contemplative aptitude.

We in the twentieth century have the benefit of generations of intensive research to help us understand ourselves. We also can draw from the ancient philosophers of Greece and from the medieval and modern scholastic philosophers to find a convenient way to link our knowledge of human beings (**anthropology**) with our search for God's interaction with us (**theology**). They simplified the approach by taking for granted the bodily reality in order to concentrate on the spiritual or non-material powers, (1) the intellect and (2) the will, as abilities which enable us to (3) transcend the human level and enter the divine.

From the Human Realm into the Divine Reign

The catechism describes our purpose in life very simply: we are made to know, love, and serve God in this life and to be happy with God in the next life. (1) Know, (2) love, and (3) serve, correspond nicely to (1) intellect, (2) will, and (3) transcendence. Although some spiritualities emphasize the **next** life to the detriment of **this** life, notice that our two purposes are equally balanced. Our goal is clear, and the very fact that God entered human history in Jesus brings the divine presence forever into our human realm. Because Jesus is among us, we are, in a sense, "halfway there." What do we have going for us that will take us the rest of the way?

If we compare human beings to animals, we notice that while we, like them, have instinct to guide us, we also have **intelligence.** We have the ability to step back from a situation, whether it be past or present, in order to view it objectively. We can also look ahead and predict possible outcomes from our actions. Because we can think and know, imagine and organize ideas, we are unique in creation. We can name both concrete objects and also abstract ideas and concepts. Within this world of imagination and thought we can travel within an ever-expanding and theoretically unlimited universe. What better forum for God to meet us?

Consider Mary, who "pondered" (Lk 1:29) and "kept all these things in her heart" (Lk 2:51) because she "did not understand what he said to them" (Lk 2:50). Yet she also questioned and interacted: "How can this be since I have no relations with a man?" (Lk 1:34); "Son, why have you done this to us?" (Lk 2:48). "They have no wine" (Jn 2:3). Mary's actions demonstrate human intelligence at work.

The second term used by the philosophers is the **will.** In the process of using our intelligence to make sense out of our lives, life doesn't just happen. We have to make decisions. Sometimes our choices are well thought out, such as (ideally!) when we get married and take up the task of raising a family. Sometimes our choices are more casual, such as deciding how to spend a weekend. At times we seem to be in a no-choice situation, manipulated by forces beyond our control, although we can still control our response. We may choose to go along or to back off, but we can't escape our human response of choice.

The will uses the information supplied by the intellect to make a decision, to act. The will is the motivational component. Consequently, it is a capacity that can make or break us. The very idea of choice implies that we could go in more than one direction and the human experience makes it clear that there are two basic directions, good or evil (as well as a great deal of room in between for the mediocre among us).

Again, consider Mary. Having questioned the angel, having received both a challenge and a promise, she makes a decision: "I am the handmaid of the Lord. May it be done to me according to your word" (Lk 1:38). At Cana, even in the face of doubtful support from her son, she instructs the waiters: "Do whatever he tells you" (Jn 2:5).

What swings our motivation to make the right choice? Could Mary have said "no" to God? Or could she have said "yes" without God's help? The third level of our description of being human is **transcendence.** In one sense this means "ever onward, ever upward"— once set on the right path, it's more likely that we'll continue. In another sense, this ability or tendency recognizes the fact that there is always something more to do. If we achieve our goal, we find a new one; if we fail, we assess our situation and look for new resources. As people of faith, we experience this restlessness as God drawing us on, challenging our growth.

However, we recognize that even the best motivation doesn't always sustain us, for we feel a double pull. On the one hand, we experience God's original blessing, God's grace, through those insights and energies which keep us on the right track. On the other hand, we experience our original sin through the familiar tendencies to drop off our efforts, to settle for less. We become comfortable in the shell of a false self in which we, not God, are the center of the universe.

The view of ourselves at the center of existence is certainly fostered by our contemporary American society with its emphasis on the rights of the individual and its tradition of rugged individualism. From this self-center, we cultivate "relationships": with our spouse, with our work group, with our study group, with our children . . . with our God. We perceive God in a polarized fashion; we are over here and God is over there—larger than life, of course—caring for me, of course . . . but still one among many relationships. With such a notion of God, it's easy for people to become so many self-contained individuals floating around in space trying to "get right with God" in isolation from each other.

The Bible corrects this concept:

Behind me and before me you have hemmed me in
   and rest your hand upon me . . .
Where can I go from your spirit?
   from your presence where can I flee?

> If I go up to the heavens, you are there;
> if I sink to the nether world, you are present there
> (Ps. 139:5, 7–8).

God is not "**a**" being separate from the human person. God simply **is**. So, God **is** everywhere, both beyond and within. There is no way we can separate from God. Which means that when we say something about God, we are also saying something about ourselves and our world because God is both at our personal inner core and also the ground and horizon within which that "I" operates. This opens the possibility of meeting God at any turn. Transcendence, our capability of being drawn on by God's power, God's grace, makes it likely (especially with spiritual training) that we will recognize God and give ourselves over to the divine design.

Once again, Mary provides an example of transcendence. Unwilling to accept the human handwriting on the wall, "Standing by the cross of Jesus were his mother . . ." (Jn 19:25). And after being seemingly abandoned by Jesus, "they returned to Jerusalem. . . . Together they devoted themselves to constant prayer. All these devoted themselves with one accord to prayer, together with some women, and Mary the mother of Jesus, and his brothers" (Acts 1:12, 14). God's grace empowered Mary to act on her best human tendencies, and even to go beyond them in such a way that God's presence was felt through her.

What Is a Life of Grace?

The title of this chapter is "Call to a Life of Grace." What does this mean? As we have seen from the description of human beings given above, we are unique in creation. We possess a body which mediates physical and spiritual realities. In the spiritual realm, our intellect and will form the essence of the human person, for it is by means of these capacities that we think and strive. To cap off this array of gifts, God gives us grace, that spiritual gift which enables us to transcend the realm of the merely human and to enter the realm of the divine.

To be called to a life of grace is to be called to train the inner eye which enables us to see the world through God's eyes. It is to take on Mary's habit of keeping "all these things in [our] hearts" so as to be alert to the God "behind, before, and within." If we are to know, love, and serve God in this life, we need to rely on God's grace, those bursts of spiritual energy which direct us toward our goal, being happy with God in the next life.

Although we acknowledge that God is everywhere, to a certain extent, there is a polarity of relationship between ourselves and God, for God is totally Other. Most of us are more conscious of distance than of closeness and look upon God more through faith than through direct mystical experience. Yet we can also testify that because of God's grace, God's spirit among us, even that small spark of faith is capable of direct union.

The word "grace" comes from the Greek word meaning beauty. The graced person is beautiful in the eyes of God. Once we gain a glimpse of God's beauty and realize that it is reflected in ourselves, we act differently. Because of our spiritual nature, we are all mystics of some sort. When we live a life of grace, beautiful before God, the reign of God gains yet another foothold through another human being who is willing to say, "I am the handmaid of the Lord. May it be done to me according to your word" (Lk 1:38).

DISCUSSION

Most of us have experienced a time when we felt like a graced person—beautiful in the eyes of God. Recall such a time. How were you aware of your human dimension? How did you feel the presence of the Spirit?

If you have not had such an experience, have you ever been in the presence of someone else who seemed to be "full of grace"?

Share one such experience with a partner.

BREAK

Enjoy refreshments and each other's company.

WRAP-UP

1. Look ahead to the "During the Week" follow-up activities. (optional)
2. Look ahead to the scripture passage and the theme of the next session. Decide on a time during the upcoming week when you will read chapter 14.
3. Participate in the Closing Prayer.

DURING THE WEEK

1. We see the results of God's grace in our own lives when our natural capacities get a special boost from the Spirit. In a sense, God enlivens, empowers, and transforms my human abilities. "God-ness" enters the world through me. Take some time to reflect on this experience in your own life.

   Nature   a. A natural talent I have is. . .
                  b. I have developed this talent by. . .
   Grace   c. God has formed me spiritually by using my
                  talent to. . .

2. Our philosophy of life is greatly informed by the Bible. Look up the following passages and note down phrases which help you answer the question: "What are God's intentions for human beings?"
   Jeremiah 29:11–15
   Hosea 2:21–23
   Romans 6:1–11
   Ephesians 1:3–10

14. Call to Conversion

Scripture Passage

Luke, chapter 3; 7:18–35: **The contrast between John's baptism of moral conversion and Jesus' baptism of God's favor and power.**

PRAYER

Introduction: A Note on the Text

Leader: Luke's third chapter begins with a complete change of scene from chapters 1–2. The children are grown up. Elizabeth's son John has fulfilled the promises implied in the strange circumstances of his birth by attracting a following of people searching for a deeper meaning in life. Like the prophets of old, John had taken up an austere life of prayer and fasting which gave him the courage to give advice on what the people needed to do.

John was aware that his ministry was temporary. His father, Zechariah, had prophesied that John would "go before the Lord to prepare his ways, to give his people knowledge of salvation . . ." (Lk 1:76–77). As we read Luke's account of John's preaching and Jesus' baptism, the transition from John to Jesus is extremely subtle. There is no mention of the cousins' conversing or even recognizing each other, only that Jesus was baptized along with others. Why? Jesus had no need to signify his conversion to a new style of life. Rather, **we** had need of the moment after this ritual, when God visibly poured out the Spirit upon him.

In this moment it is likely that Jesus achieved a new awareness of his identity. He was God's beloved, only begotten Son. No, it wasn't necessary for Jesus to be baptized, but for the sake of identity—his and ours—he submitted like the Lamb of God that he was. Through his baptism we know who we are and whose we are. Any "identity crisis" in the life of a baptized converted Christian can only occur at a human level; on a spiritual level we, like Jesus, hear the inner echo of God's voice, "You are my beloved Son/[daughter]. With you I am well pleased" (Lk 3:22).

Call to Prayer

Leader: As we do at the beginning of mass, let us recall those parts of our selves which cry out for repentance. Realizing that we too are drawn by the power of God, let us imagine ourselves among the crowd along the Jordan River listening to John, hungry for the good news. (Music, song, or a gathering gesture may be used.)

Reading

Reader: A reading from the gospel of Luke (3:7–22).

[John] said to the crowds who came out to be baptized by him, "You brood of vipers! Who warned you to flee from the coming wrath? Produce good fruits as evidence of your repentance: and do not begin to say to yourselves, 'We have Abraham as our father,' for I tell you, God can raise up children to Abraham from these stones. Even now the ax lies at the root of the trees. Therefore every tree that does not produce good fruit will be cut down and thrown into the fire." And the crowds asked him, "What then should we do?" He said to them in reply, "Whoever has two cloaks should share with the person who has none. And whoever has food should do likewise." Even tax collectors came to be baptized and they said to him, "Teacher, what should we do?" He answered them, "Stop collecting more than what is prescribed." Soldiers also asked him, "And what is it that we should do?" He told them, "Do not practice extortion, do not falsely accuse anyone, and be satisfied with your wages." Now the people were filled with expectation, and all were asking in their hearts whether John might be the Messiah. John answered them all, saying, "I am baptizing you with water, but one mightier than I is coming. I am not worthy to loosen the thongs of his sandals. He will baptize you with the holy Spirit and fire. His winnowing fan is in his hand to clear his threshing floor and to gather the wheat into his barn, but the chaff he will burn with unquenchable fire." Exhorting them in many other ways, he preached good news to the people. Now Herod the tetrarch, who had been censured by him because of Herodias, his brother's wife, and because of all the evil deeds Herod had committed, added still another to these by [also] putting John in prison.

After all the people had been baptized and Jesus also had been baptized and was praying, heaven was opened and the holy Spirit descended upon him in bodily form like a dove. And a voice came from heaven, "You are my beloved Son; with you I am well pleased."

Individual Reflection

Leader: Our understanding of baptism is that at the moment when the church gathers, through the sign of water God once again enters human life in a Trinitarian manner: the holy Spirit, the voice of the Father, and Jesus. Focus your imagination on Jesus standing in the Jordan River. See yourself standing beside him and being transformed inwardly by the impact of God's words, spoken to you as well: "With you I am well pleased." (All pause for interior reflection.)

Prayer

All: O God, thank you for calling me to be your child through baptism. Thank you for the abundant, amazing grace of your love and merciful forgiveness when, through sin, I separated myself from you. I accept the blame for my every sin. I give you thanks and praise for every moment of grace. Though I deserve nothing, you give me everything. Eternally grateful, I am yours. Amen.

LESSON

John's Baptism of Repentance

As we study this scene we are struck by the contrasts and likenesses to the prophets we considered in chapters 9, 10, and 11. That there were "crowds" looking for a "Messiah" tells us that a feeling of religious fervor was abroad in the land. We know of various movements within Judaism early in the first century, and that some of them practiced the rite of baptism. Somehow the rituals of the temple did not touch their hearts, so they were looking for something more.

Yet the tradition of the prophets is very much alive in the style John uses to speak to the people. His powerful preaching tells us of the urgency he felt, even as he risked the wrath of the current ruler.

When people came to John the Baptist they asked, "What must I do?" and according to their state in life, John gave them an answer: if you are a soldier, stop bullying people; if you are a tax collector, be honest, etc. When these same people decided to take John's advice and be converted (i.e., turn away from sinful actions and turn toward good actions), they were baptized as a sign of their commitment.

John was primarily interested in a change of behavior, as for example, when he admonished King Herod for his adulterous relationship with Herodias. But as a true prophet he must have known that only a conversion of heart (attitude) can support an authentic change of behavior leading to the transformation of the individual. For example, an alcoholic can occasionally stop drinking out of sheer will-power, but he is still a "dry drunk" and miserable until he experiences an interior change of attitude toward self, God and others.

In spite of John the Baptist's "tough love" approach, many people today would be quite happy and comfortable in being a follower of him rather than of Jesus. A call to repentance and conversion can be answered on a moral level as someone turns from a loose and easy life to a life of serious effort to do good. Such a decision is difficult in itself, and even more so during the daily grind of actually putting aside bad habits in favor of a preferred life-style. This is what John challenged his disciples to do. There is a certain appeal in this "no pain, no gain" approach, with the self-satisfaction that comes from accomplishing a goal. It's easier to rely on one's self than to follow Jesus and to rely on God's power.

Jesus' Call to Conversion

Luke recounts that after his baptism, Jesus "was led by the Spirit into the desert for forty days" (4:1–2), after which he "returned to Galilee in the power of the Spirit" (4:14). Although we can scarcely speak of his need for conversion, Jesus was himself willing to undergo the "winnowing fan," and thereafter placed himself completely at the disposal of the Spirit. When John sends his disciples to question him, he simply replies, "Go and tell John what you have seen and heard: the blind regain their sight, the lame walk, lepers are cleansed, the deaf hear, the dead are raised, the poor have the good news proclaimed to them. And blessed is the one who takes no offense at me" (Lk 7:22).

There is a new call to conversion—a call to echo the ministry of Jesus in re-creating the world.

While John the Baptist focused on a change of behavior, Jesus' call to conversion centered on a change of being. Instead of asking "What should I do?" we ask, "What should I be?" or "What should I become?" Jesus would answer, "Become a part of me like vine and branch, become one in me, as I and the Father are one." St. Paul would say, "Become Jesus, be transformed into Jesus so that you no longer live, but he lives in you." Then from this **being** flows action. What we **do** will proceed from **who we are**—part of Jesus himself. Conversion to **being** involves both the life and the person of Jesus Christ.

The prophets and John issued a call for repentance, but Jesus issues a call to **conversion,** involving a change in both behavior and attitude. Conversion begins with a grace, a free gift from God who desires to draw the beloved closer and closer. Whether it is Paul being struck down on the road to Damascus, or a college student who has an experience of God on a retreat, it is always God who takes the initiative and even gives the grace to respond. God provides an occasion or an incident that shakes us out of our self-sufficiency and brings us breathlessly into the embrace of the Divine Lover. Perhaps an example will illustrate how God invites, but never forces, an individual to turn in and find his/her real self, to discover God, and to turn lovingly toward one's neighbor.

There was once a priest who after many years as an assistant, was finally given a parish of his own. His joy over the appointment lasted but a few months because the parishioners were very independent and so was he. After several clashes and conflicts he finally resigned. On the day he left the parish with tears in his eyes and the dust literally shaken from his sandals, he vowed never to be a pastor again. Soon he was in another parish as an assistant—a very bitter and hostile man who made life difficult for those around him. Then came his conversion.

In the course of one year he attended a Marriage Encounter, a parish Renewal and the Emmaus program for priests. A triple whammy! Through these "conversion experiences" he was urged to take a good look deep within himself. What he discovered was something common to all human beings—that he was basically good, but wounded. Although he had had the advantages of years of religious study and spiritual training, and had achieved the status of an ordained clergyman, something had been missing. Through the affirmation of married couples, parishioners and fellow priests, his self-esteem was enhanced. Through the wounds of the crucified Jesus, sacramentally present, his wounds were healed. Today he is a happy, holy pastor.

Conversion to Being

While repentance starts with the intellectual awareness that something is lacking in one's life, then advances to emotions of remorse and desire to change, conversion implies a complete change of heart. Most people who experience Conversion with a capital C can recall the exact place and moment when their spiritual awakening occurred. They report that they are never again the same. While they may experience temptation, depression and anxiety, yes, and even sin, their hearts never leave their Lord. In the Christian tradition of spirituality, we need only recall names such as Paul, Augustine, Teresa of Avila or Thérèse of Lisieux to explain the meaning of conversion.

A common use of the word conversion indicates the acceptance of a new religion, as we see in the case of an adult requesting baptism. Through the *R*ite of *C*hristian *I*nitiation for *A*dults, the Catholic Christian community closely examines (scrutinizes) the sincerity of the catechumen's conversion. Only then is an individual initiated into the mystery of Christ and his church by being baptized into his death and resurrection. This process is easy to understand and a real joy to follow in the case of unbaptized adults. That is why those who are already baptized are urged to participate in the RCIA.

"By joining the catechumens in reflecting on the value of the paschal mystery and by renewing their own conversion, the faithful provide an example that will help the catechumens to obey the Holy Spirit more generously." But in reality, how many follow this advice? In reality, how many baptized, *un*converted Catholic Christians do we have? Only God knows the answer, but the church is feeling the effects of a lifeless, unenthusiastic membership (Can we dare call them "the faithful"?) who have all but stopped growing in numbers and in Spirit. And this includes not only the majority of the church, the laity, but also clergy and religious. As always, but perhaps now more than ever, the church is in need of reform and conversion.

The Paschal Mystery

If only Catholic adults could appreciate (put the proper price on) their baptism! Are they not aware that they who were baptized into Christ Jesus were baptized into his death? Through baptism into his death they were buried with him, so that, just as Christ was raised from the dead by the glory of the Father, they too might live a new life (Rom 6:3–9). Are they not aware? Are *we* not aware? Is it possible that as often as we have heard these words, we either have not understood them or we have not internalized them? One cannot do the latter without the former, so let us take a cursory look at their meaning.

The above passage from St. Paul should be familiar to many of us. It is an optional reading for funerals and baptisms, but it is a mandatory reading at the Easter Vigil—that most beautiful of all liturgical ceremonies where we celebrate the paschal mystery in all its fullness and splendor. This term, "paschal mystery," was brought to prominence in the documents of Vatican Council II, when the council fathers stated that, "by baptism, all persons are plunged into the **Paschal Mystery** of Christ: they die with Him, are buried with Him, and rise with Him (cf. Rom 6:4; Eph 2:6; Col 3:1; 2 Tim 2:11); they receive the spirit of adoption as sons and daughters "by virtue of which we cry: Abba, Father" (Rom 8:15), and thus become those true adorers whom the Father seeks (cf. Jn 4:23)." (*Constitution on the Sacred Liturgy #6*).

This is the central mystery of our faith, a "mystery" in terms of ineffable knowledge and revelation, rather than something unknowable. Someone once described a mystery as a mountain of ice cream; impossible to eat it all, but each bite perfectly delicious. That mountain of ice cream stands as an invitation to dive in (in baptism) and to take and eat (in eucharist). We respond to the invitation in faith and in a liturgical/sacramental way when we commemorate and celebrate what the Father has done for us in his son Jesus in the power of the Holy Spirit.

For Christians, baptism is just a beginning and so we refer to it as a sacrament of initiation. Whether we are baptized as infants or adults, we begin by becoming incorporated into the paschal mystery of Christ's death and resurrection. Our spiritual lives get a great kickoff with this initial outpouring of God's grace. We believe that the risen, ascended Jesus lives in glory with the Father and that there is a promise and hope of our future glory with him. We believe that the body of Christ, the church, still suffers and dies here on earth, and through the cross we also have access to the Father. We believe the holy Spirit, our advocate, is with us as gift from the Father and the Son, to give us strength in our trials, wisdom in our daily decisions and all the other gifts and graces necessary for our salvation and future glory.

Ongoing, Lifelong Conversion

After our baptism, sooner or later, we must go, as Jesus did (Lk 4:1–13), into the desert to be subjected to the trial. And what a trial it is, as we all know. The forty days Jesus spent in the desert struggling with temptation and the forces of evil reminds us of the forty years the Israelites wandered in the desert going from sin to conversion and back again. Their story is our story. Like them we face our tests at various stages of our lives. Sometimes we win, sometimes we lose. But the amazing grace of conversion is always around the next corner, challenging us to die with Christ in order to live with him in the promised land just across the river.

Those conversions (with a small "c") are the "dying daily" of which St. Paul speaks. Baptism is the initial moment, but it is the everyday union with the paschal mystery of Christ's death and resurrection which reaches fulfillment in the celebration of eucharist. Having undergone one or more major conversions, each of us is invited by God to continue the process in the thoughts, words and actions of everyday life. In a world that complains about boredom and absence of meaning, the daily conversions not only **find** meaning, but **give** meaning to our joys and sorrows. Those whose spiritual lives revolve around such conversions are the true martyrs (witnesses) who participate in the paschal mystery from the rising of the sun to its setting, from birth to death to new life.

Finally, no chapter on conversion would be complete without a few words on the sacrament of reconciliation. Suffice it to say that if anyone is really sincere about his or her spiritual formation, the regular celebration of this meeting with the merciful Jesus is imperative. And so is the penance that goes along with it, whether imposed by the priest or self-imposed. We derive tremendous consolation from a regular comparison of our lives with those of our Master. Also, many people have found that fasting, under the direction of a spiritual director, has opened them up to greater solidarity with the poor and oppressed, not to mention the symbolic value of becoming empty in order to be filled with the presence of God.

Spiritual formation never takes place in isolation. Just as the first-century Jews looked to John the Baptist and Jesus for direction, we are well-advised to seek out a regular confessor and/or a spiritual director. Such a person offers to travel as a companion on our spiritual journey toward closer union with God. But be careful—a great deal of prayer and wisdom should go into the choice of someone with whom we share the most intimate aspects of our deepest self.

DISCUSSION

Since Vatican Council II there have been many opportunities for a Catholic to experience a Conversion (capital "C") or "awakening" as it is sometimes called. These opportunities include: Charismatic Renewal, Marriage Encounter, Renew, Cursillo, Parish Renewal, Pilgrimages or some other time of special grace. As a result of participating in such spirit-filled moments, many people experience an insatiable hunger for a closer union with God and neighbor. What has been your experience? Take a few moments to respond to **either** question 1 **or** question 2.

1. Have you ever experienced a conversion or awakening? If so:
   a) What was the "after-effect" of your experience?
   b) Was there someone or some group to journey with you in your new life—a spiritual director, a "soul-friend," or a support group?
   c) If you have lost the fervor and peace experienced in your conversion, how is it possible to regain it?
2. If you have never experienced a spiritual conversion:
   a) Would you like to? Why? or Why not?
   b) What are some ways you could foster such an experience?

Share your response to one of these questions with a partner.

BREAK

Enjoy refreshments and each other's company.

WRAP-UP

1. Look ahead to the "During the Week" follow-up activities.
2. Look ahead to the scripture passage and the theme of the next session.
3. Participate in a Closing Prayer.

DURING THE WEEK

1. The greatest of all conversion experiences is the mass, the liturgy of the eucharist, when word and sacrament challenge us to turn to a more loving union with God and neighbor. Attend mass this week with the thought of conversion in mind.
2. If you have never had an opportunity to participate in a Marriage Encounter, Cursillo, etc., you might want to call your diocesan office to see if such events are scheduled in your area. Many people have found the grace of God lurking there. Be open to the gifts God has in store for you.

15. Call to Discipleship

Scripture Passage

Mark 8:22–9:52: **Jesus invites his disciples into the heart of the mystery of who he is and challenges them to follow him.**

PRAYER

Introduction: A Note on the Text

Leader: Mark's gospel is often referred to as the gospel of discipleship and this passage, central to the gospel, contains many of its key ideas. The section is "framed" by two stories about blindness; it opens in 8:22–26 by describing how Jesus cured the man at Bethsaida of his blindness by putting spittle on his eyes, and ends at 10:46–52 by relating how Bartimaeus' insistent plea for help, "Master, I want to see," received the response, "Go your way. Your faith has saved you." The stories which come in between seem to dwell on the spiritual blindness of the disciples as Jesus tries to explain who he is and what a disciple is expected to be and to do.

Jesus asks the critical question: "Who do you say that I am?" Satisfied that the disciples have grasped the basics of his identity, he relentlessly hammers home the message that the cost of discipleship is the cross. At times he is harsh, as on the subjects of divorce and riches; at other times he is gentle, as with the children he proposes as models. Patiently, three times, he explains the purpose of the journey to Jerusalem: the Son of man must suffer. There is rich symbolism in the stories of the transfiguration on the mountain, in the casting out of a violent demon, in the embracing and blessing of children.

Mark's Jesus is a teacher with authority, a Messiah to be obeyed.

Call to Prayer

Leader: Let us allow our usual concerns to fade into the background so that we may attend to the words of Jesus. (Music, song, or a gathering gesture may be used.)

Reading

Reader: A reading from the gospel according to Mark (10:35–45).

Then James and John, the sons of Zebedee, came to him and said to him, "Teacher, we want you to do for us whatever we ask of you." He replied, "What do you wish [me] to do for you? They answered him, "Grant that in your glory we may sit one at your right and the other at your left." Jesus said to them, "You do not know what you are asking. Can you drink the cup that I drink or be baptized with the baptism with which I am baptized?" They said to him, "We can." Jesus said to them, "The cup that I drink, you will drink, and with the baptism with which I am baptized, you will be baptized; but to sit at my right or at my left is not mine to give but is for those for whom it has been prepared." When the ten heard this, they became indignant at James and John.

Jesus summoned them and said to them, "You know that those who are recognized as rulers over the Gentiles lord it over them, and their great ones make their authority over them felt. But it shall not be so among you. Rather, whoever wishes to be great among you will be your servant; whoever wishes to be first among you will be the slave of all. For the Son of Man did not come to be served but to serve and to give his life as a ransom for many."

Individual Reflection

Leader: Am I, like James and John, befriending Jesus because I want a "big brother" who can arrange matters to my liking when I ask? In my heart of hearts, do I offer to help out because it makes me feel good . . . because others will approve of my efforts and look up to me . . . because I like a public role? Silently repeat to yourself: N. (my name) has not come to be served but to serve . . . N. has not come to be served but to serve . . . (All pause for silent reflection.)

Prayer

All: Jesus, Son of man, you put aside your Godhead to become one with us as a human being. You singlemindedly devoted yourself to us that we might learn the good news. Guide us to fix our minds and hearts on you. Teach us the true meaning of greatness as we look for you in your little ones. Amen.

LESSON

Discipleship in the Gospel of Mark

The title of this chapter is our "Call to Discipleship," a call about which we can learn a great deal through Mark's gospel. Who calls? Who is called? For what are they called? Answering these questions puts us squarely in the Christian tradition and gives a special stamp to our spirituality.

Obviously it is Jesus who calls, and Mark provides many strong and striking images of Jesus. He comes on the scene unflinchingly proclaiming the same message that had only recently sent his cousin, John, to jail: "This is the time of fulfillment. The kingdom of God is at hand! Repent and believe in the gospel!" (1:15). He went directly to Simon and Andrew at their workplace with the command, "Come after me" (1:17). Next he went to James and John and "called them . . . so they left" (1:20). He ignored public opinion to include a despised tax collector, Levi, among those he planned to train for the mission, knowing his power for good was stronger than the power of sin (2:13–17).

Whom did Jesus call? "Those whom he wanted and they came to him" (3:13). He looked around for people who were not afraid of hard work. Among these were "the twelve" (3:16), "his mother and brothers" (3:35), "his disciples" (6:45), and some "women" (15:40). The group of his disciples overlaps at different times, with some having more prominent roles, but Mark constructs much of his gospel by playing off the unperceptive followers against their mentor, Jesus. This enables us to come away with a clear picture of what is expected of us as disciples.

What response is expected when Jesus calls? It must be immediate. No questions asked, no psychological analysis, no hesitation— like a soldier following orders. We notice the same root, *discere:* to learn, in both disciple and in discipline. It's not that Jesus expects us to act like automatons, but rather that he expects us to understand the

urgency of the situation. We must to come to share his perspective—
that our world harbors evil in many places and that it must be
cleansed so that God will reign. What will that reign look like? As we
follow Jesus, we gain a glimpse, for he both teaches and actually
demonstrates.

Jesus Points to the Reign of God

Jesus is unquestionably at center stage, but he is not rattled by it
because his attention is not on himself, but on what he is trying to
accomplish. At times he teaches to the crowds, likening the reign of
God to scattered seed or a tiny mustard seed. Sometimes he corrects
the misguided notions of the Pharisees: fasting is not needed now, but
rather is for the time when the bridegroom is gone; the sabbath was
made for us, not we for the sabbath; the ideal of marriage is higher
than Moses' law, which allowed divorce. He shows himself to be a wise
yet canny teacher, getting out of situations where he is set up but still
getting his message across in classic forms: "Repay to Caesar . . ."
(12:17); "not the God of the dead but of the living . . ." (12:27); "Which
is the first of all the commandments? . . ." (12:28).

Most often Mark portrays him instructing his disciples: "Take
nothing for the journey . . ." (6:8); "Come . . . and rest a while . . ."
(6:31); "all these evils come from within . . ." (7:23). When they prevail on him to moderate his views about the need to suffer, he turns on
them: "Get behind me, Satan! You are thinking not as God does, but
as human beings do" (8:33). He even reiterates privately to them
teachings which have not been well-received in public: "It is easier for
a camel to pass through [the] eye of [a] needle than for one who is rich
to enter the kingdom of God" (10:25).

With Jesus, it is all or nothing. When the fig tree had no fruit, he
curses it: "May no one ever eat of your fruit again!" (11:14). When the
money-changers put their interests before those of God, he drives
them violently and singlehandedly from their place in the temple pre-
cincts. He defends "this waste of perfumed oil" (14:4) as a prophetic
sign of his claim to be the Messiah, the Anointed One. He gives himself totally: "Take it; this is my body" (14:22). While he feels fear:
"Abba . . . take this cup away from me" (14:36), he goes forth to meet
his fate: "The hour has come . . . Get up, let us go" (14:41–42). He
silently takes all the punishment his enemies mete out to him and
dies, uttering "a loud cry" (15:37).

None of this ever seemed to come clear to his disciples. They
followed because they believed in **him,** not because they understood

what he was trying to accomplish. The women seem to have been more perceptive, or at least more willing to stick it out even at the scene of his final suffering. Joseph of Arimathea had caught the spirit of self-less service, for he thought more of giving Jesus a worthy burial than of his position in the Sanhedrin. So also had the women who came to the tomb and who first heard the news that there was a point to it all—that Jesus had risen and that there was more to be done.

A Modern-Day Disciple

We have heard the gospel over and over, so it takes real concentration and prayer to allow it to move us. We know the stories and their outcomes. Preachers have thrown Jesus' one-liners in our faces to the point where we know what is coming next. Can we drop our defenses, our excuses, and truly follow the Lord? We can. We can if we are able to grasp the chasm between "God's standards" and "human standards" and do as Jesus did to make God's standards prevail. In the first half of the twentieth century we find a modern-day disciple who was able to show us the meaning of being a Christian: Dietrich Bonhoeffer.

Bonhoeffer was born in 1906 and died in 1945, not yet 40 years old. The times were tumultuous, spanning two world wars, and since he was German, and a Lutheran pastor, he found himself in the middle of controversy. A brilliant theologian and lecturer, his published writings gave him a strong reputation in academic circles. He taught at Berlin University and at Union Theological Seminary in New York. Unfortunately, his career got underway at the same time as Hitler's gained ascendancy. The contrast between God's standards and Hitler's was too much for Bonhoeffer, who spoke out against the abuses of the Third Reich.

To protect him from retaliation, his friends persuaded him to move to London, where he left academia and worked as a pastor for two years. However, he could not shake off the call to enter the struggle, so moved back to Germany. There he took up the direction of an illegal Church Training College, living among the students and young ministers as they formed a community. Threatened, he left Germany once again, but could not stay away, writing to his mentor, Reinhold Niebuhr, "I shall have no right to participate in the reconstruction of Christian life in Germany after the war if I do not share the trials of this time with my people. . . . I cannot make this choice in security."

Back in his native land, Bonhoeffer contributed his strong spiritual views to the underground opposition. This time he was arrested in

1943 by the Gestapo, and spent the rest of his life in prison and concentration camps. He was an inspiration to his fellow prisoners and to his guards because of his calmness and self-control, even during the Allied bombings of Berlin, and for his kindness and concern for his fellow prisoners. In the final chaotic months of the war, he was transferred from one concentration camp to another. A few days before the camp at Blossenburg was liberated by the Allies, Bonhoeffer was executed there by special order of Himmler on April 9, 1945.

Against this backdrop of heroic conviction, we read Bonhoeffer's writings with special attention. It is to him that we are indebted for the Christian classic, *The Cost of Discipleship*. In a famous passage he contrasts human standards and God's standards with the terms "cheap grace" and "costly grace": "Cheap grace is grace without discipleship, grace without the cross, grace without Jesus Christ, living and incarnate. . . . Costly grace is the gospel which must be **sought** again and again, the gift which must be **asked** for, the door at which a person must **knock.** Such grace is **costly** because it calls us to follow, and it is **grace** because it calls us to follow **Jesus Christ.**"

We who feel ourselves called to foster a spiritual life would do well to study the meaning of discipleship as described by this twentieth-century martyr. He makes a great deal of gazing steadily at the Lord, of following **him,** not some formula for holiness. He reminds us that there is no content to this call, no specific task to which we can address ourselves. We must put our efforts to whatever is at hand, not to a specific career that we have mapped out for ourselves. We must resolutely cut ourselves off from any person or situation which prevents us from living a life of faith. Our call is to stand face-to-face with Jesus and to view all of life from that perspective.

A Spirituality of Discipleship

In our endeavor to identify signposts to direct our spiritual formation, what characteristics of discipleship should we look for? Three stand out: (1) a single-minded attention to Jesus and his efforts to bring about the reign of God, (2) an urgency of purpose, and (3) service of others, even at personal cost.

Right at the outset of his ministry, the Spirit sent Jesus to the desert (Mk 1:12) and even after he was active in ministry, he continued this habit of prayer (1:35). But when his disciples "pursued him," he does not hesitate: "Let us go on to the nearby villages that I may preach there also. For this purpose have I come" (1:38). To keep our attention fixed on Jesus means that we must be willing to "go on." While we rely on prayer for solace and for direction, we are ready to go with him to proclaim the good news.

Like Jesus, our proclaiming is both in word and in deed. We become rooted in gospel standards so that when we are questioned we can respond with the same surety as he did. We become skilled at detecting falsehood. We become less tolerant of sinful situations and more willing to take the initiative to change them. Without expecting dramatic results, we come to rely on God's power and, like the disciples who "drove out many demons . . . and anointed with oil many who were sick and cured them" (6:13), feel God at work in us.

Secondly, a spirituality of discipleship is one of urgency. Jesus says "let us go on." John the Baptist had felt this urgency and had spoken out; so had Bonhoeffer; both of them landed in prison. As for us, most of us are relatively safe, not at risk in a life-and-death sense. We need to take ourselves to situations where we **feel** an urgency—to a soup kitchen or a hospital, to a prison or homeless shelter. We need to listen to those who bore us with their hard-luck stories. We need to associate with those who are culturally different to remind ourselves that it's a big world out there, this world that Jesus came to save. And then we need to **do** something, whether it takes the form of direct assistance or of political action designed to change inhumane and discriminatory situations.

Finally, our spirituality must be one of service: "For the Son of Man did not come to be served, but to serve and to give his life as a ransom for many" (10:45). We cannot settle for a comfortable "Jesus and me" spirituality which stops at the level of personal enjoyment, such as the stimulation we gain from study groups such as this, or from our aesthetic appreciation of liturgical services with beautiful music and inspiring homilies. Like the disciples, we work in community, but we don't settle for cozy coffee-klatches or committees where we talk about what needs to be done and then recruit others to do the dirty work.

A novice director once told her charges, "The definitions of a lady and a saint are the same—others first, and self last." Social psychologists tell us that this philosophy can be carried to extremes when people become co-dependent, feeling worthless unless they are needed; they manipulate situations so they will be regarded as good people because they take care of others. Such a martyr "role" is a far cry from the selfless giving Bonhoeffer witnessed to us. Service implies a certain stamina, a willingness to do for another even when it isn't convenient, even when it isn't for someone who is loved, or is perhaps for someone who isn't even attractive. It is for the sake of the **other,** not for my sake or to get the job done.

DISCUSSION

1. Jesus asked the disciples the question, "But who do you say that I am?" (Mk 8:29). How each of us answers that question is influenced by our personal religious history. One may reply, "my Savior," or "my Lord." Another may use a scriptural title: Jesus is "the Good Shepherd," or "the Son of God." A hymn may influence my response: "I know that my Redeemer liveth," as might a devotion, "Most Sacred Heart of Jesus, have mercy on me."

    1. Take a few quiet moments to allow a favorite title for Jesus to surface in your consciousness. How does this compare to the way Jesus is portrayed in Mark's gospel?
    2. Share your impressions with a partner.

BREAK

Enjoy refreshments and each other's company.

WRAP-UP

1. Look ahead to the "During the Week" follow-up activities. (optional)
2. Look ahead to the scripture passage and the theme of the next session. Decide on a time during the upcoming week when you will read the chapter.
3. Participate in the Closing Prayer.

DURING THE WEEK

Take time for a study of the discipleship theme in Luke's gospel:

1. What impresses you most in the following stories of Jesus calling his disciples?
   Luke 5:1–11   Luke 6:12–16
   Luke 5:27–32   Luke 8:1–3
2. What becomes clear through Jesus' instructions to the disciples?
   Luke 9:1–6   Luke 10:1–20
   Luke 9:23–27   Luke 14:25–35
   Luke 9:46–50
3. How did Jesus' fate create a crisis for his disciples? How did they handle this crisis?
   Luke 22:54–62
   Luke 24:36–53
4. What caused a transformation among them?
   Acts 1:1–2:47

16. Call to a New Covenant of Loving Union

Scripture Passage

John 6:22–71, and chapters 14–17: **The evangelist, John, gathers Jesus' sayings to his disciples in the Bread of Life Discourse and a "Last" Discourse at the Last Supper that stresses who God is and how the disciples are consecrated to God's mission of establishing a covenant of unity and peace.**

PRAYER

Introduction: A Note on the Text

Leader: When we pick up John's gospel after reading the synoptic gospels, we notice a definite change of style and tone. While Matthew, Mark, and Luke prefer to present Jesus' message in the form of short vignettes, John frequently gathers this message into long speeches or discourses. His account of the Last Supper omits the familiar narrative describing how Jesus transformed the Passover symbols of bread and wine into his very self. Earlier, in chapter 6, John used a discourse or monologue format to tell us how Jesus described himself as "the Bread of Life." Now, at the Passover meal, when Jesus is on the brink of his own passing over from this life to the next, he pours out his heart to his friends, and indeed to us.

He layers image upon image in his attempt to make it clear to us how intimate is the union between divine and human. His words take on additional significance, for they are like a farewell speech that was traditionally given by ancient Hebrew or Greek heroes. From time immemorial, the words of someone on his or her deathbed have always been filled with special meaning and importance. And so, what Jesus prayed for and the actions he performed on this occasion, were memorable and eternal in light of the paschal mystery that was taking place. He was fulfilling the original plan of God in creating us—to enter, along with the Father and the holy Spirit, into complete union (communion) with us. Nowhere in the New Testament is this unity spoken of so hopefully as in the gospel of John. We become very aware that the old covenant is passing away as the new covenant, with its promises of unprecedented intimacy between divine and human, is announced. While "loving union" is only one aspect of the eucharist, it could easily be the most formative aspect of our spirituality.

Call to Prayer

Leader: Let us place ourselves in the presence of God—Jesus, the Father, and the Advocate—and unite ourselves with all those who are gathered to celebrate mass at this moment throughout the world. (Music, song, or a gathering gesture may be used.)

Reading

Reader: A reading from the gospel of John (17:20–26).

[Jesus said:] "I pray not only for them, but also for those who will believe in me through their word, so that they may all be one, as you, Father, are in me and I in you, that they also may be in us, that the world may believe that you sent me. And I have given them the glory you gave me, so that they may be one, as we are one, I in them and you in me, that they may be brought to perfection as one, that the world may know that you sent me, and that you loved them even as you loved me. Father, they are your gift to me. I wish that where I am they also may be with me, that they may see my glory that you gave me, because you loved me before the foundation of the world. Righteous Father, the world also does not know you, but I know you, and they know that you sent me. I made known to them your name and I will make it known, that the love with which you loved me may be in them and I in them."

Individual Reflection

Leader: Let us reflect not only on Jesus' Last Will and Testament, but our own as well. Picture yourself at the end of your life, on your deathbed, with your family and friends around you. At this moment of parting, what do you wish for, pray for—for them? Is there anything you want them to do "in remembrance" of you? What do you say to them? (All pause for silent reflection.)

Prayer (from Eucharistic Prayer II for Masses with Children)

Lord our God, listen to our prayer. Send the holy Spirit to all of us who share in this meal. May this Spirit bring us closer together in the family of the church. . . . Gather us all together into your kingdom. There we shall be happy forever with the Virgin Mary, Mother of God and our mother. There all the friends of Jesus the Lord will sing a song of joy. Amen.

LESSON

Jesus' Last Discourse

Those of us who are striving to develop a deeper spiritual life would be well-rewarded to return over and over again to a reading of Jesus' **Last Discourse** in John's gospel (chapters 14–17). Its richness lies not only in its consoling words, but also in its capsule theology of the meaning of life. In the opening verses, Jesus states the aim and goal of our lives: "And if I go and prepare a place for you, I will come back again and take you to myself, so that where I am you also may be" (14:3). In the closing verses, he explains why we are here at all: "As you sent me into the world, so I sent them into the world" (17:18).

As noted above, John often gathers his material into a discourse. In the first part of his gospel, these discourses are addressed to the crowds, but here the audience is different. Only his close friends are with him. The message is tailored to those who are prepared and able to be initiated into the intimate realities of communion between divine and human. In order to understand what Jesus is saying in this Passover meal setting, we need to recall his discourse about the Bread of Life (Jn 6:22–71).

At that time, his listeners had been shocked and scandalized at Jesus' statement: "I am the living bread that came down from heaven; whoever eats this bread will live forever; and the bread that I will give is my flesh for the life of the world" (6:51). Not only do "the Jews" quarrel among themselves (note that John uses the term "the Jews" to categorize those people who constantly questioned and harried Jesus), but even his disciples were murmuring. In fact, "as a result of this, many [of] his disciples returned to their former way of life and no longer accompanied him" (6:66). Those disciples who were at the Last Supper were the ones who chose to remain with Jesus because even though it wasn't clear to them either, they believed Jesus had "the words of eternal life" (6:68). We, like the disciples, gather closely around Jesus as we try to understand this mystery.

The New Covenant

In the first section of this book, we examined the various ways Yahweh took the initiative in establishing a covenant with the people of Israel. Always there was a sign. At times the sign was visible, as in the case of Abraham and circumcision, or of Moses and the Law; sometimes the sign was invisible as with the Law written on people's hearts described by the prophet Jeremiah. These signs verified and validated the covenant relationship. Insofar as the people of Israel responded positively to the covenant, and even in their failures they were formed spiritually both as individuals and as a nation. They themselves became a sign to all nations, especially the powerful ones, of God's preferential love for his chosen people.

Now we come to a new covenant, ratified in the blood of Jesus Christ. We call it eucharist. In this covenant, too, there are visible signs—bread and wine, and signs often invisible to the naked eye—such as a loving union with God, neighbor and indeed, the whole cosmos. This loving union is a sign of our being formed and transformed into Christ who gives us his body and blood for our spiritual nourishment unto eternal life.

Father Ignacio Larranaga writes beautifully about the relationship between covenant and unity. "Because God created us in His image and likeness, the final goal of the Covenant is to become one with Him without losing our identity (the tendency of love, its intrinsic strength, is to unite those who love each other); and I would almost dare to say that the final end and perfection of the encounter lies in the disappearance of all duality between God and ourselves, and in the arrival of total unity."

Nothing in this world has the potential of transforming us in the image and likeness of God as much as the eucharist, the new covenant in Christ's blood. It is true that we are made in the image and likeness of God, and that is why human life is so precious, even from the first moment of conception. But because of the sin of the world into which we are born, things of nature and nurture happen to us which impede the realization of the God-life within us. Baptism initiates us into a new life in God and Christ's life in the church, his body. This is the beginning of actualizing to a greater degree the potency of the "image and likeness of God." But if baptism is just the beginning of this journey, we need strength and food to sustain us until we have reached our destination, which is union with the God who made us and from whom we came. Until we return to him, our hearts are restless for complete union—Union.

Our Human Longing for Union

Perhaps this desire for Union can be traced back to the Garden of Eden. In the beginning, Adam and Eve were united with God in friendship and obedience. They were also united with one another—"bone of my bone and flesh of my flesh . . . and the two of them become one body" (Gen 2:23–24). Their unity with God and with one another, however, was broken by sin. Through disobedience their friendship with God was lost and with one another they experienced shame. And so, deep within each one of us, is that long-lost desire to restore the broken unity with God and one another.

Or perhaps the desire for Union can be traced back to life within our mother's womb. Before we were born we were closely united with our mother in every way, not only physically, but emotionally and spiritually as well. In her bestseller, *Necessary Losses,* Judith Viorst writes:

> For before we begin to encounter the inevitable separation of everyday life, we live in a state of oneness with our mother. This ideal state, this state of boundarylessness, this I-am-you-are-me-is-she-is-we, this harmonious interpenetrating mix-up, this gloating "I'm in the milk and the milk's in me," this chill-proof insulation from Aloneness and intimation of mortality: This is a condition known to lovers, saints, psychotics, druggies and infants. It is called bliss.
>
> Our original bliss connection is the umbilical connection, the biological oneness of the womb. Outside the womb we experience the gratifying delusion that we and our mother share a common boundary. Our lifelong yearning for union, so some psychoanalysts say, originates in our yearning to return, if not to the womb, then to the state of illusory union called symbiosis, a state "for which deep down in the original primal unconscious . . . every human being strives.

The Role of the Holy Spirit, Our Advocate

Regardless of the many psycho-bio-spiritual reasons for the desire for unity, we must recognize the fact that the need is there, and if God put it there, then God must meet the need. And this God does through various ways such as friendship, marriage, mysticism and the eucharist. More specifically, we can attribute the work of creating unity to the person of the holy Spirit. Jesus told the disciples: "But I tell you the truth, it is better for you that I go. For if I do not go, the Advocate will not come to you. But if I go, I will send him to you" (16:7). The work which the Advocate was sent to do is brought out clearly in the words and gestures of the sacraments. One sign that indicates the presence of the holy Spirit bringing about unity is the invocation of the holy Spirit along with the imposition of hands. This latter gesture is similar to the "overshadowing" of Mary by the holy Spirit which brought about the most spectacular unity of divinity with humanity in the mystery of the Incarnation.

Each of our sacraments gives us a special insight into some form of union with God. In baptism the holy Spirit brings about a union of the child with God and with the church. Confirmation, another sacrament of initiation, completes our entry into the church and fortifies us with the gifts of the Holy Spirit, making us mature witnesses to God's kingdom. In the sacrament of holy orders, men are "ordained for the church's ministry by the laying on of hands and the gift of the Holy Spirit." Priests are instructed to unite the spiritual sacrifices of the faithful to the eucharistic sacrifices of Christ, and to unite themselves more closely every day with Christ. There is also a unity of love, respect, service and obedience among deacons, priests and bishops. In matrimony, the union of husband and wife images the covenant between God and his people and is the sign of special union of Christ and the church. In the sacrament of reconciliation, the penitent is reunited with the church by the holy Spirit, "sent among us for the forgiveness of sins." In the anointing of the sick, the priest prays that the infirm person may be helped with the grace of the holy Spirit. This is a prayer for spiritual and physical well-being and wholeness or unity.

Finally there is the sacrament of the eucharist. During the celebration of the eucharistic liturgy, there is an invocation of the Spirit which shows that while the eucharist is the action of the risen Christ among us, it is also the action of the holy Spirit. From our Western liturgy we have the words found in Eucharistic Prayer II: "Let your Spirit come upon these gifts to make them holy, so that they may become for us the body and blood of our Lord, Jesus Christ." And from the Divine and Holy Liturgy of John Chrysostom (Eastern rite), we have the invocation of the Spirit as follows: "So that, those who partake of them (holy bread, holy chalice), they may be for the cleansing of the soul, for the remission of sins, for the communion of the holy Spirit, for the fullness of the kingdom of heaven, for intimate confidence in You, and not for judgment or condemnation."

Going beyond the blessing of the bread and wine, the Western rite makes it clear that we, along with the gifts, receive the transforming Spirit: "May all of us who share in the body and blood of Christ be brought together in unity by the holy Spirit." This union of us, one to the other, is clearly taught by St. Paul with his theology of the body of Christ—Jesus as head and we as members—with all its implications for how we live our lives. Paul had no doubt that the bread and wine was the body and blood of Jesus Christ, but for him it was the "whole Christ," the risen, glorified Christ united to all who believed in him and lived in him.

That is why a right relationship was called for among the members of each Christian community. No wonder Paul got so upset when the wealthy members did not provide for the needs of the poor before celebrating the eucharistic meal. Perhaps that is why he warned that those who eat and drink without recognizing the body, are eating and drinking unto damnation. Paul saw the body of Christ in all its mystical and cosmic dimensions, not simply "receiving Jesus," the head of the body.

In a sermon on the mass, Father William McNamara, O.C.D. once said that we go through the three classical stages of spiritual and mystical life in the eucharistic liturgy itself. First of all, we go through the **purgative** way at the penitential rite when we examine our sinfulness before the presence of God and his church, throw ourselves at his feet and beg "Lord, have mercy." We are "purged" of our guilt. Next, we pass through the **illuminative** way as our minds and hearts are enlightened by the Word of God, and as we offer our total selves to the Father with Jesus. Some of the darkness of our lives falls away as God's light helps us to realize how close we are to God. Finally, during the eucharistic prayer we experience the **unitive** way as we come into "holy communion" with God and all creation. Often a feeling of deep peace accompanies this moment of union.

To this helpful insight of Fr. McNamara's we could add that the mass is a foretaste of the things to come in heaven and indeed we go through the same process when we come to die, although in heaven all is one and there is no need of one thing following another in sequence. Our encounter with God at the moment of death will first of all be **purgative,** from which we get the notion of purgatory. Call it what you will, purification will take place as our lives are replayed before our eyes and God's.

The Jesuit theologian Karl Rahner believed that at death we become "pan-cosmic" or capable of a totally expanded consciousness. As we realize the cosmic consequences of our faults, failings and sins, there will be intense pain and embarrassment. The old, sinful self will be burned away as the **illumination** of who we really are and what God meant us to be is clear. It is here that the Word is both judge and light, illuminating God's providential plan for us so that we will know, even as we are known. Now the mystery unfolds and disappears along with faith. Now there is only knowledge and **union,** the fulfillment of our deepest longings.

The faith and hope which carried us through the times for which we were "sent into the world" (Jn 17:18) have disappeared, and only love remains. We experience total union between lover and the beloved, indescribable, ineffable union, known only in human terms as spousal (and dare we say, orgasmic) union. An eternal ecstasy awaits us, and the eucharist, the "Sacrament of the Conquest of Death," is a foretaste of that heavenly union. Jesus made all of this clear in his last words to his disciples, words spoken while he stood in the shadow of the cross.

DISCUSSION

Take a few moments to reflect on this situation. It wasn't too many decades ago that black Catholics, when they attended mass in a "white church," had to wait until all the whites had received holy communion before they approached the altar rail. St. Paul would have had a field day with that practice.

What went wrong? What prevents people from recognizing the body of Christ? Can you think of similar instances? What can be done about these situations?

BREAK

Enjoy refreshments and each other's company.

WRAP-UP

1. Look ahead to the "During the Week" follow-up activities. (optional)
2. Look ahead to the scripture passage and the theme of the next session. Decide on a time during the upcoming week when you will read the chapter.
3. Participate in the Closing Prayer.

DURING THE WEEK

1. When you attend mass this week, listen for words that speak about unity and look for gestures which express unity. Try going to mass at a different parish and bring your sense of unity with you to share with the strangers you meet there. After the mass is over, spend a few minutes in silence reflecting on how you can share the living union of the eucharist with your close relatives and friends.
2. Many Catholics say that the eucharist is the center of their prayer. Think about the way you have been formed spiritually by the eucharist. Do you remember your first holy communion? What impressed you the most on that memorable day? As a youth, did the eucharist make any difference in your daily life? Does it today?

17. Call to the Cross

Scripture Passage

Matthew, chapters 26–28: **Jesus gives himself over and undergoes his passion for the sake of the kingdom.**

PRAYER

Introduction: A Note on the Text

Leader: As we listen to the gospel each week at Sunday mass, we probably don't notice much difference from Matthew to Mark to Luke. In fact, as a group they're called **synoptic** because they seem to "see with the same eye." However, a closer look at Matthew's gospel shows us that he frequently quotes the Hebrew scriptures and always takes care to point out that what happened in Jesus' life fulfills a prophetic saying. He even constructed the gospel around five major discourses of Jesus, modeled on the Torah, or Law, which forms the first five books of the Bible. Scholars agree that Matthew was a Jew who converted to Christianity and that he probably lived in Antioch, a thriving city about 300 miles north of Jerusalem where many Jews had settled.

One of the most difficult problems for these early converts from Judaism was the crucifixion of Jesus. As they struggled to understand why Jesus had to undergo such a shameful death, stories of the passion were often read during the liturgy. As the stories were collected, they took the form of the "passion narratives," which then became the core of the gospels. The question of these early converts to Christianity, "Why did Jesus suffer?" still causes us to ponder. In fact, the passion narrative is read in its entirety twice each year during Holy Week. The passage read on Palm Sunday is the one we consider today.

161

To contemplate Jesus' suffering is to understand God's "love beyond all telling" in a special way.

Call to Prayer

Leader: Let us turn our eyes to Jesus on the cross and our thoughts to his inner struggle. (A crucifix should be displayed in the center of the group. Music, song, or a gathering gesture may be used.)

Reading

Reader: A reading from the gospel according to Matthew (26:25–46).

> Then Jesus came with them to a place called Gethsemane, and he said to his disciples, "Sit here while I go over there and pray." He took along Peter and the two sons of Zebedee, and began to feel sorrow and distress. Then he said to them, "My soul is sorrowful even to death. Remain here and keep watch with me." He advanced a little and fell prostrate in prayer, saying, "My Father, if it is possible, let this cup pass from me; yet, not as I will, but as you will." When he returned to his disciples he found them asleep. He said to Peter, "So you could not keep watch with me for one hour? Watch and pray that you may not undergo the test. The spirit is willing, but the flesh is weak." Withdrawing a second time, he prayed again, "My Father, if it is not possible that this cup pass without my drinking it, your will be done! Then he returned once more and found them and withdrew again and prayed a third time, saying the same thing again. Then he returned to his disciples and said to them, "Are you still sleeping and taking your rest? Behold, the hour is at hand when the Son of Man is to be handed over to sinners. Get up, let us go. Look, my betrayer is at hand."

Individual Reflection

Leader: Jesus, afraid and vulnerable, goes back and forth between his Father and his friends. When have I felt fearful and helpless, begging that I might not have to "undergo the test"? Let me join my moment of pain with that of Jesus. (All pause for silent reflection.)

Prayer

Leader: (holding up the crucifix for all to see) Behold the wood of the cross, on which hung the Savior of the world.

All: Come, let us worship.

(The leader reverently venerates the crucifix, then passes it to the next one, and so on around the group.)

All: (Stand.) Holy is God! Holy and strong! Holy immortal One, have mercy on us! Amen.

LESSON

Suffering As A Theme of Spirituality

Over and over through these sessions we have come up against the problem of human suffering and how a spiritual viewpoint enables us to gain the perspective we need to deal with life's problems. The contribution scripture makes to this aspect of spirituality is immense, since we have God's revelation given over a period of many hundreds of years to many individuals who were seeking the same answers. If we recall the story of Ruth, we are reminded that human fidelity is far outdistanced by God's fidelity. Jeremiah's cries were from a heart torn apart by grief at the sight of a people willing to abandon their God. Job had no recourse, no defense but to abandon himself to the will of a God far superior to his multi-millionaire status.

Jesus is the direct revelation of God, yet he does not brush away the problem of suffering, deep-rooted as it is in human nature. Rather, he undergoes the test. He suffers. Because of his passion, suffering has a different meaning. As we hear the call to the cross, we look to him for that meaning, examining Matthew's gospel for insights.

When Matthew wrote his gospel around the year A.D. 80, the Israelite people had sunk to a low point in their history. During Jesus' active ministry in the 30's, a great deal of religious unrest was apparent through the various parties: the Pharisees, the Sadducees, the Zealots, the Essenes. In the years after his death, famine sapped the energies of the people, while their internal squabblings led to political murders, even of high priests. The Roman procurators became persecutors, restricting civil rights. Finally, open rebellion broke out, prompting the Romans to siege Jerusalem, slaughter the rebels, and finally, raze their temple in A.D. 70.

Amidst the rubble, the Jewish leaders, known as Pharisees in the gospel, regrouped. They withdrew from the ruins of Jerusalem and began to study and reflect. Besides these external disasters, they recognized the steady diminishment of their numbers as some Jews joined what had originally appeared as a mere schismatic branch, but was now strongly identified as "Christian," or followers of the Messiah. What did Moses' law, the Torah, mean in these new circumstances? They began to write the Mishnah, a detailed explanation of the Torah. Meanwhile, Matthew, a Jew who had converted to Christianity, countered by writing his gospel as an explanation of how Jesus fulfilled the Torah.

Matthew followed Mark's gospel closely, adapting it to his Jewish-Christian audience. He views the disciples in a more favorable light than Mark, but retains high, demanding standards. He quotes Jesus as saying: "Foxes have dens and birds of the sky have nests, but the Son of Man has nowhere to rest his head," and "Follow me, and let the dead bury their dead" (Mt. 8:20, 22). Doubtless reflecting the problems of his situation around A.D. 80, Matthew gives special force to the warning Jesus gives the disciples: "But beware of people, for they will hand you over to courts and scourge you in their synagogues. . . . Brother will hand over brother to death . . ." (10:17, 21).

Why must our spirituality include the cross? Matthew makes it very clear with these words of Jesus: "Whoever does not take up his cross and follow after me is not worthy of me. Whoever finds his life will lose it, and whoever loses his life for my sake will find it" (10:38–39). Together with Mark and Luke he includes this difficult but incontrovertible passage:

> Then Jesus said to his disciples, "Whoever wishes to come after me must deny himself, take up his cross, and follow me. For whoever wishes to save his life will lose it, but whoever loses his life for my sake will find it. What profit would there be for one to gain the world and forfeit his life? Or what can one give in exchange for his life?" (16:24–26)

Jesus Lives Out the Truth of His Own Words

The disciples had reason to remember these words of Jesus, for they recalled them against a background of how he himself had lived them out. Why did Jesus suffer? The answer may be found partly by looking at the circumstances of his life and partly by attempting to understand God's plan.

The whole of the gospel leads to the passion in the same way as a plot demands resolution. Jesus, in the circumstances of his life as a Palestinian Jew in the first century, lived by two laws. The first was the Torah, which directed him to observe the Jewish religious practices and feasts. The second was Roman law, administered by the procurator and enforced by the occupation troops. Since Roman policy was to follow regional customs and law as much as possible, they allowed the puppet king, Herod, and the ruling council, the Sanhedrin, a great deal of leeway in handling local affairs. In Matthew's retelling of the events of Jesus' last days, it is clear that Jesus' sharp criticisms of the religious leaders and his popularity as a preacher and healer had brought him into direct opposition to the Sanhedrin.

There were many factions among the Jews in Palestine, so control of the council had become a political football. The Sadducees and High Priest were in charge and were determined to remain so. They are portrayed as ruthless, willing to stop at nothing to get rid of Jesus. They solicit a traitor, Judas. They find witnesses willing to twist their testimony to make Jesus appear as a blasphemer. With more regard for traditional treatment of blasphemers than for courtroom dignity, they resort to physical abuse of the accused, Jesus. They enter into collusion with the Roman authorities to carry out the execution, planting rabble-rousers in the crowds to instill fear of a riot in their overlords. Why did Jesus die such a terrible death? On a practical human level, it was because he spoke out against abuse of power and became a victim of that same power.

A second reason for Jesus' suffering may be found by viewing his death as a Passover. The gospel stories do not elaborate on the sufferings, but simply state what happened in a simple, straightforward style. After detailing the intense inner struggle of Jesus in Gethsemane, the description shifts to an exterior perspective. Once Jesus has somehow sensed that this is the moment for which the Father has been preparing him, he takes firm hold, rebuking the friend who would defend him with a sword, remaining silent before his judges, calmly announcing his expected vindication. Whatever they do to him, he endures. Finally, at the moment of his death, "Jesus cried out in a loud voice" the last words of the prayer which had apparently continued inside him all along, Psalm 22: "My God, my God, why have you forsaken me?" (Mt 27:46).

Why did Jesus die such a terrible death? On a cosmic and theological level, Jesus needed to fulfill the Father's will, to pass beyond human limitations into the full potential of his unique divine-human self. We finally come to understand God's plan at the scene of the empty tomb when Jesus met his old friends Mary and Mary Magdalene outside his empty tomb. "Peace!" he says. God's plan is peace. He directs the whole crowd of disciples to gather in Galilee, where they see him once again. Astonished, they believe. Jesus had to die, but only to take his place among us in a new way, a way which makes peace possible.

The Impact of Jesus' Death

There can be no doubt that the dramatic details of Jesus' death caught the imagination of the faithful over the centuries. This was especially true in Europe during the middle ages. Almost all of our greatest artists contributed a rendition of Jesus in one of the situations described in scripture and brought forward into popular devotion by the sorrowful mysteries of the rosary—the Agony in the Garden, the Scourging at the Pillar, the Crowning of Thorns, the Carrying of the Cross, and the Crucifixion. The Pietà was also a popular subject, while the Stations of the Cross provided a further occasion to depict the suffering of Christ and to invite the reflection of Christians.

Certain cultures, such as the Spanish and their colonial offspring in Latin America, foster a spirituality centered on the passion. Processions, and costumed pageants are elaborately staged to enable participants to enter into the experience of their Lord. The visions related by medieval mystics provide detailed descriptions of the suffering Jesus. Even so peaceful and joyful a saint as Francis of Assisi is remembered for having received the gift of the stigmata.

Perhaps the fact that the human body with arms outstretched in the posture of an **orans** takes the form of a cross, tells us something about the power of this symbol. We can only take this form while standing upright, at attention, and extending ourselves as far as possible. This posture is the first part of an enthusiastic hug through which we embrace others and gather them close. Even tracing the sign of the cross from forehead to breast to shoulders reminds us to know, love and serve God.

Whether its expression be maudlin and sentimental or sturdy and thoughtful, the cross has the power to move us. We come to a sense of our own small sinfulness over against the "love beyond all telling" of a God who didn't hesitate to lay down his life for us. Seeing the cross gradually exposed during the Good Friday liturgy, joining ranks with other Christians who silently venerate the feet of the corpus, listening to the "Reproaches"—"My people, what have I done to you? In what have I offended you? Answer me!"—all strike a chord of sorrow in our hearts.

Simply gazing at the face of "the Crucified" renews our sense of courage and stamina. Faced with his gaze, we become willing to acknowledge our guilt for our sin. Sidestepping our psychological and emotional barriers, in a moment of truth, we recognize that we have joined the crowd which yells, "Crucify him!" We resolve once again to take up our own cross, to step beyond our mean-spirited measuring of life's tasks and to strive once more to become the person God intended at the moment of our creation.

The Paschal Mystery

Many preachers who urge us to take up our cross do us a disservice by dwelling only on the negative side of the message. If we describe our cross as a drunken husband who beats us, the proper response is not, "Offer it up." During the middle ages St. Anselm developed a theory that Jesus had to suffer because the Father demanded that some human "make up" for all the sin in the world; it took a divine-human person to fully atone, but we still had to chip in our little bit by putting up with the sorrows life dealt us. This is not the call to the cross.

Suffering is not simply a fact of human existence which is to be borne uncritically. Some suffering results from sin and has natural consequences, such as a hangover which I experience after abusing alcohol. But other suffering is unexplainable, such as the accidental drowning of a child. Also, suffering can occur just because of our human limitations—we are simply not able to have everything we need or want, to be on friendly terms with everyone, to please everyone. After all, "we're only human." Then again, suffering is likely to occur when we stand up for what is right. The point of Christian suffering is to really **feel** the discrepancy between what **is** and what **should be** and to work, with God's help, to overcome the difference.

There is a great difference between the world we know and the world God has in mind. A world over which God reigns is our goal because it is the reign of God that Jesus came to bring about. This goal was not unattainable because Jesus died; rather, Jesus reappeared in risen form to say, "Peace." He was able to speak of peace because he had personally stretched out his arms to bridge the gap between earth and heaven. He had overcome the discrepancy between what is and what should be. So reconciled within himself, he knew peace.

As for us, we know that he lived a full human life and died a courageous death and is once more among us. We know it and yet we continue to ponder its mystery. A mystery is a mystery because we can't explain it but we can plumb its depths. The cross is such a challenge to us that we devote ourselves to it each year during Lent and the **Triduum,** those traditional days of Good Friday, Holy Saturday, and Easter Sunday which recall this central, paschal mystery.

The call to the cross means the call to die to self and to rise to Christ on a daily basis. How many occasions can we think of where "man" proposes and God disposes? Such occasions of frustration may become the opportunity to put aside our own interests (die to self) and rise to the occasion (rise in Christ). It's a constant challenge to remember that we are not the center of the universe, nor is our little domestic world, or our close-knit work world. Dying to self and rising in Christ calls on us to stretch our horizons. We need to continue to try to take **God's** viewpoint in the face of opposite evidence from a **human** standpoint. Like Jesus, we want to join earth to heaven. It isn't easy.

Peace in the Face of Violence

Take violence for example. One of the biggest problems in our society today is violence in the home. People take out their inner sufferings on those closest to them. They pollute their language with obscenities. They yell at their husbands. They molest their children. Some persons are so afflicted with violence that they carry it into the community. They fight. They rape. They murder. On an international level, they become terrorists or soldiers of opportunity or make violence "legal" in the name of war or public control.

What is God's viewpoint? How does a Christian deal with this? Pope John Paul II gave us an example. In May, 1981, he was being driven in an open car through a packed St. Peter's Square. A shot rang out. The pope slumped back, his body in shock from the bullet that sliced through his tissues. Unconscious, only the help of his assistants got him out of the chaotic crowd to the hospital in time to allow the healing hands of a physician to minister to his gunshot wounds.

Pope John Paul recovered. Gradually his physical wound healed. But what of his interior wound? Not only would the world not give peace, but it lashed out in terror at a pope who symbolized God's peace. All that Pope John Paul held dear was shattered. How could this wound be healed? Two and a half years later, in January, 1984, Pope John Paul performed a remarkable gesture. He visited his would-be assassin, Mehmit Ali Agca. Writing in *Time* magazine, Lance Morrow described the scene:

In a bare, white-walled cell in Rome's Rebibbia prison, John Paul tenderly held the hand that had held the gun that was meant to kill him. . . . The Pope brought the photographers and the cameramen because he wanted the image in that cell to be shown around a world filled with nuclear arsenals and unforgiving hatreds, with hostile superpowers and smaller, implacable fanaticisms.

Surely one of the toughest demands of a Christian spirituality which embraces the cross as it attempts to speak "Peace" is Jesus' directive, "Therefore, if you bring your gift to the altar, and there recall that your brother has anything against you, leave your gift there at the altar, go first and be reconciled with your brother, and then come and offer your gift" (Mt 5:23–24). Any spirituality which claims the name "Christian" must be willing to leap the chasms created by our wounded human nature. We live in the "now" and view Jesus in the "not yet." The example of Pope John Paul II is only one of many which inspire us to realize that Jesus brings us a portion of the "not yet" as he comes to us in communion. Since it is the nature of God to love to the limit, we who strive for union with God will need to stumble on the cross as we make our way Home.

DISCUSSION

Jesus' first word to the women outside the empty tomb was, "Peace." This was the fruit of his suffering. In our daily struggle to be faithful to God's view, to live the paschal mystery of dying and rising, we too need to take the first step to "Let Peace Begin with Me."

1. Take a few moments to recall an incident in your life when you have experienced peace after a time of suffering.
2. Find a partner and share your stories.

BREAK

Enjoy refreshments and each other's company.

WRAP-UP

1. Look ahead to the "During the Week" follow-up activities. (optional)
2. Look ahead to the scripture passage and the theme of the next session. Decide on a time during the upcoming week when you will read the chapter.
3. Participate in the Closing Prayer.

DURING THE WEEK

Reflect on the following excerpts from **The Challenge of Peace: God's Promise and Our Response,** the 1983 pastoral letter of the United States Bishops.

1. "We readily recognize that we live in a world that is becoming increasingly estranged from Christian values. In order to remain a Christian, one must take a resolute stand against many commonly accepted axioms of the world." (#277)
   Reflect: Give some examples of "commonly accepted axioms of the world" against which we, as Christians, need to take a stand.
2. "Interior peace becomes possible only when we have a conversion of spirit. We cannot have peace with hate in our hearts." (#284)
   Reflect: What experience in my life proves this to me?
3. "Therefore we encourage every Catholic to make the sign of peace at Mass an authentic sign of our reconciliation with God and with one another. This sign of peace is also a visible expression of our commitment to work for peace as a Christian community. We approach the table of the Lord only after having dedicated ourselves as a Christian community to peace and reconciliation." (#295)
   Reflect: Does sharing the sign of peace at mass help your family's recurring need for reconciliation?
4. "As a tangible sign of our need and desire to do penance we, for the cause of peace, commit ourselves to fast and abstinence on each Friday of the year. We call upon our people voluntarily to do penance on Friday by eating less food and by abstaining from meat." (#298)
   Reflect: Try this. Speak about your experience to someone else.

18. Call To Witness

Scripture Passage

John, chapter 20 and chapter 21; Matthew 28; Mark 16; Luke 24: **The resurrected Jesus appears to his disciples and commands them to go forth to carry on his mission.**

PRAYER

Introduction: A Note on the Text

Leader: We have already examined John's gospel in chapter 16, so we recognize its uniqueness as compared to the synoptics. However, all four gospels are alike in that the final chapters form what are called the "Resurrection Narratives." The gospels took their content from the stories about Jesus which circulated within the communities of Christians that gathered in the house churches and synagogues of cities throughout the Roman Empire. The stories about the resurrection show a great many variations from one evangelist to the other. However, each gospel has two types of stories. Although no evangelist tells of anyone who actually saw the resurrection, they all tell about someone who visited the tomb and found it empty, thus witnessing to the fact that Jesus must have risen from the dead since no corpse remained. The second type of story tells about a witness—always someone well-known in the community of disciples—who actually experienced a face-to-face appearance with the risen Lord.

Our passage for prayer is one of the second type, the poignant appearance of Jesus to Mary Magdalene in the garden in which the tomb was located. We know of Mary from other gospel passages, where she is seen to be a disciple of Jesus, following him and attending to his needs. She has seen him and has come to love him and to believe in him. On this occasion, under the stress of the extraordinary events, Mary struggles to find a lead, a direction. Then, in one touching moment of recognition, she moves from sight to in-sight.

Call to Prayer

Leader: Let us take a moment to release ourselves from our daily cares and concerns, to quiet our active energies, and to go into the garden at the time when morning has broken. (Music, song, or a gathering gesture may be used.)

Reading

Reader: A reading from the gospel according to John (20:11–18).

But Mary [of Magdala] stayed outside the tomb weeping. And as she wept, she bent over into the tomb and saw two angels in white sitting there, one at the head and one at the feet where the body of Jesus had been. And they said to her, "Woman, why are you weeping?" She said to them, "They have taken my Lord, and I don't know where they laid him." When she had said this, she turned around and saw Jesus there, but did not know it was Jesus. Jesus said to her, "Woman, why are you weeping? Whom are you looking for?" She thought it was the gardener and said to him, "Sir, if you carried him away, tell me where you laid him, and I will take him." Jesus said to her, "Mary!" She turned and said to him in Hebrew, "Rabbouni," which means Teacher. Jesus said to her, "Stop holding on to me, for I have not yet ascended to the Father. But go to my brothers and tell them, 'I am going to my Father and your Father, to my God and your God.'" Mary of Magdala went and announced to the disciples, "I have seen the Lord," and what he told her.

Individual Reflection

Leader: As I consider Mary in her grief, I recall incidents in my own life when I have been on the edge, vulnerable. Such a moment is often a time for the Lord to make his presence felt. Close your eyes and try to visualize the moment of recognition. Beseech the Lord to make his presence felt to you. (All pause for silent prayer.)

Prayer

All: Rabbouni Jesus, I plead for your presence in my life. Make my blindness fall away so that I might recognize you hidden in the guise of my family, my friends, my co-workers. Even as I grow close to you and come to savor your presence, give me the vigor and confidence to tell others about you, my Lord. Amen.

LESSON

The Significance of the Resurrection

When I was a child, my father used to announce Easter Day by proclaiming that it was "the greatest feast in the Christian calendar!" Most Christian people do indeed mark the importance of this day with new spring clothes, church attendance, Easter baskets with candy and eggs, and family gatherings. Why is the feast of the resurrection so highly celebrated? The details of the scripture accounts provide us with helpful information.

In John 20:6 we learn that the wrappings which had covered Jesus were lying on the ground of the tomb. This contrasts with the account of the raising of Lazarus in 11:44, where "the dead man came out bound head and foot with linen strips, his face wrapped in a cloth." Lazarus was alive—but because he had been resuscitated; he had not actually completed the passage from life to death, so eventually, later, he would die. Jesus was alive—but because he had been raised by the Father; he had actually already died, so could not die again. Yet he was, in fact, alive! What kind of life was this?

Jesus must have had a somewhat different appearance than what he had before because Mary Magdalene didn't recognize him at first. Yet when he spoke her name, she immediately knew him and apparently ran over and hugged him in some manner. (Matthew tells us that the women embraced Jesus' feet.) This action prompted Jesus to tell her, "Stop holding on to me. . . ." No longer held back by human limitations, Jesus is free to move out about at will. Because he can do this, he can be there for us always, so there is no need to cling to him. And apparently Jesus did just that in the days after his resurrection—moved freely among his friends, reassuring them with his presence.

Mary Magdalene's Conversion

Mary's reaction helps us to understand another specifically Christian stamp to our spirituality. Something happened inside her when she realized Jesus' identity. Her cry of recognition was an acknowledgment that here was Someone who could claim her complete devotion. Her apparent move to embrace him demonstrated her desire to transcend herself and her surroundings in order to be united with him. At that moment, she experienced conversion.

Such an experience is a frequent one among those who attempt discipleship. As with Mary, it is not as though they have not already been following the Lord. In fact, conversion often does not occur until later in life, when in one small instant something is different inside. The natural human and social ties shake loose a little as one's values are reshuffled and the divine claim is strengthened. Our natural direction, which is to become spiritualized, takes a more definitive form, a more compelling force.

With Mary, the inner shift is described in the words by which Jesus describes the last phase of his mission: "I am ascending to my Father **and your Father,** to my God **and your God.**" Somehow Mary too has entered into this life-beyond-life of Jesus. Now Jesus' Father is Mary's Father as well. His God is accessible to her. The words of Jesus in the Last Discourse are fulfilled—at his going, the Advocate comes. Human beings can communicate with God in a new and immediate way and humanity becomes the media God uses to communicate with other human beings. Mary's next task becomes the call of every Christian—the call to **witness.** She must have done her job well, for it is remembered in all four gospels. We can close our eyes and imagine this energetic and attractive woman, her eyes shining with the glow of inner enlightenment, announcing to the disciples, "I have seen the Lord!" The gift that is given becomes a gift to others.

The New Form of Jesus' Body

The appearances of Jesus which are recorded in the five gospel chapters which tell the events of the resurrection help us get a glimpse of Jesus alive in this new way. Each evangelist includes one chapter, with an additional chapter appended to John's gospel. They also help us understand what that "new life" means for us. To be linked to Jesus implies two imperatives: (1) community; and (2) commission.

Jesus had spent his public life journeying about with his disciples teaching and healing. He had taken great care to train them, to make sure they understood what the reign of God was like and what it would take to bring it about. At his death it looked like all that training was wasted, for the teacher was dead and the disciples scattered. However, the news that Jesus had been seen spread like wildfire and brought the old gang back together.

The resurrection chapters include almost a roll call: Matthew names Mary Magdalene and the other Mary (28:1) as well as "the eleven disciples" (28:16). Mark also names Mary Magdalene as well as Mary the mother of James, and Salome (16:1), while the appendix to Chapter 16 mentions two of the disciples (16:12) and "the Eleven" (16:14). Luke refers to Mary of Magdala, Joanna, and Mary the mother of James, as well as "the Eleven" (24:9–10) and "two of them" (24:13) who join "the eleven and those with them" where they learn that Jesus had appeared to Simon (24:34). John lists Peter and "the other disciple" as investigating Mary Magdalene's report; within the gathering, Thomas and Peter are subjects of special scrutiny. John lists the names of the disciples: "Together were Simon Peter, Thomas called Didymus, Nathanael from Cana in Galilee, Zebedee's sons, and two others of his disciples" (21:2). There can be no doubt that we are among a **community!**

The time during which Jesus appeared in his resurrected body among his disciples was very limited. Nonetheless these brief encounters had a phenomenal effect. The community found itself once again. They began to gain the first glimmers of the idea that they themselves would become the new form of Christ's resurrected body.

Jesus used these opportunities to make it clear that, just as he had a mission from the Father, his disciples had a mission from him. It is to this fledgling community that Jesus gives the **commission** that dictates the shape of his body. All four of the evangelists include Jesus' command. Matthew's wording has come to be called "the great commission":

All power in heaven and on earth has been given to me. Go, therefore, and make disciples of all nations, baptizing them in the name of the Father, and of the Son, and of the holy Spirit, teaching them to observe all that I have commanded you. And behold, I am with you always, until the end of the age (28:18–20).

The appendix to Mark's gospel is brief but strong:

> Go into the whole world and proclaim the gospel to every creature (16:15).

Luke includes the command in the beginning of Acts:

> But you will receive power when the holy Spirit comes upon you; and you will be my witnesses in Jerusalem, throughout Judea and Samaria, yes, and to the ends of the earth (Acts 1:8).

John phrases it:

> "As the Father has sent me, so I send you." And when he had said this, he breathed on them and said to them, "Receive the holy Spirit. Whose sins you forgive are forgiven them, and whose sins you retain are retained" (Jn 20:21–23).

Though each evangelist uses different words, the common thread is clear: go . . . make disciples . . . proclaim the good news . . . be my witnesses . . . I send you. . . . The community is not a static, self-sufficient group, but a dynamic, Spirit-filled church which is commissioned to continue what Jesus has begun.

Evangelization Fulfills Christ's Command

The word "gospel" is derived from the Greek word *evangelion,* meaning "good news" or "good tidings." We have already noted that the four who wrote the gospels are called evangelists. Accordingly, it's easy to see why a community which has been commissioned to proclaim the good news came to be called **evangelizers.** Those of us who have been formed in the Catholic tradition tend to think of evangelization as a "Protestant" activity. However, since we proudly claim our origin with the apostles, we can scarcely sidestep Jesus' own imperative.

In 1975, ten years after the close of the epochal Second Vatican Council, Pope Paul VI issued an "Apostolic Exhortation" entitled *On Evangelization in the Modern World.* In it, he strongly affirms: "We wish to confirm once more that the task of evangelizing all people constitutes the essential mission of the church." (#14) Those of us who are striving to strengthen the link between our spirituality and the Bible have already identified the scriptural basis of that papal pronouncement. Let's consider three aspects of Pope Paul's message: (1) What it means to be a witness; (2) various methods of evangelization; and (3) the qualities of evangelizers.

First, what does it mean to **witness?** We have seen that Mary Magdalene, transformed by her encounter with the risen Christ, is an excellent model. She conveyed such total conviction to the disillusioned disciples that they too were willing to take the chance of once again meeting their Teacher and Friend. Our human criteria of judgment is often limited to scientifically verifiable data. A witness is able to take people where they are, but goes on to help them believe in possibilities they haven't considered. Evidence based on personal knowledge is offered in a manner that appeals to another's sense of what is true, right, and good.

Secondly, what **methods** can we use to evangelize? For most of us, personal witness is obviously the most important method. Taking the opportunity in conversation to express our religiously-based values to our associates helps them realize that there are "good people" who take religion seriously. This method can be as simple as remarking, "Our family is going to the church fiesta this weekend," or, "Our priest said in his homily last Sunday that gossip is a form of 'killing,' so just remind me!" To motivate ourselves toward such a confident approach, we need to evangelize ourselves continually by prayer, study and worship so that our vision of the Lord and his kingdom does not grow dim.

Active involvement in one's parish as a catechist or liturgical minister gives a public character to evangelization. Some parishes sponsor outreach programs to invite non-Catholics to participate in pre-baptismal R.C.I.A. classes or to invite non-practicing Catholics to become involved in the church community. Serving as a sponsor for a catechumen both activates one's own faith and also evangelizes someone else. Simply attending church functions and programs gives us a chance to associate with others who share and reinforce our values. Civic or social involvement increases our range of contacts and our opportunities to influence others in a Christian manner.

Some people feel a definite call to preach, the classic method of evangelization, through which someone directly proclaims the meaning of Jesus' life and teaching. They may experience this as a call to the ordained ministry or perhaps to be a missionary to persons in a non-Christian culture. Those who feel called to life as a religious sister or brother seek a life devoted to evangelization. It is evident that methods of evangelization are limited only by the imagination and enthusiasm of Christians.

Finally, what **qualities** make a good witness? A witness must be authentic. He or she must feel and believe deep down the truth of his or her message, then go on to live out these beliefs, as we realize through the old adage, "What you are speaks so loudly that I can't hear what you're saying." In addition, a good witness is a joyful, even enthusiastic person. Because Christian faith tells us that what we see isn't necessarily what we get, a witness keeps an eye out for those aspects of the reign of God which are already visible, rather than getting bogged down in the trials and troubles of daily life. Not that he or she is a Pollyanna, but that a witness can manage the balance between ideal and reality, maintaining humor and perspective.

Certainly anyone who makes the effort to evangelize must have the quality of humility, because no one can win respect from everyone, and we will at times be rebuffed. We need to remember that we don't evangelize because we want attention and praise, but because we want to make people think about deeper issues. We will also want to foster the ability to discern good from evil, and to pray for prudence to know when to speak and when to keep silent.

Who Needs Evangelization?

To ask, "Who needs evangelization?" is to ask, "Who needs good news?", and we would all agree that we all need good news. But this is a question worth considering, because evangelization doesn't come easily to us. If we can be convinced of the need, perhaps we will be more ready to attempt it.

First of all, we ourselves, as the church, need evangelizing. We form a subculture of the larger society in the sense that there are rituals of initiation, as well as a language which only members can speak comfortably. While on a business trip to Miami, a man called home to tell his wife that his plane had circled the airport because of a hurricane in the Gulf of Mexico. "Did you say your Act of Contrition?" she inquired. Since he was not a Catholic, this approach to helping him express any fears fell flat.

For us who belong to what we believe is the "one true church," it's easy to forget that we haven't yet exhausted God's revelation. So we need to start with ourselves, trying to see what we look like to outsiders. At times that can be a discouraging exercise when we encounter people who have written us off as irrelevant or arrogant or misguided. Such information is most helpful in identifying our weak points and in trying to address these, purifying our "churchy" culture so it more clearly shows forth its Founder.

And how can we be sure that the Christ we are trying to share is the Christ of the universal church's faith? Simply because we are who we are, we have a certain image of Christ. To some extent that image is distorted by our limited experiences. We need to evangelize each other's image of Christ by challenging one another, by holding up that image to the scrutiny of the scriptural testimony as we study together each week.

Who needs good news? Surely the outsiders of society. We need to look around for those for whom the American dream is likely to remain a dream. Usually such persons are poor—lacking money, or education, or a pleasing personality, or the drive to better themselves. They may, in fact, have many things going for them, but have a poor self-concept that prevents them from making the most of their talents. They may be poor in qualities such as generosity and justice, because instead they have developed selfishness and greed. Yes, the poor have many faces. In many respects, the poor are always with us.

Since Jesus claimed that he could be recognized as the Messiah because "the poor" have the good news preached to them, it should be clear to us who are attempting to link spirituality to "real life" that a call to witness, to evangelization, is inescapable. Surely people will be able to look at us and see something special. How can we not share a word that will help them get in touch with their own spiritual nature? On this point, let us give the last word to Pope Paul: "It is unthinkable that a person would accept the Word and give himself or herself to the Kingdom without becoming a person who bears witness to it and proclaims it in his or her turn." (#24)

DISCUSSION

1. The way we fulfill our call to witness will depend on our life setting. Take a few moments to consider how you would advise persons in each of the following situations to witness to their faith:
   —a young mother in an African-American ghetto
   —a middle-aged priest
   —a Catholic Hispanic man who is approached by a Jehovah's Witness

—a college student living in a dorm
—someone in similar circumstances as your own
2. Form groups of three to discuss any of these situations.

BREAK

Enjoy refreshments and each other's company.

WRAP-UP

1. Look ahead to the "During the Week" follow-up activities. (optional)
2. Look ahead to the scripture passage and the theme of the next session. Decide on a time during the upcoming week when you will read chapter 19.
3. Participate in the Closing Prayer.

DURING THE WEEK

Think ahead to the situations you will be likely to encounter this week. Decide on one which could provide a likely moment for you to inject a word of witness to your faith. Rehearse what you might do or say. Take the opportunity and try your plan. Later, reflect on what happened. How did you feel? How did the other person react? What might you do another time?

19. Call To Be Church

Scripture Passage

Acts, chapters 1–15; **Following the command of Jesus and filled with the Spirit, the apostles become witnesses "to the ends of the earth" and in so doing, become church.**

PRAYER

Introduction: A Note on the Text

In the Acts of the Apostles, Luke gives us an inspiring account of life in the early days of the church. From the beginning we see how the holy Spirit forms a fearful band of men and women into a courageous community that Paul would call "The Body of Christ." They were also known as "Followers of the Way," later on in Antioch they were called "Christians," and not until centuries later, "Catholics." Acts is not documentary history as we know it today, but rather follows the genre of that time, combining actual incidents with statements of faith, while retaining several versions of stories considered to be of major importance. It is our prime resource for understanding how God formed the apostles and disciples into a remarkable combination of social institution and mystical body that we call church.

To become church was no easy task. We see how the apostles borrowed some traditions from their Jewish heritage, but also developed new practices. They did not always agree on how to form themselves, how to set up ground rules which would enable them to "teach all nations." Our reading today gives evidence that they were off to a good start. Part of the solution was to assemble and pray, invoking the Spirit to guide them. Another approach was to authorize certain leaders, such as presbyters. Yet another practice was to visit the churches in other towns. However, a major problem unsolved at that time, was that the covenant Law did not allow Jews to eat with uncircumcised persons, Gentiles. How then could they "take and eat" as Jesus had commanded them? Let us see how they settled this situation.

Call to Prayer

Leader: Let us call upon the holy Spirit who forms us into church. (Pause. Music, song, or a gathering gesture may be used.)

Reading

Reader: A reading from the book of Acts (15:1–32).

Some who had come down from Judea were instructing the brothers, "Unless you are circumcised according to the Mosaic practice, you cannot be saved." Because there arose no little dissension and debate by Paul and Barnabas with them, it was decided that Paul, Barnabas, and some of the others should go up to Jerusalem to the apostles and presbyters about this question. . . . When they arrived in Jerusalem, they were welcomed by the church, as well as by the apostles and the presbyters, and they reported what God had done with them. But some from the party of the Pharisees who had become believers stood up and said, "It is necessary to circumcise them and direct them to observe the Mosaic law."

The apostles and the presbyters met together to see about this matter. After much debate had taken place, Peter got up and said to them, "My brothers, you are well aware that from early days God made his choice among you that through my mouth the Gentiles would hear the word of the gospel and believe. And God, who knows the heart, bore witness by granting them the holy Spirit just as he did us. . . . The whole assembly fell silent, and they listened while Paul and Barnabas described the signs and wonders God had worked among the Gentiles through them.

After they had fallen silent, James responded, "My brothers, listen to me. . . . It is my judgment, therefore, that we ought to stop troubling the Gentiles who turn to God. . . ."

Then the apostles and presbyters, in agreement with the whole church, decided to choose representatives and to send them to Antioch with Paul and Barnabas. [They were to deliver a letter which said:] "It is the decision of the holy Spirit and of us not to place on you any burden beyond these necessities, namely, to abstain from meat sacrificed to idols, from blood, from meats of strangled animals, and from unlawful marriage. If you keep free of these, you will be doing what is right. Farewell."

And so they were sent on their journey. Upon their arrival in Antioch they called the assembly together and delivered the letter. When the people read it, they were delighted with the exhortation. Judas and Silas, who were themselves prophets, exhorted and strengthened the brothers with many words.

Individual Reflection

Leader: Recall that although this account describes a peaceful settlement, other passages in the New Testament advise us that the decision was difficult to implement. The Spirit is able to work only where we attend closely to the divine promptings. As I reflect on my own experience of decision making in the life of the church, how and when have I been able to recognize the presence of the Spirit?

Prayer

All: Come holy Spirit, fill the hearts of the faithful. Kindle in them the fire of your love. Send forth your Spirit and they shall be created. And you shall renew the face of the earth.

O God, who by the light of the holy Spirit, did instruct the hearts of the faithful, grant that by this same Spirit we may become truly wise and ever rejoice in his consolation. Through Christ our Lord. Amen.

LESSON

The Formation of the Church

The gospels hardly mention "church" but rather tell us of Jesus and his preaching. It is evident that Jesus did not come among us simply to found a church, but rather he came to lead us to the kingdom of God. Yet it is equally obvious that Jesus' plan was to bring about the goal of the kingdom by means of people whom the Spirit would empower. It is these people who populate the pages of Acts, and it is from them that we learn about the formation of the church. It is our story as well, because Vatican Council II has finally drilled into each and every Catholic the battle cry, "*We* are the church! We are eager to help build the kingdom!"

It is true that in many places the battle cry is only a whimper. All the more reason for us who love the church to practice what might be called "reciprocal ecclesial formation," which is another way of saying "the church forms us and we form the church." This formation, started on the first Pentecost by the power of the holy Spirit, has continued ever since. The Acts of the Apostles shows us how this reciprocal formation took place in the primitive Christian community.

We see the spiritual formation and development of people such as Peter and Paul, and the formation of whole communities such as Antioch and Jerusalem. Formation takes place in peace time and under persecution. Jews, who converted to Christianity, are formed in one way, Gentile Christians in another. And when problems and disagreements arise, the whole church is formed into a closer image of Jesus Christ because of their openness to the holy Spirit working among them and healing their divisions.

As we read through the Acts of the Apostles we discover that from the beginning, the church was not perfect. Yes, most of the members were open to being formed and transformed by the Spirit of Jesus, and that's what made the difference. In Acts 1:15–26 we see Peter proposing that they needed to replace Judas, the prayer of the group, the selection of two candidates and the casting of lots for the final decision in reconstituting "The Twelve." The bilingual, bicultural conflict between the Hellenists and Hebrews regarding the "daily distribution" is described in 6:1–7; here the solution was to expand the ministries to include Greek deacons. In chapter 10 we gain insight into how the Spirit inspired Peter to overcome his firmly entrenched religious and cultural upbringing in favor of the more universal call of the Lord to the centurion Cornelius.

Many people who are seeking a deeper spiritual development see no need for a church. They find inspiration and a higher power in nature, contemplation, or a strict ethical life-style. They prefer to avoid the hassle of working out our human differences for the sake of a community approach. For us who look to the Bible for direction, the Acts of the Apostles makes it clear that our path is not intended to be that of an individual and God, but that God forms us through others in the church.

"Models" of the Church

Some years ago, in a very significant book, *Models of the Church,* Father Avery Dulles, S.J., gave his readers a deeper understanding of what "church" was all about. By "model" he doesn't mean "ideal," but rather a framework around which to gather the various activities of a particular church community. Just as sociologists use the term "life-style," he might have coined the term "church-style." His initial five models or "styles" (Institution, Mystical Communion, Sacrament, Herald, and Servant), along with an image developed subsequently by Dulles (Community of Disciples), can be used to analyze a certain mode in which the Spirit works in the church.

For example, in the study of church history, every ecclesiastical epoch can be examined in light of these models. Invariably, one model will predominate in every historical period and in every geographical location. These models can also be used to study the various styles of leadership and ministry in parishes and dioceses, and will often explain why tensions exist between a group of people who follow one model and another group who subscribe to a different model.

Something should be said at this point about tensions between the advantages and disadvantages within each model, and the antithetical conceptions among the various models themselves. This apparent "creative conflict" can actually be a moment of grace at the time and point where the opposites intersect. It is the moment of paschal mystery being acted out within the framework of the church. Sometimes the grace is present in the healing of the conflict, and at other times it is present in the unresolved struggle which involves a "dying daily." The church is a living organism and thus requires some "stretching" in order to grow.

Now, after 2000 years, we as church are still being formed by the scriptures, church teachings, the sacraments, lives of the saints and so forth. Our lives and the lives of every Catholic throughout the world continue to form the church, for better or worse. We are not yet the spotless Bride of Christ described so poetically in Revelation 21:2— far from it—but hopefully and lovingly we are moving in that direction. There is always room for improvement, and even criticism, but we must keep in mind that when we criticize the church, we criticize ourselves. Any criticism we engage in should be done out of love.

Our particular interest in this chapter is the reciprocal formation that takes place between church and faithful, so we will use Dulles' models as the framework for this endeavor. Each model has its own strengths and weaknesses which impact on the formation of individuals and groups within the church.

The Church As Institution

According to Dulles, the prevailing image of the church is the institutional one. It is a hierarchical, organizational model based largely on juridical authority, administration and chain of command. It is the one model familiar to most people throughout the world, regardless of their religious affiliation. The advantage is that people know who is in charge and, indeed, the fact that someone **is** in charge. The disadvantage is that strong pressure for perfection falls **on** the top person of one level **from** the top person at the next level; a dictatorship is possible at every level of administration, from pastor to pope.

If the institutional church is the most familiar model, so it is with her formative dimension. Most of us, whether clerics, religious or laity, were formed spiritually by the institutional church, within its structures and under its authority. Some were formed in a novitiate or seminary, others in a parish church or as lay missionaries or in CCD programs or in Catholic schools. And it wasn't all that bad. The church has formed some pretty wonderful saints, most of whom have never been formally canonized.

But we have also formed the institutional church, especially if we have lived out our prophetic mission given to us at baptism. It is the prophet who most often comes into conflict with the institutional church. Faithfulness to his or her God-given vision has frequently brought about every sort of punishment from a cautious hierarchy, as is seen when the twentieth-century Jesuit scientist Pierre Tielhard de Chardin was silenced, or the fifteenth-century visionary Joan of Arc was burned to death at the stake. The church, however, has become richer because of their prophetic lives. Whenever we strive to do God's will, especially by fulfilling our baptismal commitment to be priests, prophets and leaders, we form church for the better. When we fail to do so the church is de-formed and we are de-formed.

The Church As Mystical Communion

The image of the church as mystical communion or community of the people of God is a model based largely on the gifts of each member, but also as the action of the holy Spirit in each one. We oversimplify this when we take the attitude that "everyone is equal and we do everything to be a happy community." Yet, the advantage of this model is that many people are involved in the life of the church and the contributions of each one are respected. The disadvantage is that decision making takes a long time and individuals who want to relinquish responsibility can "pass the buck."

This is the model of community and/or fellowship (*koinonia*) which was recognized by Pope Pius XII in his encyclical letter *Mystici Corporis* and later developed in the 1964 Vatican II document *The Dogmatic Constitution on the Church*. Many of us were formed by the former popular model as we were taught that in order to be a healthy member of the mystical body of Christ we had to keep the commandments and participate fully in the sacramental life of the church. The latter model made us proud to be numbered among the People of God and many became open to the possibility that folks from other Christian denominations were a pilgrim people with us in some undefined way. Ecumenism was high and the holy Spirit was found at the center of a charismatic revival. People were being formed spiritually through ecumenical dialogue, charismatic renewal, cursillo and many other small-group based movements and organizations.

Those who grew spiritually because of their involvement in this fellowship model of the church made the institutional church aware of the need to decentralize and informalize if the demand for familial closeness was to be met. For example, among Hispanic Catholics, there are many for whom the church is too impersonal and for whom leadership opportunities are limited. And so they join a small fundamentalist sect where they feel more "at home."

On the other hand, many informal groups within the Catholic Church, such as the base christian communities, were, and are today, training grounds for lay leaders in the church, and there they contribute to the formation of the church. No one could possibly measure, for example, the valuable contribution of the Polish people to a vital theology of work, or the Latin American laity to Liberation Theology.

The Church As Herald

The model of church as herald is one based on the strong preaching of the gospel and viable religious education programs offered to the faithful. In parishes where this model predominates there is greater stress on preaching, education and missionary activities. The advantage of such a model is that people of all ages and backgrounds participate in the educational mission of the church and its consequent thrust toward evangelization. For instance, the role of the lay catechist in Africa is greatly responsible for the phenomenal growth of the church on that continent. The disadvantage is that some ministers, both clerical and lay, impose their personal religious practices and beliefs on the people they were sent to serve. Priests and deacons are expected to be great orators. And "church" could easily mean "Sunday celebration" and "Sunday school."

Outside of the family, the greatest formative influence in our lives is the school, from pre-K to Ph.D. Many people fear that the decline of the Catholic-school system will contribute to the loss of Catholic culture. How many of us owe our spiritual formation to priests, sisters, brothers and dedicated laity who taught us by word and example. Having heard the good news, we were challenged to go out and proclaim it ourselves. We helped form the church by our adherence to and proclamation of gospel values in our daily lives.

The Church As Sacrament

The church as sacrament is a model centered on the liturgical times in people's lives, that is, the sacraments and worship. So often we can focus on the church as a place, holy as it might be, where we go for prayer and the sacraments. For many it is a place of peace, for some a place of escape. The advantage of this image is that liturgy and worship can be meaningful experiences which bring us into contact with the divine. The celebration of the feasts of the church provides spiritual formation opportunities for well-disposed participants. The disadvantage is that liturgy can sometimes become theatrical and an end in itself instead of the means to union with God. It is even possible that the needs of the poor can be overlooked when a parish budget is concerned primarily with buildings, vestments and holy objects.

There is no doubt that all of us were formed by the sacraments and prayer life of the church. These sacred, memorable moments often led to a true encounter with God—Father, Son and holy Spirit. Today, more and more people are recording these events on video, much to the chagrin of many liturgists. But at least it indicates that there is something important going on at that moment. For the properly disposed person, spiritual formation is taking place through the words and actions of Christ alive in the church. It is Christ who nourishes us with his body and blood; it is Christ who forgives us; it is Christ who heals us, and so forth. Through the sacraments we come to share in his divinity. And by our sharing in the holiness of God, we make more visible the holiness of the church. With Christ, we help form the church into a "chosen race, a royal priesthood, a holy nation, a people set apart" (1 Pet 2:9).

The Church as Servant

The church as "Servant" is a model based on Jesus as the savior of the poor, downcast, underprivileged, sick and oppressed. We oversimplify this when we say "all our buildings and material goods should be available to the poor who need them." The advantages are that, following Matthew 25:31–46, social justice concerns become priorities, parishioners are people-centered and aware of the needs of the times; clergy are close to families at times of sickness, death and tragedy. The disadvantages are that ministry goes into overtime, often resulting in burnout; and single issues sometimes block out everything else.

Just as Jesus' disciples had to become servants before he called them friends, so we are called to servanthood/ministry as a precondition to divine friendship. To minister is to serve. Today we find a proliferation of ministries in the church, especially in the United States. Some ministers were "called," others volunteered; but regardless of how they arrived at ministry, they soon realized that unless they were engaged in continuing spiritual formation, they were mere functionaries performing various tasks.

Volunteers, especially, were challenged by the idea of commitment when they realized that ministry meant serving "in season and out of season," when it was both convenient and inconvenient. All ministers—clerical, religious or lay—are formed spiritually when they are faithful to the services they perform, because they are dealing with charity or love, which in itself is formative. It is not a complete formation, but will stand in good stead on judgment day when, as St. John of the Cross said, "We will be judged on love."

By our loving service we form the church. Everywhere in the world the Catholic Church can be found ministering in parishes, schools, hospitals and agencies of relief for the poor through the dedicated service of clergy, religious and laity. Over the past 2000 years a proud history of service has been written by the church. The goal of "every member a minister" is still a lofty ideal, but more progress toward this end has been made in the past generation or two than since the days of the early Christian community.

The Church as a Community of Disciples

Finally, the most recent model developed by Fr. Dulles in his book, *A Church to Believe In,* is the image of church as a community of disciples. Drawing heavily from Pope John Paul II's encyclical, *Redemptor Homines,* from the Acts of the Apostles, and from the gospels,

Dulles sees the church made up of disciples who have broken from the world and its values and who follow Jesus "on the way to full conversion and blessedness of life . . . in new and ever changing situations." This model adds a scripture-based spirituality to the other models while preserving what is valid in them. It is the most appropriate because it speaks about forming disciples as Jesus formed his own disciples:

> Membership in that body has for its source a particular **call,** united with the saving action of grace. Therefore, if we wish to keep in mind this community of the People of God, which is so vast and so extremely differentiated, we must see first and foremost Christ saying in a way to each member of the community: "Follow me." It is the **community of the disciples,** each of whom in a different way—at times very consciously and consistently, at other times not very consciously and very consistently, is following Christ." (Pope John Paul II in *Redemptor Hominis*)

We who are participating in this study together are certainly seeking to be a community of disciples. As the church moves forward ever so slowly towards the model of "spotless bride," she will continue to form and be formed by her members like ourselves who are advancing in holiness. In a way, each one of us is a model of the church in that we present to the world a unique image of Christ, the bridegroom. Our growth and development in the spiritual life will make that image glow with clarity and brilliance.

DISCUSSION

Having looked at the various models of the church in light of the mutual formation process, perhaps one model has surfaced as being the most appealing for you based on your experience of church. On the other hand, one particular model might have caused difficulties for you.

1. Take a few moments to look back over the various models and to write a brief response to this question:
   Which of these models has been most significant in your own spiritual formation?
2. Form groups of four to discuss your responses.

BREAK

Enjoy refreshments and each other's company.

WRAP-UP

1. Look ahead to the "During the Week" follow-up activities. (optional)
2. Look ahead to the scripture passage and the theme of the next session. Decide on a time during the upcoming week when you will read chapter 20.
3. Participate in the Closing Prayer.

DURING THE WEEK

Regardless of which image you prefer, there is one problem that has been present in the church from the beginning—discouragement. Why not write a letter this week to one or more of the following: pastor, school principal, director of religious education, parish council president, bishop, prison chaplain, etc., thanking them for their ministry and encouraging them to remain steadfast in the faith. Warning: do not complete this exercise if your local cardiologists are on strike!

20. Call To Be Lovers

Scripture Passage

1 Corinthians: **Paul instructs his beloved community with practical applications of a Christ-centered spiritual formation.**

PRAYER

Introduction: A Note on the Text

We have surely all heard it expressed that the New Testament is a covenant of love, and indeed, each book is shot through with references to love in its various forms. Of these books, Paul's first letter to the Corinthians is of special interest to us. Written a mere twenty years after Jesus' death, it gives us special insight, not only into the first exciting days of our Christian church experience, but also into the universal human experience of trying to live life from a spiritual viewpoint.

Paul was a man who took life seriously and lived it passionately. While we think of him as an itinerant preacher, moving restlessly from town to town to spread the gospel of Jesus' presence among us, his stay with the Corinthians lasted about 18 months, during which time he had ample opportunity to test out his ideals among a community. Later, on his third missionary journey, having heard of the problems within the church he had founded there, he wrote them a letter exhorting them to keep their eyes fixed on the goal and to live accordingly.

What is the goal? Our passage today helps us to know Paul's view on this, for it is the classic hymn of love. Often when we hear these beautiful words, we experience a nagging sense of guilt, feeling that this kind of love is beyond us and that we'll never be able to achieve it.

But Paul presents love as a gift, God's gift to each of us, the love that is God's own self. Because God's creation is dynamic, this gift is partial, fitted to our human pattern of gradually activating our potential as we mature. Rather than feeling discouraged because we are not yet patient, kind, and so on, let us listen to the goal, our gradual transformation into God. At the moment when we see "face-to-face," God will have finished the work. We, like God, will be love.

Call to Prayer

Let us gather our scattered energies so that we may focus our attention on God's word with its power to transform us. (Pause. Music, song, or a gathering gesture may be used.)

Reading

Reader: A reading from the first book of Corinthians (13:1–13).

If I speak in human and angelic tongues, but do not have love, I am a resounding gong or a clashing cymbal. And if I have the gift of prophecy, and comprehend all mysteries and all knowledge; if I have all faith so as to move mountains, but do not have love, I am nothing. If I give away everything I own, and if I hand my body over so that I may boast, but do not have love, I gain nothing.

Love is patient, love is kind. It is not jealous, (love) is not pompous, it is not inflated, it is not rude, it does not seek its own interests, it is not quick-tempered, it does not brood over injury, it does not rejoice over wrongdoing but rejoices with the truth. It bears all things, believes all things, hopes all things, endures all things.

Love never fails. If there are prophecies, they will be brought to nothing; if tongues, they will cease; if knowledge, it will be brought to nothing. For we know partially and we prophesy partially, but when the perfect comes, the partial will pass away. When I was a child, I used to talk as a child, think as a child, reason as a child; when I became a man, I put aside childish things. At present we see indistinctly, as in a mirror, but then face to face. At present I know partially; then I shall know fully as I am fully known. So faith, hope, love remain, these three; but the greatest of these is love.

LESSON

The Early Church Both Lacked and Possessed Love

In the first century, Corinth was the major city in Greece, a bustling seaport, a cultural center. Here a city boy from Tarsus could both ply his tentmaker's trade and also find many persons eager to hear a word of spiritual leadership which would help them make sense of their lives. Paul was familiar not only with his own Jewish heritage, but also with the Greek culture and idiom, so was well-suited to provide such leadership. Profoundly changed by his personal encounter with Jesus Christ, he was eager to explain and demonstrate that "the way" was no pie in the sky, but life worth living.

His vision is all-encompassing: "All belong to you, and you to Christ, and Christ to God" (3:22–23). So grand a view requires total commitment: "So whether you eat or drink, or whatever you do, do everything for the glory of God" (10:31); "Your every act should be done with love" (16:14); "Only one receives the prize. Run so as to win" (9:24); "Strive eagerly for the greatest spiritual gifts" (12:31). For Paul, it is all or nothing, surely the agenda of a lover.

Paul's opening words make it clear that love was a much-needed agenda for his old friends: "I urge you, brothers, in the name of our Lord Jesus Christ, that all of you agree in what you say, and that there be no divisions among you, but that you be united in the same mind and in the same purpose" (1:10). At how many church meetings would we have wanted to make this speech! If we perceive cliques among us, Paul too had to contend with factions, with leaders more concerned about their own glory than with God's. The letter is almost a textbook on love as it explains, case by case, what love is not.

Nonetheless, Paul recognizes the gradual nature of God's gift, the fact that we need to mature spiritually. "I could not talk to you as spiritual people, but as fleshly people, as infants in Christ" (3:1). He is especially concerned about the church's liturgical assembly, for it is at such times that we, in a sense, rise above our limitations and provide a clear witness of the heavenly banquet which awaits us in the kingdom. He recalls the revelation which he himself received and which he passed on to them that Jesus is truly present, "This is my body" (11:24). Then he extends this reflection further: "Because the loaf of bread is one, we, though many, are one body, for we all partake of the one loaf" (10:17). Such mystical union almost staggers our human notions of love, but Paul does not shy from a detailed explanation (12:14–31).

Maturing in Love

"Make love, not war," was a very catchy slogan during the '60s. But how many of the "flower children" really knew what they were talking about when they used their favorite word, "love"? These idealistic young people thought that establishing peace and love throughout the land would be as easy as placing a flower in a soldier's rifle barrel. They joined movements and organizations such as the Peace Corps with every good intention of making this world a better place to live for all people. What happened to their dreams can be illustrated by the following story.

There was once a medical doctor who was at one heart with the '60s generation. He, too, was interested in joining the Peace Corps in order to bring a better quality of life to third world people. He made his application and was summoned to Washington for an interview. He was accepted without the slightest problem, but was informed that his responsibilities would entail the normal range of medical care for Peace Corps volunteers, including treatment of mental illness and venereal diseases when necessary. The doctor was shocked. "I thought these young people went overseas to do good, out of love for their fellow human beings. Why are they getting into so much trouble?" he asked a close friend. "Most of the volunteers are not getting into trouble," his friend replied, "but there are a lot of idealistic kids who don't know what true love of neighbor is all about. And until they find out, we can expect problems like these at home and abroad."

To discover what love is all about takes a lifetime for each of us. Too many people are concerned about the end product, feeling loved, rather than the process. It is the process that is most important; that's why Eric Fromm refers to the "art" of loving and why Paul refers to it as the greatest of the gifts. In 1 Corinthians, Paul helps us to understand the process and gift of Christian love by: (1) describing various Christian virtues; (2) describing ethical standards; and (3) giving his preference about how the various states of life help one to live a life of love.

Christian Virtues Which Assist Love

"Now it is of course required of stewards that they be found trustworthy" (4:2). **Trust** is certainly a basic requirement for one who wants to grow in love. Psychologists tell us that the first years of a child's life are most significant for this very reason. From the care we receive as an infant we learn whether we can expect care and concern or whether we must earn it by certain modes of behavior. Children who suffer from physical or verbal abuse have great difficulty in trusting others. In order to grow in intimacy, we need to trust another person and to share our deep feelings.

Friendship is a form of love that flourishes in an atmosphere of trust. There is at least the implicit commitment between friends that trust will never be betrayed, that confidences will be kept, and that the mutual concern for life and growth, even when it means amicable correction, will be the hallmark of their relationship. Trust fosters spontaneity, that ingredient which makes for peace and joy. With my friend I can be who I am and relax in his or her presence. What a privilege it is to have a friend "in the Lord," a soul friend, who helps to form me in my life as a Christian. And I, in a reciprocal way, form my friend with my love.

"The body . . . is not for immorality, but for the Lord" (6:13). **Chastity** is not well understood today, probably due to the widespread belief that sexual activity is a natural part of developmental growth. However, when we define chastity as self-control in the area of sexual activity, we see that it is integral to the meaning of love, since our natural inclination is to express with our bodies the affection we feel in our hearts. Any healthy person finds out quickly that self-control in this area isn't easy. But the experience of unexpected sexual arousal is complemented by the observation that lack of self-control leads to some big problems: unwanted pregnancies, abortions, murder by a wronged lover, venereal disease or possibly AIDS.

On the other hand, we observe happily married couples and realize that God's intention is for man and woman joined in marriage to be a sign of the intimate spiritual union which is possible not only between human beings, but also between God and us. The act of "making love" to one's deeply loved life partner, culminating in the ecstasy of genital union, is both the reality that fosters further love and also a metaphor of ideal love. Experience teaches us that not every act of sexual union is equally rewarding, but married persons practice chastity by going beyond moods and being available to respond to one's spouse, or even (as God does with us) taking the initiative in creating times and moments for sexual expressions of love.

Marriage is, of course, a great school of **fidelity.** The marriage vows themselves express this: "I promise to have you as my spouse, to be true to you in good times and in bad, in sickness and in health; to love you all the days of my life." To be faithful means more than not committing adultery. It means keeping a lifelong commitment of love, one day at a time. The words "lifelong commitment" can be very frightening in this age of disposable and dispensable objects (and people), but approaching it on a day-to-day basis can make it less awesome.

The Christian view of marriage is that it is a sacrament. At the moment when the two persons pledge their lives to one another, God's love touches them in a special way. As they seek holiness, likeness to God, they do so through one another. They receive the strength to be faithful and to bring up their children. Couples who are able to talk about their spiritual feelings or religious beliefs have a definite extra dimension to their marriage since the daily ups and downs are seen in a different dimension. However, even when beliefs differ, ". . . the unbelieving husband is made holy through his wife, and the unbelieving wife is made holy through the husband" (7:14).

Another virtue associated with love is **patience.** "No trial has come to you but what is human. God is faithful and will not let you be tried beyond your strength; but with the trial he will also provide a way out, so that you may be able to bear it" (10:13). As twentieth-century Americans who have grown up on a regimen of instant self-gratification, patience doesn't come easily. A spiritual outlook prompts us to realize that God has certainly been patient with us and we need to expect growth slowly. Those of us who are parents are especially in need of patience in the love we show our children.

The concept of patience implies that we foresee an outcome that has not yet been realized. Our ultimate vision is that God's kingdom will come, but as we pray in the "Our Father," meanwhile we also forgive trespasses, with the expectation that ours too will be forgiven. Christian love is always ready to extend forgiveness and to strive for reconciliation.

Paul's letter makes much of that basic ingredient of love, **respect.** While he refers to social conventions as a basis for his admonitions regarding the attire which is appropriate for liturgical gatherings (11:7–16), it is his spirituality of the body which prompts strong utterances. "If you pronounce a blessing [with] the spirit, how shall one who holds the place of the uninstructed say the 'Amen' to your thanksgiving, since he does not know what you are saying?" (14:16). Respect calls for consideration of other worshippers and their ability to participate. Another common problem at these gatherings, bad manners in not waiting for others at table, indicates a lack of respect for one's fellow Christians (11:33–34).

When we go beyond our family, where "blood is thicker than water," to the community, we need strong underpinnings for showing respect. Our cultural biases are usually stronger than our Christian beliefs, as we see when we find ourselves muttering racial and ethnic slurs. Another indicator of lack of respect is the low level to which we often allow our language to slip. On the other hand, love prompts us to pay attention to social skills, showing consideration by posture, eye contact, providing a chair or a cup of coffee. For someone with a Christian spirituality, such actions are more than politeness, but actually honoring Christ's presence in the other person.

Ethical Standards

Just as we can explain our call to be lovers by describing certain virtues which characterize Christian love, we can also recognize certain ethical standards which regulate the behavior of Christian lovers. As always, Paul's standard is Christ, and the other person viewed as a member of Christ. "Everything is lawful for me," but not everything is beneficial. "Everything is lawful for me," but I will not let myself be dominated by anything (6:12). He goes on to apply this standard to sexual conduct and later (10:23), to a knotty problem for people of that time—whether or not to eat meat sold in the market when it might have been purchased from a supplier who bought from the temples where animals were offered to idols.

Paul bases his judgment as to whether or not something is "beneficial" on the neighbor. His listing of judgments tells us that sexual infidelity was in no way beneficial because "your bodies are members of Christ" (6:15). In the case of the meat, "Eat anything sold in the market, without raising questions on grounds of conscience, for 'the earth and its fullness are the Lord's' " (10:25). However, if your companions would be scandalized because it is against their conscience, but not against yours, don't eat it (10:28). As for behavior in liturgical assemblies, since the purpose is to honor God, unusual clothing and speaking in tongues draw attention to oneself rather than God, so should be avoided, because "everything must be done properly and in order" (14:40).

Although Paul deserves financial support from the church, he forgoes this right. "On the contrary, we endure everything, so as not to place an obstacle to the gospel of Christ" (9:12). He rebukes those who seek their rights in court: "Why not rather put up with injustice? Why not rather let yourselves be cheated?" (6:7). In fact, he admits he is a "fool on Christ's account" (4:10) because, "the message of the cross is foolishness to those who are perishing, but to us who are being saved it is the power of God" (1:18).

We in the twentieth century find ourselves with many moral dilemmas common in first-century Corinth, but we face many more that he didn't dream of. However, for someone seeking a spiritual basis for ethical guidance, his principles of love are valid across time: love of Christ, concern for the other, and the cross.

Love Within Our State of Life

One wonders if Paul was ever married, and would certainly pity the poor woman, if so. He is totally single-minded and single-hearted and doesn't (in this letter at least) seem to need any emotional support. His advice regarding marriage is to simply remain as one is—if married, fine, if not, avoid the hassle. However, if you need sex, do get married. His opinion is, of course, based on his view that "time is running out . . . For the world in its present form is passing away" (7:29,31). Since Jesus had promised to "come again," people of that time thought it meant soon. Now that many centuries have passed, we've adopted the viewpoint that we should live as fully human a life as possible, whether married or single.

Priests and vowed religious promise to live celibate lives, that is, to give up the genital expression of love in order to witness, with Paul, to the total universal love of Christ which we will all experience in heaven. The purpose of the vow is to achieve freedom, both from family cares so one can be of service to others, and also freedom of heart. It is a sign of the "hundredfold," another reward promised by Jesus to those who "give up" spouse and family. It is a sign of the paschal mystery—the celibate dies daily, but his or her death is a source of daily new life for himself or herself and for others. Celibacy is not easy, but for an individual who knows how to love, it can be a joyful burden, like pregnancy. By following the example of Mary, ever virgin, in pure, total abandonment to God, the celibate can expect her special intercession.

We have considered married life in the preceding section, but what of those who simply do not marry? In order to avoid becoming mere bachelors or spinsters, such persons need to find persons to love, persons who will take them out of narrow selfish concerns and help them discover the love of friendship and the companionship of a community.

Love is a many-splendored thing, so the song goes. As each person sings his or her love song called life, the words and notes and rhythms are all different. That's because no two individuals love or are loved in exactly the same way. But all will admit that there is a "higher love" worth striving for in life. Made in the likeness of one who comes into our lives "with love beyond all telling," we are all called to be lovers.

DISCUSSION

1. Write a brief response to this question: "What do you regard as the most essential characteristic of a lover?"
2. Form groups of four and compare your responses.

BREAK

Enjoy refreshments and each other's company.

WRAP-UP

1. Look ahead to the "During the Week" follow-up activities. (optional)
2. Look ahead to the scripture passage and the theme of the next session. Decide on a time during the upcoming week when you will read chapter 21.
3. Participate in the Closing Prayer.

DURING THE WEEK

Extend your reflection on your call to be a lover by writing out your response to the question below which best fits your life circumstances:

1. The most significant experience in making my marriage **Christian** has been ... because ...
2. Although my marriage cannot be considered Christian in the fullest sacramental sense, it is significant in my spiritual growth because ...
3. Although I am not married, I find myself moving toward ideal Christian love through my relationships with others, especially ...

21. Call To Be Healers

Scripture Passage

The book of Ephesians: **Through the power of Christ, God gives those who take on the Son's name—Christians—the blessings of the Spirit: insight and the ability to make a broken world once again whole.**

PRAYER

Introduction: A Note on the Text

Leader: The book of Ephesians is a rich and inspiring source for those of us who are striving to deepen our spiritual lives. It is one of the latest of the **Pauline** letters (those probably not written directly by Paul, but rather by disciples who were converted and trained by him), so it repeats many of the themes and even the actual phrases of the earlier letters. Some scholars believe it to be not so much a letter to a specific Christian community, as an instruction given to catechumens at their baptism. We know that frequently persons seek baptism because they feel a spiritual restlessness, a desire to achieve integration or a sense of wholeness. Ephesians speaks to their deeply felt needs, pointing to Christ as the goal and the community of his followers as the place where reconciliation is possible.

As we listen to the passage in our prayer today we can imagine the first-century catechumens standing in a tiny cluster before a congregation of mostly Jewish converts. From what we know of first-century baptisms, they are probably in a secluded place during the midnight Easter Vigil, feeling as fearful as a cancer patient facing the technology of a hospital room. Should they have come this far? What are they getting themselves into? Can this experience heal their inner insecurities? Is God's "love beyond all telling" great enough to embrace such different people as Jews and Gentiles?

Call to Prayer

Leader: Let us take a moment to recall those hidden areas of our life which are in need of healing. (Pause.) Now let us attend to the inspired words of scripture. (Music, song, or a gathering gesture may be used.)

Reading

Reader: A reading from the epistle to the Ephesians (2:11–22).

Therefore, remember that at one time you, Gentiles in the flesh . . . were at that time without Christ, alienated from the community of Israel and strangers to the covenants of promise, without hope and without God in the world. But now in Christ Jesus you who once were far off have become near by the blood of Christ.

For he is our peace, he who made both one and broke down the dividing wall of enmity, through his flesh, abolishing the law with its commandments and legal claims, that he might create in himself one new person in place of the two, thus establishing peace, and might reconcile both with God, in one body, through the cross, putting that enmity to death by it. He came and preached peace to you who were far off and peace to those who were near, for through him we both have access in one Spirit to the Father.

So then you are no longer strangers and sojourners, but you are fellow citizens with the holy ones and members of the household of God, built upon the foundation of the apostles and prophets, with Christ Jesus himself as the capstone. Through him the whole structure is held together and grows into a temple sacred in the Lord; in him you also are being built together into a dwelling place of God in the Spirit.

Individual Reflection

Leader: Let us take a moment to recall a time when we experienced great physical or emotional pain—a time when we felt "far off . . . a stranger . . . behind a barrier of hostility. . . ." (Pause.) How did I get through it? Was it a person God sent into my life? A book I read at the time? An event which shook me up? (Pause.) As I look back, how was I able to grow from this experience? How was I helped to heal?

Prayer

All: Lord Jesus, we who were once far off have been brought near by your blood. We have been healed. We praise you for this good work in us. We thank you for those who have helped us to understand the meaning of pain. We ask that your Spirit remain with us as we continue to be formed into your holy temple. May we come to know your peace. Amen.

LESSON

A Trinitarian Worldview for Healing

We live in a world which is in need of healing, so we often experience conflict, alienation, and illness. Much of our energy is devoted to patching up quarrels or recovering from various types of trauma. Even then, we often realize that our hard-won solutions are necessarily partial and short-term. Nonetheless, our faith tells us that God is mindful and merciful. Our cries of pain are heard. It is through us, who continue Christ's work, that "a broken world is once again made whole." This is the meaning of "heal"—to make hale, sound, or whole. The very word implies that all is not well, and our experience of the world agrees with this assessment. But what **should** things be like? What is "whole"?

The book of Ephesians helps us get a handle on this question in that it summarizes many of the themes of spirituality which we have considered throughout this book and points to a worldview which integrates many disparate aspects of our lives. Central to this worldview is God as Trinity, or a communion of persons. "Blessed be the **God** . . . who has blessed us . . . as he chose us . . . to be holy . . . and destined us for adoption to himself . . ." (1:3–5). "In [**Christ**] we have redemption . . . forgiveness . . . the riches of his grace . . . wisdom and insight . . . a plan for the fullness of times, to sum up all things in Christ, in heaven and on earth" (1:7–10). And finally, we "were sealed with the promised holy **Spirit** . . ." (1:13).

The centerpiece of this worldview is Jesus Christ. The author uses language common to the late first century when many people exhibited a craving for "gnosis," or secretly revealed knowledge about

God and the origin and destiny of the world and humankind. The "mystery religions" were popular because they promised such knowledge to their initiates. Christianity corrects this elitist notion: "[God] put all things beneath [Christ's] feet and gave him as head over all things to the church, which is his body, the fullness of the one who fills all things in every way" (1:22–23). While it is a mystery, the secret is out. As members of Christ, members of the church, **we** contribute to the wholeness of the world, and yes, even the cosmos.

The author hammers home this Trinitarian worldview both by prayer and by exhortation:

> For this reason I kneel before the Father, from whom every family in heaven and on earth is named, that he may grant you in accord with the riches of his glory to be strengthened with power through his Spirit in the inner self, and that Christ may dwell in your hearts through faith . . . (3:14–17). And do not get drunk on wine, in which lies debauchery, but be filled with the Spirit, addressing one another [in] psalms and hymns and spiritual songs, singing and praying to the Lord in your hearts, giving thanks always and for everything in the name of our Lord Jesus Christ to God the Father (5:18–20).

The Church As the Ideal of Unity and Wholeness

The message of the risen Christ was "Peace!" This was a message which took root among Christians, as the mature reflections of Ephesians indicate: "For he is our peace, he who made both one and broke down the dividing wall of enmity . . ." (2:14). As we saw in our prayer, church becomes the place for bringing together those who are "far" with those who are "near" for, "through him we both have access in one Spirit to the Father" (2:18).

However, these brave words were formed in the crucible of conflict within that very church, which had struggled to determine how "old" and "new" covenants should interact, how Jews and Gentiles could possibly blend their cultural and religious heritages. Paul describes himself as a "zealot for my ancestral traditions" (Gal 1:14). Later, after receiving a revelation from the Lord, he understood how his Jewish beliefs formed a backdrop for Jesus. Still, he had no hesitation about preaching to the Gentiles and did not require them to be circumcised. Naturally he was challenged on that point. The harsh words he uses to describe his challengers—"false brothers secretly brought in, who slipped in to spy . . ." (Gal 2:4), give us an idea of the acrimonious nature of the dispute. However, there is another side to the story.

The leader of the "opposition" was Peter. Peter is familiar to us from the gospel stories, for he had been among those chosen and trained as a disciple by Jesus. He is shown to be chief among the apostles, even though the tradition includes a story which shows him in a very bad light:

> . . . one of the bystanders said to Peter once more, "Surely you are one of them; for you too are a Galilean." He began to curse and to swear, "I do not know this man about whom you are talking." And immediately a cock crowed a second time. Then Peter remembered the word that Jesus had said to him, "Before the cock crows twice you will deny me three times." He broke down and wept (Mk 14:70–72).

Just as Paul's history of persecuting Christians haunted him in later life, Peter's betrayal of his own best friend, his Lord and master, left a scar to remind him of his personal weakness. Like Paul, he accepted forgiveness, put this behind him and went on, relying on the grace of God to use him for the upbuilding of the church. Both leaders of the early church needed and found healing from personal sin. Perhaps it was this experience which made them open to the Spirit.

Like Paul, Peter too had a revelation that convinced him that "God shows no partiality" (Acts 10:34), and persuaded many in the church that Jesus wanted to include even Gentiles. But the issue didn't die. It took a formal Council where all the church leaders assembled to discuss this problem, and then issued a letter, which set down the church's policy of inclusiveness (Acts 15:1–35). Later, the controversy persisted as the church tried to put the policy into practice, with Paul giving Peter a tongue-lashing for his inconsistency (Gal 2:11–14).

Nonetheless, God's power prevailed, through him "who is able to accomplish far more than all we ask or imagine, by the power at work within us . . ." (Eph 3:20). God makes no apologies for selecting such apparently inadequate leadership as Peter and Paul; rather, God expects to "show the immeasurable riches of his grace in his kindness to us in Christ Jesus" (Eph 2:7), by using these very men to accomplish the phenomenal growth of the church.

Limits to Human Wholeness

Well, it's all very well and good to acknowledge the truths that the towering rhetoric of Ephesians brings before us, but if God's intentions are so lofty, why do we feel so miserable? Why do we continue to need healing? As we filter the daily news, or study works of art, music, and literature, we can identify at least three sources of human misery: sin, our finite nature, and natural disasters.

Sin occurs when there is a clash of wills between my desires and God's designs. Even when we don't consciously have God in mind as an adversary, but merely decide matters in a self-centered or immature way, we can inflict suffering on ourselves or on others. A selfish cause usually has a painful effect somewhere. Recall the threefold effects of sin from chapter 3: (1) We experience tension because we're not at peace with ourselves; (2) We damage our relationships with others; (3) We weaken our relationship with God. Even when we ourselves do our best to avoid actual sin, we can still suffer at the hands of others who sin.

A common source of pain is the fact that **to be human is to be finite.** We can't do it all or have it all. Our energies and resources often do not match our appetites. We can't completely control our environment and we have even less control over our family, friends, and associates, all of whom have minds of their own. Our physical limitations often constrain us, as we catch colds, break bones, or are struck with serious disease. As we age, we endure numerous losses: our work and its status, the death of loved ones, perhaps loss of hearing or memory. Eventually we face that ultimate deprivation, the loss of life as we know it. We can complain about things being unfair, inopportune, or downright unnecessary (I don't need this!), but we still must endure our human limitations.

In addition, there is the possibility of accidents and **natural disasters.** As we saw in the case of Job, such events put our belief in God to the test, since there is no humanly logical response to this type of suffering. Yet, if God is patient with this imperfect world, we have no choice to be otherwise. Our psyches must accommodate the realities of life. Yes, we are a people in need of healing.

The Wounded Healer

History gives us examples of people whose sufferings forced them to come to terms with pain. We can think of an Ignatius Loyola who, wounded in battle, used his lengthy recuperation as a spiritual retreat;

later, he founded the Jesuit Society, which has contributed so much to the betterment of humankind through education and missionary work. Because he was healed spiritually as well as physically, he was able to help others. We have already considered the similar experiences of Peter and Paul. Father Henri Nouwen describes this process in his book, *The Wounded Healer*.

First, he acknowledges that we are all wounded in some way, an observation confirmed by our experience. Whether someone grows up in an environment of terror such as in Lebanon or Central America, or in a dysfunctional family in the United States, people with childhood trauma need to heal inwardly. No one, in fact, goes through life without some bad times, and these can affect us deeply. We need to expect such events to take an emotional toll, but then we need to deal with our pain so that we can live "well" or in a healed manner.

Nouwen proposed the image of **hospitality** as the "virtue which allows us to break through the narrowness of our own fears and to open our house to the stranger. . . . [It is] the ability to pay attention to the guest." Perhaps we have had the experience of someone who paid attention to us when we were down and out, or suffering somehow. If we were treated in such a sympathetic manner that we felt safe and able to express our feelings of fear or anger, we were probably able to look at the situation more objectively. Anyone who has been fortunate enough to be treated in such a compassionate manner can appreciate what a healing experience it is.

When the situation is reversed and we encounter someone who is suffering, are we able to take the role of host, of listener? Nouwen suggests that what makes it difficult for most people to listen is that we each have our own agenda, and our self-centered preoccupations prevent us from paying attention. First, one "has to be at home in his own home—that is, he has to discover the center of his life in his own heart." Many people are afraid to do this because they are afraid of what they might find within themselves. They are too afraid of loneliness to seek the solitude they need. So they keep themselves "busy."

"Many people suffer because of the false supposition on which they have based their lives . . . that there should be no fear or loneliness, no confusion or doubt. But these sufferings can only be dealt with creatively when they are understood as wounds integral to our human condition." Rather than ignoring our feelings or denying that there is a problem, we need to pay attention to what's going on inside.

The more we acknowledge our own wounds, without dwelling on them, the better we can respond to our call to be healers for others. We need to feel secure and at home as "members of the household of God"

(Eph 2:19). We need to come to terms with our finite nature, with our capacity for sin, and with the possibility of unexpected disaster. Then, at home with ourselves and our God, we are able to extend hospitality to others, to arrange a setting where we are approachable and they sense a possibility of receiving our undivided attention. We don't need a medical or psychology degree to practice this kind of healing. We only need a peaceful heart.

Also, we cannot shrink from our challenge to join hands with others who organize themselves to heal the ills of society. Somewhere in our lives we must find time to take action on behalf of those whose condition is so deprived that they are, even if only temporarily, incapable of self-help. Whether it be a world-wide effort such as "Habitat for Humanity," or a national network like "Meals on Wheels," or a local group lobbying to improve our community's response to the addicted or homeless among us, we must extend our horizons to match God's limitless view, the fullness of the cosmic Christ.

The Sacraments As Healing Actions

Just as a small child who is ill with a fever doesn't understand what is the matter with her, but appreciates her mother's gentle stroking of her head with a cool cloth, persons who are in pain appreciate another's healing touch. Jesus, fully human as well as divine, demonstrated his understanding of that basic human need over and over in his healing ministry. He even gave up his life for us to heal our sinful nature, becoming the preeminent "wounded healer." His followers, the church, recalled his instructions and repeat his actions and words, knowing that in this action he will once again be present.

In the sacrament of reconciliation, a Christian honestly faces up to his sin—whether it be a lack of love or an outright act of carelessness or defiance. Then, in the spirit of penance and the sorrow of Peter when he heard the cock's crow, honestly admitting his guilt, he feels the priest's hands placed in blessing on his head, and hears the words, "I absolve you from your sins in the name of the Father, and of the Son, and of the Holy Spirit." Most people who receive this sacrament with an open heart come away feeling healed interiorly.

The other "sacrament of healing" is the anointing of the sick. Under the burden of physical or mental pain, the Christian experiences the care and concern of the community. In preparing the oil, the priest prays, "God of all consolation . . . make this oil a remedy for all who are anointed with it; heal them in body, in soul and in spirit, and deliver them from every affliction." As she feels the hands of the priest on her head and the oil on the skin of her forehead and hands, the Christian hears these prayers: "Through this holy anointing may the Lord in his love and mercy help you with the grace of the Holy Spirit" and "May the Lord who frees you from sin save you and raise you up." The comfort and healing experienced by people who receive this sacrament at times actually assists their cure.

Each of the sacraments has some physical sign by which our bodies are touched, and a scriptural word which touches our hearts. When a sacrament is well celebrated, the Christian comes away feeling that he or she is important in the church community, that someone has paid attention to him or her, and that something within has been healed.

DISCUSSION

1. Take a few minutes to consider your own family, your workplace, and the community in which you live. Jot down some "ills" that need healing.
2. Which "ill" do you consider the most urgent? What professions, institutions, agencies, or self-help groups are available to help? Is there anything you can do to help?
3. Form groups of four to discuss your findings.

BREAK

Enjoy refreshments and each other's company.

WRAP-UP

1. Look ahead to the "During the Week" follow-up activities. (optional)
2. Look ahead to the scripture passage and the theme of the next session. Decide on a time during the upcoming week when you will read chapter 22.
3. Participate in the Closing Prayer.

DURING THE WEEK

1. Our own families are often in need of healing. Read Ephesians 5:25–6:20 and note down any advice which you feel would be especially healing if you implemented it. Target one area and make at least two attempts to see if you can practice being a "wounded healer."
2. Review the "rules" for listening given in chapter 1:
   a) Pay attention to the other person.
   b) Test your reception by rephrasing what is said.
   c) Tell the other person how you feel about the topic.
   d) Aim for redemptive listening—looking past the person's "filter" and seeing Christ.

How do you feel our group is doing as regards our listening skills? Can we make any improvements?

22. Call to Ministry

Scripture Passage

Paul's letter to the Romans: **Paul summarizes his beliefs, his faith in Christ rather than the Law, together with advice on how to live the Christian faith.**

PRAYER

Introduction: A Note on the Text

Leader: Paul's letter to the Romans was most likely written from Corinth around the middle of the first century, towards the end of his ministry of founding churches in cities across Asia Minor. We recall that Paul had been in the center of the controversy about how to include both Jews and Gentiles within the same church. Since the emperor had expelled the Jews from Rome in A.D. 49, it was Jewish converts to Christianity who had remained behind. Left without the synagogue structure to support their gatherings, they had developed "household" churches and had evangelized many Gentiles who had joined them. Because they were well-organized, Paul did not see that he was needed there, but simply planned to stop by on his way to Spain.

Realizing that his reputation has probably preceded him, Paul writes a lengthy treatise explaining his views, particularly his position on how Jesus has replaced the Law. It was very clear to Paul that all was not right with the world and that Jesus Christ had done something about it by his acts of teaching and healing. From this it followed that those who have been transformed by Jesus must do as he did— serve their fellow men and women. Our passage today reminds us of our call to ministry, to service according to the gifts we were given, and goes on to highlight some of the members of Paul's community who are an example to us of such ministry.

Call to Prayer

Leader: Let us reflect on our life as members of the 20th-century body of Christ, begging for the wisdom to recognize our gifts and the strength to exercise them. (Pause. Music, song, or a gathering gesture may be used.)

Reading

Reader: A reading from the book of Romans (12:3–8; 16:1–27).

For by the grace given to me I tell everyone among you not to think of himself more highly than one ought to think, but to think soberly, each according to the measure of faith that God has apportioned. For as in one body we have many parts, and all the parts do not have the same function, so we, though many, are one body in Christ and individually parts of one another. Since we have gifts that differ according to the grace given to us, let us exercise them: if prophecy, in proportion to the faith; if ministry, in ministering; if one is a teacher, in teaching; if one exhorts, in exhortation; if one contributes, in generosity; if one is over others, with diligence; if one does acts of mercy, with cheerfulness. . . .

I commend to you Phoebe our sister, who is [also] a minister of the church at Cenchreae, that you may receive her in the Lord in a manner worthy of the holy ones, and help her in whatever she may need from you, for she has been a benefactor to many and to me as well.

Greet Prisca and Aquila, my co-workers in Christ Jesus, who risked their necks for my life, to whom not only I am grateful but also all the churches of the Gentiles; greet also the church at their house. Greet my beloved Epaenetus, who was the firstfruits in Asia for Christ. Greet Mary, who has worked hard for you. Greet Andronicus and Junia, my relatives and my fellow prisoners; they are prominent among the apostles and they were in Christ before me.

[Now to him who can strengthen you, . . . to the only wise God, through Jesus Christ be glory forever and ever. Amen.]

Individual Reflection

Leader: Now let us call to mind those persons who would be on our roster of people who have given noteworthy service to build up the body of Christ. (Pause.) At this time, let me also recall with thanks those times when I have been able to use my gifts in service to others ... in my family ... at work ... in my church community. (Pause.)

Prayer

All: Lord Jesus Christ, you call us to build up your body. We praise you for your good works through us. We thank you for your power in us. We ask that you continue to move us to see the needs of a hungry world, and to answer them with a ready heart. Amen.

LESSON

Ministry in Paul's Community

It is easy for us to understand how Peter and the other apostles got into ministry, for they were trained by the Lord himself! But what of Paul? He tells us of his call to ministry in his letter to the Galatians:

> Now I want you to know, brothers, that the gospel preached by me is not of human origin. For I did not receive it from a human being, nor was I taught it, but it came through a revelation of Jesus Christ. . . .
> But when [God], who from my mother's womb had set me apart and called me through his grace, was pleased to reveal his Son to me, so that I might proclaim him to the Gentiles, I did not immediately consult flesh and blood, nor did I go up to Jerusalem to those who were apostles before me; rather, I went into Arabia and then returned to Damascus.
> Then after three years I went up to Jerusalem to confer with Kephas and remained with him for fifteen days (Gal 1:11–12; 15–17).

So it seems that Paul too had a "call" and that he had some very lengthy "spiritual formation" in Christ! We are not the first to set out on this path.

Unlike us, however, who have inherited centuries of tradition on how to organize ourselves for ministry, Paul's community was on the cutting edge. For them, there was an obvious and compelling link between God and the world. **God** has a plan: "For from him and through him and for him are all things" (Rom 11:36); **Jesus** shows us how the plan is to be accomplished: "by sending his own Son in the likeness of sinful flesh and for the sake of sin, he condemned sin in the flesh . . ." (Rom 8:3); and the **Spirit** moves us to do it: "For you did not receive a spirit of slavery to fall back into fear, but you received a spirit of adoption, through which we cry, "**Abba,** Father!" (Rom 8:15)

This triune approach is significant. It's the nature of triangular construction to provide strong support, with the angles and sides leaning into each other, as can be seen by studying a geodesic dome. As for us, simply looking heavenward to our God provides a frail, two-way image. By grounding it horizontally with our relationships with other humans who are also linked to God, we feel much more stable. The more humans join this "body," the stronger is the witness and the more likely that others who are outside the link will be able to see the possibility of an alternative to the world we experience on our own, without God.

Paul was convinced of this. "If God is for us, who can be against us?" (8:31)—"**us**"! This means church, and church means people, and people cannot come together to reach a goal without some type of organization. This requires service, both to keep the group together, and to help it reach out. The community with which Paul was familiar had developed ministries to fit the needs of their situation. Based on their gifts, the members took certain roles. In our prayer, we heard a listing of gifts—a favorite theme of Paul's, as we noticed in 1 Corinthians.

What were some of the roles of service which they identified? The sixteenth chapter of Romans seems to have been added on to this letter since, unlike the church to which he addresses the letter, the people who make up the list are obviously very well known to him. It is the roles he associates with them that help us gain some knowledge of the early church's approach to ministry. Phoebe is called a "minister" (a term which other translations render "deaconess"). She seems to have devoted herself to ministry, for Paul introduces her to another community, which leads us to believe that she may be relocating and relying on him for a letter of reference.

The Christians need a meeting place, so the role of hospitality was provided by those who had large enough houses to accommodate the group, such as the couple Prisca and Aquila. Another couple, Andronicus and Junia, are "prominent among the apostles . . ." (16:7), so apparently "apostle" was a role. It is certainly a role which Paul proudly claims: "Paul, a slave of Christ Jesus, called to be an apostle and set apart for the gospel of God . . ." (1:1). The so-called "Pastoral Letters" (1 Timothy, 2 Timothy, Titus) were written later in the first century and from them we notice further development of roles. We find descriptions in 1 Timothy: bishops (3:1–8), presbyters (5:17), deacons (3:8–13), widows (5:3–16).

Ministry in Contemporary Times

Over the centuries between Paul's time and ours, the church's understanding of ministry has tended to settle into the institutional categories already spoken of in 1 Timothy. We easily recognize hierarchical ministers: bishops, priests, and deacons. Jesus was recognized because he "taught them as one having authority" (Mt 7:29), and we too look towards someone to have the authority to keep us on track. Our stable, responsible leadership has traditionally been composed of those who are called forth by God from among the community and designated for leadership by the laying on of hands in holy orders. Their role in presiding over the eucharistic assemblies and preaching the Word has a central place in our formation.

In addition, just as the early church had its "widows" and "deaconesses," women formed themselves into religious orders of sisters. After the eighteenth century such women have taken more public roles of service in the church, particularly in schools and hospitals. Likewise, men who wanted to devote themselves to works of service formed themselves into communities of brothers. The presence of priests, sisters, and brothers historically resulted in the laity taking a back seat with the attitude, "Let the priests and nuns do it."

The Second Vatican Council changed all that, with a renewed theology of church, as we saw in chapter 19. What are the implications for ministry? This is a point that has received a great deal of discussion. If Jesus founded the church in order to help us bring the world into the kingdom of God, it would seem that two types of ministry are required: (1) ministry to build up the church, or "ecclesial" ministry, and (2) ministry in the world itself. As in Paul's time, the role we take depends on our gifts. Those who receive gifts of leadership and preaching are asked to discern if they are called to the priesthood or religious life.

At the same time, those who receive gifts of prophecy, teaching, exhortation, administration, etc., can be called to use these to build up the church as "lay ministers." This is, of course, a recent term, and can refer either to volunteers or to those who prepare for professional careers and are employed by the church. As in the beginning days of the church, the type of ministry is determined by the needs of the church in a particular area. In some cases, the need for ministry arises because priests are few and far between, as in Latin America, where the role of catechist has become dominant. In other cases, ministries long associated with the laity, such as visiting the sick or feeding the hungry, have been recognized in a more formal manner.

Many people feel no call to use their gifts for ecclesial ministry, for they have their hands full with the second category listed above, ministry in the world itself. This is what Paul calls "spiritual worship": "Do not conform yourself to this age but be transformed by the renewal of your mind, that you may discern what is the will of God, what is good and pleasing and perfect" (Rom 12:2). In other words, with our head on straight about the plan of God for the world and our part in it, we consistently apply this point of view as we go about our work as homemakers, lawyers, mechanics, etc. Granted, some jobs are more likely to be seen as God's work—that's why the early Christians screened out the likes of prostitutes and even soldiers! But the point is the motivation. We're not out to make big bucks but to develop a world which is likely to match God's kingdom.

Twentieth-Century Developments

Prior to the Second Vatican Council there was very little written or understood about the role of the laity in the church. What did develop from the early 1900s until the council was a gradual deepening of the awareness of the laity's rights and duties regarding the liturgical and sacramental life of the church. This canonical or juridical approach to the role of the laity considered the pope, bishops, and priests as official leaders, with the laity as their assistants. The lay apostolate and "Catholic Action" were looked upon as an arm of the hierarchy. While this had a strong advantage in integrating lay ministry with the already established church structures, it overlooked the fact that it was normal to be laity and only by a special call of vocation did a relatively few number of men become clergy. By sheer weight of numbers, the laity were deserving of an ecclesial or church identity of their own.

The 1964 document, *The Dogmatic Constitution on the Church* in fact did treat the issue of the laity from a theological point of view. More recently, in 1980, the United States Bishops issued a statement on the role of the laity, *Called and Gifted: The American Catholic Laity.* In 1989, Pope John Paul II issued an apostolic exhortation with the Latin title *Christifidelis Laici,* in which he addresses the dignity of the lay faithful and their participation and co-responsibility in the life of the church. This document gives us a more universal approach to lay ministry, much appreciated in a church which, like the world, is becoming more international and intranational each day. Just as Paul looked beyond his local churches toward Rome, neither can we afford to become provincial in our outlook in ministry. All of the particular churches have gifts to contribute which will benefit the entire church.

As we consider our call to ministry, let's draw from *Christifidelis Laici.* Here Pope John Paul II lists two temptations which face laity today: (1) getting so involved in church ministry that they don't "become actively engaged in their responsibilities in the professional, social, cultural and political world;" and (2) separating faith from life. (In all fairness, we must admit that some clerics face these same temptations. One bishop recently exclaimed, "Deliver us from priests and deacons who get high on incense!") In order to resist these two temptations, it is necessary for lay Christians to know: (1) their identity and vocation; (2) the nature of their mission in the church as communion, and (3) their needs regarding evangelization, collaboration, and formation.

Identity and Vocation

The laity's **identity** flows from their baptism; recall, "The Spirit itself bears witness with our spirit that we are children of God . . ." (Rom 8:16). Likewise, the laity discern their **vocation**—namely, to come to a deeper knowledge of what it means to be graced by God and to live out one's responsibilities in the light of that knowledge; recall, ". . . and if children, then heirs, heirs of God and joint heirs with Christ, if only we suffer with him so that we may also be glorified with him" (Rom 8:17). From this identity (who we **are**) and vocation (what we are **called to be**) flows our sharing in the mission of Jesus Christ to build the kingdom (what we are called and sent to **do**).

Before leaving the topic of identity and vocation, we might take note of the fact that Pope John Paul II's *Christifidelis Laici* favors the model of church known as **koinonia** or communion. This model is a very mystical one in the sense that "mystical" refers to an experience of God. Perhaps he realized that we live in a very experiential-oriented world that wants to hear about God only from people who have "touched" God. The Christian who is incorporated into the life of

Christ and has reached the "unitive way" has eminent qualifications and credentials to communicate that life to the church and the world. Those of us still going through the "purgative way" also communicate loving service, although our words and deeds will be recognized as less authentic than those coming from a mystic.

In theory then, every minister will eventually become a mystic, although in practice it doesn't always work out that way. The theory is true, however, because our **charisms,** or gifts given by the Spirit for service, are a sharing of God, a communion with God. Whatever our gifts may be, they all share in Jesus' own ministry and mission. Nonetheless, many people still feel hesitant to use these gifts. Pope John Paul II points out three areas which, if implemented, might encourage such hesitant Christians.

The Need for Re-evangelization, Collaboration, and Formation

In chapter 18, we explored the notion of evangelization, or the announcing of the good news. This is the heart of the church's ministry, so it has been taken up on many fronts in our own country. The Paulists use the field of publishing to put books like this one in the hands of the faithful, while the Josephites work in the Afro-American community, the Glenmarys in "no priest land, U.S.A.," and so forth. Lively parish evangelization efforts have brought thousands of non-practicing Catholics "back home" as well as new inquirers into R.C.I.A. programs.

In spite of such efforts, as a mass movement in the church, evangelization is still trying to get off the ground. Some experts claim that what was needed was pre-evangelization through catechesis and social action on the grounds that, "You can't preach the gospel to someone with an empty stomach." Others complained that the faithful themselves had never been truly and authentically evangelized and therefore were not prepared to evangelize others. Pope John Paul II states that the time has come for **re-evangelization,** especially in the First World, where the good life enables many to live "as if God did not exist!"

In the United States it is estimated that over the past thirty years, mass attendance has dropped 50%, and that of those who do attend on a regular basis, many are nominal or cultural Catholics who simply go along with the externals of traditions and rituals. Therefore, the pope calls for a "remaking" of the Christian fabric, not just a "mending," because of the urgency of the problem. His exhortation calls upon the Christian faithful "to testify how the Christian faith contributes the only fully valid response . . . to the problems and hopes that life poses. . . ." (#34)

A second area Pope John Paul II targets is the need for **collaboration,** which he expresses mainly in terms of marriage and the family. He sees that man and woman are willed by God "to be the prime community and at the same time to be a 'sign' of that interpersonal communion of love which constitutes the mystical, intimate life of God, Three in One." (#52) We should note that another common use of this word arises from women religious in the United States who were tired of being treated like second-class citizens in the church. They simply wanted to collaborate—work with—clergy and laity as equal partners and laborers in the Lord's vineyard. While the document does not address this issue, it does give considerable space to the dignity of woman from an anthropological and theological perspective, and to her role in the mission of the church and in the world.

In an ironic twist, the pope laments "the absence or scarcity of the presence of men, some of whom abdicate their proper church responsibilities, allowing them to be fulfilled only by women. Such instances are participation in the liturgical prayer of the church, education and, in particular, catechesis of their own sons and daughters and other children, presence at religious and cultural meetings, and collaboration in charitable and missionary initiatives." (#52) Sad but true. Just as racism can be an obstacle to evangelization, so sexism can be an obstacle to the lay faithful in presenting their charisms to the church, whether it be men unwilling to do what has come to be seen as "women's work" or women who are excluded from "men's ministries."

The final need that must be met for the full impact of the charisms of the lay faithful is that of **formation.** Until recently this word was used almost exclusively for clergy and religious, but since Vatican II and the proliferation of lay ministries in the church, total and ongoing Christian formation is a necessary responsibility for the laity. It is described as, "a continual process in the individual of maturation in faith and a likening to Christ, according to the will of the Father, under the guidance of the holy Spirit." (#57)

Formation gives the lay faithful a clearer understanding of their vocation and the mission which flows from their baptism. It takes place in such a way that it integrates their "spiritual" and "secular" lives in order to avoid a split between faith and daily life. Although spiritual formation has a privileged position, the laity ought to receive doctrinal formation and catechesis "geared to age and the diverse situations in life." (#60) In chapter 19 we talked about the "reciprocal" formation of church and members. *Christifidelis Laici* agrees:

"The more we are formed and the more we feel the need to pursue and deepen our formation, still more will we be formed and be rendered capable of forming others." (#63)

Such has certainly been the purpose of this book and group study —to assist you in your process of formation. It would be hard to imagine that you would not have experienced growth after completing 22 chapters to date! As authors, we are grateful to supply a catalyst for uniting the sincere desire for formation on the part of the participant with the ever-present desire of God to form us as the potter forms the clay.

DISCUSSION

1. Write a brief response to the following question: Do I feel more at home as an "ecclesial minister" or as a "minister in the world"? Why?
2. Share your response with a partner.

BREAK

Enjoy refreshments and each other's company.

WRAP-UP

1. Look to the "During the Week" follow-up activities. (optional)
2. Look ahead to the scripture passage and the theme of the next session. Decide on a time during the upcoming week when you will read chapter 23.
3. Participate in the Closing Prayer.

DURING THE WEEK

One often wonders what people in Paul's day thought when they read or heard one of his letters for the first time. Did they find it complex and confusing? Did they find it necessary to reread it many times before they even began to understand it? Were some people overwhelmed by his theology, sometimes dogmatic, often mystical?

Perhaps our reactions are the same when we sit down to read a document such as *Christifidelis Laici*. (By now we should know not to read it before bedtime unless we suffer from insomnia!) And yet these documents are part of the living tradition and teaching of the church. They should be read by literate Catholics who can grasp the content and apply it to their lives. How many couples would approach family planning in a much more spiritual way if they took time to inform their consciences by reading *Humanae Vitae*.

One of the best ways to tackle a church document is to read it with a highlighter in hand and mark the passages which have special meaning. Look for definitions, explanations, and concepts which are the "meat" of the document. Then, at a later time, review the document which you have marked up for your personal use. Anyone who takes some time for this will be well rewarded with spiritual insights which become food for thought.

During this week, obtain a copy of *Christifidelis Laici* and give this method a try.

23. Call to Holiness

Scripture Passage

Revelation 3:20–7:17; 21:1—22—21: **From a final judgment viewpoint, we come to understand the holiness of God and how we humans participate in that holiness.**

PRAYER

Introduction: A Note on the Text

For our prayer today, we will reflect on God's word as presented in the book of Revelation. More so than with most biblical books, it's difficult to select from this complex text a suitable passage which helps us raise our minds and hearts to God. The purpose of the book is to impress upon us that the stakes for the spiritual journey are high. Not only has the author, John, been exiled to the rocky island of Patmos for his beliefs, but he has seen his associates martyred. Undoubtedly, for him, the stakes are high. It is clear to him that God is holy and we are called to be like God, but he also sees that this cannot be done without a struggle. To drive home his point, the author writes in **apocalyptic** style, taking a futuristic, end-of-the-world point of view and multiplying fantastic, at times terrifying, images.

As we listen to the reading in our prayer, we are led gently into John's visions through a famous text which shows how God takes the initiative, and then awaits our response before sitting at table with us in the most intimate of manners. We glimpse the reward of divine intimacy which awaits us. Then the scene changes as John takes us with him to the exalted throne room of the Most High, populated with creatures which rival the *Star Wars* trilogy for imaginative detail. He draws heavily from the Hebrew scriptures, particularly Daniel, for his setting. We get a taste of God's wrath toward those who thwart the divine design, and also experience the consolation of those who have withstood the test.

As we listen to the reading in prayer, it's well to put on hold any questions which occur about the meaning of the symbolism, but simply to allow the power of those symbols to challenge our spiritual sensibilities.

Call to Prayer

Leader: Let us close our eyes, and imagine all our cares cupped in our hands. Now let us open our hands to allow these concerns which so occupy our attention to fall away as we prepare to go with John into the realm of Revelation. (Music, song, or a gathering gesture may be used.)

Reading

Reader: A reading from the book of Revelation (3:20–21; 4:1–2; 5:6–7; 6:1—7:17).

Behold, I stand at the door and knock. If anyone hears my voice and opens the door, [then] I will enter his house and dine with him, and he with me. I will give the victor the right to sit with me on my throne, as I myself first won the victory and sit with my Father on his throne. (Pause.)

After this I had a vision of an open door to heaven, and I heard the trumpetlike voice that had spoken to me before, saying, "Come up here and I will show you what must happen afterwards." At once I was caught up in spirit. . . . (Pause.)

Then I saw standing in the midst of the throne and the four living creatures and the elders, a Lamb that seemed to have been slain. He had seven horns and seven eyes; these are the [seven] spirits of God sent out into the whole world. He came and received the scroll from the right hand of the one who sat on the throne. . . .

Then I watched while the Lamb broke open the . . . fourth seal . . . I looked, and there was a pale green horse. Its rider was named Death, and Hades accompanied him. They were given authority over a quarter of the earth, to kill with sword, famine, and plague, and by means of the beasts of the earth. . . . (Pause.)

After this I had a vision of a great multitude, which no one could count, from every nation, race, people, and tongue.

They stood before the throne and before the Lamb, wearing white robes and holding palm branches in their hands. They cried out in a loud voice:

"Salvation comes from our God who is seated on the
    throne,
and from the Lamb. . . ."

Then one of the elders spoke up and said to me, "Who are these wearing white robes, and where did they come from? I said to him, "My lord, you are the one who knows." He said to me, "These are the ones who have survived the time of great distress; they have washed their robes and made them white in the blood of the Lamb.

"For this reason they stand before God's throne
    and worship him day and night in his temple.
The one who sits on the throne will shelter them.
They will not hunger or thirst anymore,
    nor will the sun or any heat strike them.
For the Lamb who is in the center of the throne will
    shepherd them
    and lead them to springs of life-giving water,
    and God will wipe away every tear from their eyes."

Individual Reflection

To be holy is to be like God. How do I see myself like God in: first, the invitation to sit at table? second, in the face of the rider of Death? and third, in the number of those in white robes in the heavenly throne room?

Closing Prayer

God Most High, teach me the meaning of "fear of the Lord." As I grow closer to you, I come to trust your wisdom and actions, even though I am too small to grasp your plan. I long for the time when you will wipe away my tears as easily as my troubles fell from my cupped hands. Strengthen me for the struggle by a clear vision of your day of triumph. Amen.

LESSON

The Biblical Notion of Holy

Throughout this book we have tried to form an idea of the holy through our consideration of the various books of the Hebrew and the Christian scriptures. However else God comes across to us, we can never doubt that when we say God is God and we are human, we mean that God is in charge, because the divine perspective is simply beyond our grasp. Nonetheless, along the way, our flashes of insight have given us to understand that holiness is the most intimate essence of the Godhead. The book of Revelation presents God's holiness in a most awesome manner.

The **apocalyptic** style was popular among people in ancient times who were being oppressed by powerful governments, because it can be read on more than one level. An outsider or spy would consider the text to be simply a fantastic tale. An insider would know the significance of the names and numbers. To understand the book is a challenge to us today because we need quite a bit of study to qualify as an insider, one who appreciates its literary structure and the meaning of its symbolism, as well as the customs of the first-century Roman Empire and the biblical allusions. That is far too large a task for a course of this nature, but some small explanation will help us acknowledge the inspiration it can provide.

By using the device of a vision, John can say anything he wants. However, there is more to his choice of style than that, for in a day when everyone believed in gods of some description, a visionary was respected for being able to mediate the mysteries of the other world. The mystery is gradually revealed through other literary techniques, such as the scroll with its seven seals, each disclosing a further misery, or the elder who explains the identity of those wearing white robes. Numbers are significant: seven as perfection, four as universal since it indicates the four directions of the world.

The Lamb would recall the paschal lamb which was slain at the Passover; for a Christian this would identify Jesus, while the horns and eyes show the unlimited scope of his power. The throne symbolizes the awesome power of the Most High God, while the living creatures and the elders let us know that all of creation and humanity are subject to this God. The author borrows the idea of the four horsemen from the prophet Zechariah (1:7–11), and the punishments from the prophet Ezekiel (14:21). The white robes and palms signify victory.

A careful scrutiny of the visions throughout the book show that John alternates spectacles of wrath and punishment with scenes in the heavenly court. Those are rewarded who have stood their ground, maintained their loyalty to Christ, and separated themselves from a pagan society where honoring the emperor superseded honoring God. They belong to God and are possessed by God in surroundings which far surpass any mere human luxuries. God's holiness is perceived both through the power with which the enemies are crushed and also through the splendor of the court. The holy people praise God for their "salvation"—a word derived from the Greek, meaning total well-being. The idea of salvation, so central to the spiritual search, is beautifully expressed in 7:15-17, as well as in the verses from chapter 3 which opened our prayer.

Although the book of Revelation provides a wealth of images which help us understand holiness, we must remind ourselves as well of the many stories and lessons we have considered in the course of these chapters. God has no limits, so can express and share holiness with such diverse personalities as Jeremiah, Ruth, Mary, Paul, and (yes!) even you.

Holiness in the Christian Tradition

As we moved through the stories from the Hebrew scriptures in the first part of this book, we were constantly aware of the covenant: God promised to be the God of the Israelites and the Israelites promised to be God's people. Since God is holy, so too were the Israelites. "You shall be a kingdom of priests, a holy nation" (Ex 19:6). As Christianity became established, they appropriated that claim: "But you are 'a chosen race, a royal priesthood, a holy nation . . .' " (1 Pet 2:9). To belong to the people of a holy God is to be holy oneself.

Paul uses the same word as the title of our chapters, "call"—a call to be holy: "To all the beloved of God in Rome, called to be holy" (Rom 1:7); "To you who have been sanctified in Christ Jesus, called to be holy . . ." (1 Cor 1:2). He, like John of Patmos, treats of the contrast between good and evil, often in strong language. As we know, for Paul, the role of Christ is central in transforming us from simple humanity to a new status: "For if we have grown into union with him through a death like his, we shall also be united with him in the resurrection" (Rom 6:5). This union is a partaking in God's holiness: "Do you not know that you are the temple of God, and that the Spirit of God dwells in you? If anyone destroys God's temple, God will destroy that person; for the temple of God, which you are, is holy" (1 Cor 3:16-17).

We affirm in the Apostles' Creed that we believe in the "communion of saints." This belief developed as Christians gathered in assembly to celebrate the liturgy, perceiving themselves to be the body of Christ. It gained strength during times of persecution, when many of them suffered, even to martyrdom. As they worshipped, they felt joined to both their Hebrew ancestors and also to these recent martyrs as to a "cloud of witnesses . . . [who inspired them to] . . . persevere in running the race that lies before us" (Heb 12:1). This belief is echoed in the words of the Third Eucharistic Prayer: "From age to age you gather a people to yourself."

It is, of course, at the liturgy of the eucharist that we are privileged to experience holiness in a special way for it is there that we partake of the holiness of Christ himself. We recognize Christ's presence in the Word which is proclaimed, in the consecrated bread and wine, in the person of his minister, the priest, and in the people who gather to pray and sing. (*Constitution on the Sacred Liturgy, #7*). We hear the priest invoke the Spirit, not only to transform the bread and wine into the body of Christ, but also to transform those present into the body of Christ. Anyone who has served as a eucharistic minister and has seen the devotion with which people receive this sacrament can testify to the real presence of the holy.

The holiness experienced through membership in the church was described in the *Dogmatic Constitution on the Church,* approved in 1964 by the bishops who formed the Second Vatican Council. Two features of this document are noteworthy here. First, for centuries, persons who experienced the call to holiness in a personal manner frequently followed a "vocation" to the priesthood or religious life. The laity took a back seat as far as special helps for cultivating holiness, relying on sermons and their confessor for spiritual direction. This document repudiated the notion that holiness was for an elite few: "Thus it is evident to everyone that all the faithful of Christ of whatever rank or status are called to the fullness of the Christian life and to the perfection of charity." (#39)

Secondly, a popular notion prevailed that "outside the church there is no salvation." This was in spite of observable evidence that many good people were not only not Catholics, but not even Christian. It was also against the inspired word of God: "In truth, I see that God shows no partiality. Rather in every nation whoever fears him and acts uprightly is acceptable to him" (Acts 10:34–35). In chapter 2, "The People of God," the council document clarifies this point: "They could not be saved who, knowing that the Catholic Church was founded as necessary by God through Christ, would refuse either to enter it, or to remain in it." However, it goes on to describe a chain of linkage based on the degree of revelation persons receive: Catholics are "fully incorporated"; Christians are "joined in many ways"; Jews are "that people to which the covenants and promises were made"; Moslems "acknowledge the Creator"; and finally, "Nor is God remote from those who in shadows and images seek the unknown God." God, being God, cannot be prevented from standing at anyone's door and knocking. On the contrary, God never ceases to surprise us by who is invited to holiness!

Saints through the Ages

When people are asked to name someone they regard as holy, some mention a canonized saint, such as St. Francis of Assisi; some mention prominent contemporary people, such as Mother Teresa; and some tell of individuals they know personally. Rarely, if ever, has anyone mentioned his or her own name! When we contemplate the holiness of God, we may find ourselves uncomfortable, as did Moses and Jeremiah, who begged to be let off from such close association with the divine. Even Jesus, though he walked among us, may at times seem too holy to be our model. Yet, the example of another human being who has successfully "run the race" often inspires us. From earliest times, such example has caught the imagination of the faithful and prompted them to "devotions" or prayer that such a holy one would act as an intercessor for others of us. Mary, under her many titles, is the prime example.

Prominent among the list of the early saints were the martyrs, who were honored as "witnesses" because their convictions took them to the ultimate threshold of holiness. Some persons gained reputations for holiness in a particular geographic area and were honored locally. It wasn't until almost the year 1000 that an official "canonization" occurred. Today, even without such official approval, people such as Archbishop Oscar Romero fire the imagination of people and motivate them to honor these individuals. This is as much to remind themselves of their own call to holiness as to revere the memory of those who have gone before us.

Then there are the hidden saints, our family, friends, and neighbors into whose faces we can look and somehow feel that we are in God's presence. When asked to list characteristics of persons regarded as holy, we hear comments such as: "She's got her priorities straight." "He lives the gospel." "She's weathered the storm, with all that she's gone through, and still keeps her cheerful spirit." "He sees Christ in others, yet in a very human way." "I think she's a very prayerful person because she seems to take things in stride." A sense of humor is often mentioned, perhaps because smiles and jokes remind us that we who are in the care of Providence need not take our situations overly seriously.

Our Personal Call to Holiness

We read in the book of Genesis: "God created man in his image; in the divine image he created him; male and female he created him" (1:27). Since to be human is already to be in the image of the divine, our nature is to be holy. Persons who are magnificent human beings are holy just by mirroring their Creator. Those of us who are baptized have a special privilege. "The followers of Christ are . . . justified in the Lord Jesus, and through baptism sought in faith they truly become sons and daughters of God and sharers in the divine nature. In this way they are really made holy." (*Dogmatic Constitution on the Church,* #39)

When we take our humanity seriously, and add to that a realization of what the marvelous gift of grace can bring about, we find ourselves living the kind of lives which show forth "the fruit of the Spirit . . . love, joy, peace, patience, kindness, generosity, faithfulness, gentleness, self-control" (Gal 5:22–23). The effort we have been making to advance our spiritual formation by participating in this study group is undoubtedly rooted in the call to holiness which we have experienced personally and will surely be blessed with such growth.

DISCUSSION

Realize that a desire for holiness is not bragging, but simply a statement of God's call and favor; then reflect on these questions:

1. Have you ever felt holy? Describe the circumstances.
2. Do you feel that holiness is possible for you? Why or why not?

Select a partner and discuss either one of these questions.

BREAK

Enjoy refreshments and each other's company.

WRAP-UP

1. Look ahead to the "During the Week" follow-up activities. (optional)
2. Look ahead to the scripture passage and the theme of the final session. Decide on a time during the upcoming week when you will read chapter 24.
3. Participate in the Closing Prayer.

DURING THE WEEK

Reflect on Revelation 3:20–21. How have you responded to God's initiative? Make a list of all the good qualities which you have developed in your struggle to be faithful to God's call.

24. Call To Celebrate

Scripture Passage

Luke 9:1–11:13: **By his control over the forces of evil, Jesus demonstrates that the kingdom of God has come and that his followers have cause to celebrate as they too contribute to the coming of the kingdom.**

PRAYER

Introduction: A Note on the Text

Leader: As we end our spiritual "journey" together, we return once more to Luke's gospel and its description of Jesus' journey. These chapters deal with "the Twelve" and the "Seventy-two" being missioned—sent into the world to proclaim the Good News, to preach, to heal, and to cast out demons. The apostles and disciples are given certain requirements to fulfill in terms of their mission; for example, they are to travel light, to waste no time with unbelievers, to trust in divine providence, and to avoid looking back. Evidently they obeyed the words of Jesus because they returned to him rejoicing over their successes. Then the Master rejoiced in the holy Spirit with his disciples. Here is a gospel picture of a laughing, joyous Christ.

God had sent Jesus on a journey into the world so that it would be completely clear to us that God is not only Creator, but also "Savior King" in the oriental sense of a ruler who continuously works to ensure the well-being of his people. In his gospel, Luke uses the symbols of Satan and serpents and scorpions to portray the power of the devil being subject to God's power, not only through Jesus, but through the disciples. He uses the term "kingdom of God" to describe both the "good times" when Jesus' followers personally experienced this power

231

and well-being and also the future situation when the struggle will be over.

We too have our moments—moments which help us experience the reality and the possibility of the kingdom of God. And so, as we arrive at the conclusion of this book, we will focus on the joy that is ours in this life and the next as a result of the love we have for God, self and neighbor. It is a love beyond all telling, modeled by Mary, the most perfect of human lovers. All of the previous chapters of this book have led to this moment—a moment of joy which is the reward for being disciples and servants of Jesus. Having answered all the other "calls," it is now time to answer the call to celebrate.

Call to Prayer

Leader: Let us place our concerns in the hands of our Lady as we devote our energies to the praise of God. (Pause.) From our hearts, let us offer a prayer of thanksgiving for the joy in our lives. (Music, song, or a gathering gesture may be used.)

Reading

Reader: A reading from the gospel according to Luke (10:17–21).

The seventy[-two] returned rejoicing, and said, "Lord, even the demons are subject to us because of your name." Jesus said, "I have observed Satan fall like lightning from the sky. Behold, I have given you the power 'to tread upon serpents' and scorpions and upon the full force of the enemy and nothing will harm you. Nevertheless, do not rejoice because the spirits are subject to you, but rejoice because your names are written in heaven."

At that very moment he rejoiced [in] the holy Spirit and said, "I give you praise, Father, Lord of heaven and earth, for although you have hidden these things from the wise and the learned you have revealed them to the childlike. Yes, Father, such has been your gracious will. All things have been handed over to me by my Father. No one knows who the Son is except the Father, and who the Father is except the Son and anyone to whom the Son wishes to reveal him."

Individual Reflection

Leader: During our final session, we do well to ask ourselves, "Formation for what?" and to recall a response prompted by the catechism answer—we are formed for greater knowledge, love, service, and happiness in this world and the next. Our "calls" have led us to reflect on knowledge, love, and service. Now we ask ourselves, "What is happiness? Where does it come from? From whom do we get it?" Think of the happiest moments in your life. What was their cause and source? How long did the happiness last? Is it still with you in some way? (All pause for silent reflection.)

Prayer

All: It was a joy to me, O God, in the midst of the struggle,
    to feel that in developing myself,
    I was increasing the hold that you have upon me.
It was a joy to me, too, under the inward thrust of life
    or amid the favorable play of events,
    to abandon myself to your providence.
Now that I have found the joy of utilizing all forms of growth
    to make you, or to let you, grow in me,
    grant that I may willingly consent to this last phase of
      communion,
    in the course of which I shall possess you
    by diminishing in you. Amen.

(Pierre Tielhard de Chardin)

LESSON

Ultimate Happiness

Our reflections on happiness were prompted by the gospel scene when the disciples returned in jubilation and then Jesus rejoiced in the holy Spirit and praised the Father. What a happy sight Luke portrays! It is a celebration of victory, and all victories deserve to be celebrated. But notice that Jesus quickly pointed out to his followers that the reason for their joy should not be the power they had over sickness and Satan, but that their names were inscribed in heaven. This, then, is the ultimate cause of our ultimate joy—the "beatific vision"—to be happy with him forever.

Do we understand what is meant by "beatific vision"? One young person recently said, "When I die, I don't want to go to heaven and sit around all day and look at God. That's boring." And true—an eternity like that would be boring. But it's hardly a good description of heaven. As a matter of fact, there is no good description of heaven. "Eye has not seen, and ear has not heard . . . what God has prepared for those who love him" (1 Cor 2:9). The virtue of hope allows us to believe in and live for what is promised, if not fully understood—an eternity of joyful loving union with God and all creation. The amazing thing is that we don't have to die in order to experience that happiness and glory because we can have a foretaste of it here on earth.

Our passage from Luke recounts incidents from Jesus' life which are full of those images of hospitality which help us appreciate our ultimate goal. Much of our human happiness comes in those respite moments when we find shelter and share food with one another. Jesus instructs his disciples to look for and expect such situations. "Into whatever house you enter, first say, 'Peace to this household.' . . . Stay in the same house and eat and drink what is offered to you, for the laborer deserves his payment" (10:5,7). Failure to offer such hospitality is a sign that the Kingdom is not present: "And as for those who do not welcome you, when you leave that town, shake the dust from your feet in testimony against them" (9:5). We definitely get the idea that such moments are a foretaste to be savored, but not a steady diet. During the moment of the transfiguration, when Peter suggests putting up tents for Jesus, Moses, and Elijah, the vision moves to its climax and disappears. Later, Jesus comments, "Foxes have dens and birds of the sky have nests, but the Son of Man has nowhere to rest his head" (9:58).

Sharing food is a deeply-rooted symbol of well-being that crosses cultures and time. This section of the gospel tells us of Jesus feeding the five thousand, to the point that, "They all ate and were satisfied . . ." (9:17). Jesus tells the disciples, as you spread the good news, "Eat what is set before you" (10:8). He instructs us to pray, "Give us each day our daily bread" (11:3), and uses examples of a parent giving food to a child to illustrate the generous nature of God. Yet the story of Jesus at the home of Martha and Mary reminds us that the food is a symbol of much more—the "better part."

The sharing of oneself in love is at the root of our happiness, as we see through the story of the Good Samaritan (10:29–37). This message is consistent throughout the New Testament. In John's account of Jesus' Last Discourse we read that our joy will be complete if we live in the love of Jesus. Paul says that joy comes from the holy Spirit, the Spirit of indwelling love (Rom 14:17). The great Christian philosopher/theologian, Josef Pieper, wrote: "Joy is an expression of love. One who loves nothing and nobody cannot possibly rejoice, no matter how desperately he craves joy. Joy is the response of a lover receiving what he loves."

Highways to Heaven

If eternal bliss is our goal in life, then all roads of this journey should lead to joy in this life and the next. Love is the super expressway, but there are some two-lane roads and four-lane highways that are just as important in reaching our final destination. Let us look at several of them, but first, let's mention **humor,** which might be thought of as a road sign—an indication that we're on the right road.

A good sense of humor goes a long way in maintaining a spirit of joy. The person who takes himself or herself too seriously will find it difficult to be happy, whereas the person who can laugh at his or her mistakes, foibles and limitations will gain a true humility. It's interesting to note that both humor and humility come from the same "down to earth" root-meaning. It is this kind of humor that produces happiness which is contagious. We love to be with someone who is so gifted as to make everyone laugh without poking fun at others or resorting to ribaldry.

Closely associated with humor is a four-lane highway which is **leisure,** in the forms of recreation, entertainment, and art. It takes time withdrawn from utility and profit to be happy. In our society we place so much importance on being productive that many people become workaholics. Have you ever met a workaholic who was happy? No more than alcoholics or drug addicts who *appear* to be happy when they indulge their addictions or compulsions. Even those who are caught up in "spiritual" compulsions are not happy until they get everyone in the world to believe as they do.

Leisure, on the other hand, allows the joys of life to settle in. Persons who are able to be refreshed by time off from work are also able to enjoy their work, for they understand harmony and balance in the use of time. Some spiritual writers suggest "wasting time" in the presence of God, which is the prayer of contemplation—surely no waste of time at all. Planned or spontaneous leisure affords the opportunity for our souls to be nourished by the "divine milieu"—God, nature, the intellectual life, creative arts, and so forth.

Recreation is one way to use our leisure time to enjoy a balanced and happy life. Physical exercise and play open us up to the spiritual and cosmic influences in our environment, not to mention their importance for a healthy body, which so greatly affects our outlook on life. Recreation does what it says—re-creates us so that we can live our lives with greater enthusiasm and joy. Play teaches a child-like dependence on others, a quality admired by Jesus when he said that we must become like little children (Lk 9:47).

Wholesome **entertainment** has a way of lifting us out of ourselves through the power of words, music, drama, or spectacle. Grand opera, for example, is one of the most powerful forms of entertainment, but not everyone has the taste for it, or even the price of a ticket. We in the 20th-century United States can choose from a tremendous variety of entertainment available to suit everyone's taste and pocketbook. As persons open to the Spirit, we'll avoid anything which chips away at our true humanity by catering to our baser nature. And we'll also try to avoid getting into a rut, but rather will be willing to try something new; we might find ourselves pleasantly surprised at the joy that new forms of entertainment can bring.

The same applies to **art.** Art appreciation can be most uplifting and inspiring because artists communicate a vision that gives us a new or renewed insight into reality. Even when it does not make us happy (standing in front of Picasso's "Guernica," for instance), still there is a feeling of being present to something majestically transcendent. By taking advantage of the tours and lectures at local museums we can expand our limited perspective and learn to appreciate "the work of human hands."

The Festivals of Life

The next road we'll consider is a three-lane road, really two lanes with a middle turning lane. One lane is celebrating feasts, the other lane is celebrating sabbath, and the middle lane is liturgy.

For believer and non-believer alike there is sheer exuberance in the **celebration of feasts,** whether sacred or secular. The festivals of life, especially, are occasions for joy today just as they were two thousand years ago at Cana in Galilee, for example. There is a primordial happiness in the celebration of a new birth or a marriage in the family. Many primitive cultures still celebrate rites of passage for their young. How happy is the individual who after an even painful ritual, can say, "Now I am a man!" or "Now I am a woman." This is a privilege unknown to most youth in "advanced" cultures.

One of the most outstanding examples of festivity in our times is portrayed in the film, *Babette's Feast,* an Academy Award-winning foreign film. Here we see the selfless love involved in the preparation of a festive banquet and the power of love which melts frozen hearts. It is truly a eucharistic story, without trying to be so. In a culture where "feedings" of convenience often replace prepared family meals, viewing this film could be a wonderful catechesis for an understanding of eucharist as a paschal meal. Is it any wonder that Jesus in his preaching and parables so often uses examples of feasts, food, wedding banquets, and meals to tell us about the kingdom? He chose the Passover meal as the last supper with his disciples and the opportunity to share himself with them so as to bring them joy when he could no longer be physically present with them. "Happy are those who are called to his supper."

The Jews regard **Sabbath** as a special day for leisure and festivity, a practice which Christians observe on Sunday. But how many today treat it with the respect and reverence it deserves? Instead, it has become a day on which we do all the things we didn't have time for during the previous week. As we reflect on our "call to celebrate," we will want to consider how we can take advantage of our culture's "weekend" to get on the road to leisure by taking time for recreation, entertainment, and art. The old slogan, "The family that plays together, stays together," gives us a good lead. Just as tithing is an ideal way to give our treasure to the Lord, so Sabbath is the best way to give our time to the Lord, sacred time for us to be formed by God through our joyful celebration with family and friends.

The "turning lane" between feasts and Sabbath is **liturgy.** Feasts, like liturgy, are the "work of the people," and when they are sacramentalized as in the eucharist, they become like the Sabbath, a celebration of the work of God. Sacred liturgy brings the work of people and the work of God together. Its purpose is to make God present to the people and the resulting joy can range from the deep, peaceful joy experienced in "high church" liturgy to the ecstatic, exuberant shouts of joy at an Afro-American gospel music mass.

Did you ever notice the faces of people leaving the church on Sunday morning? If they were sad, vacant, or simply the same as before the mass began, then something was missing from the liturgy, either on the part of the presiding minister, or the people, or both. Experiencing God in the liturgy cannot but help bring about a sense of joy, whether internal or external. What kind of witnesses to the world are we if our hearts are not filled with joy?

We might take a turnoff along a scenic route to happiness in the form of **devotion to Mary,** the Mother of God, and our mother. In the Litany of the Blessed Virgin Mary, she is given the title "Cause of our joy," and so she is in the sense that she gave us Jesus, who tells us, "Come to me, all you who labor and are burdened and I will refresh you." Mary is the scenic route because along the way to happiness we stop by all those vistas and parks where we can gaze at the grandeur of the mountains and seaside, and pick wildflowers to place in her hands; for such can we consider all her feast days, with their masses, prayers, novenas, as well as the processions, songs, rosaries, pilgrimages, shrines and cathedrals dedicated to her.

Catholics have long practiced Marian devotions as a way of allowing one's self to be formed by the one who formed the Word Incarnate in her womb. During his life her influence was formative, from the crib to the cross. The road called Mary is best traveled on foot, in the humble way of a pilgrim. As with many other Christian practices and beliefs which have perdured over the centuries, there has collected a residue of fanatical, superstitious, and otherwise inordinate devotion, but a gospel spirituality can still invite us to explore the path and find our way.

The Road of Suffering and Death

The last road to happiness is a dead end, literally. It is the rough and bumpy road of suffering and death. There is no real happiness in this life that does not intersect with this road, for it is the paschal mystery lived out in daily experience. The signs that greet us with "Detour" or "Closed for Repairs" are God's way of saying that there is no lasting happiness in this life. But that doesn't mean that we can't have a deep-down peaceful joy in spite of (and perhaps because of) pains and sorrows in our lives.

Recently, a Gallup poll was taken to determine which population group in terms of age, race, and sex was the happiest. The results showed that elderly Afro-American women were in first place, followed by elderly Hispanic women. Yet, of all the population groups in the United States, these two groups have suffered the most. They have watched their husbands struggle for steady employment and just wages; they have seen their husbands die at an early age; some have witnessed their sons and grandsons caught up in a life of drugs and crime, visited them in prison and cried at their funerals; others have had to care for the babies born to their teenage grandchildren. They have had to endure poor medical treatment, substandard housing, low wages, second-hand clothes and cheap food.

But these are the women you find in somebody's church every Sunday. They might be poor and in pain, yet they experience an inner peace and happiness because they know how to take their troubles to Jesus and unite their sufferings with his. The Negro spirituals are a perfect example of this type of spirituality. The *Roman Martyrology* is filled with stories of saintly people who were happy in the midst of suffering. Even in our time, St. Maximilian Kolbe, when he was in the starvation bunker of Auschwitz shortly before his death, could be found singing hymns until his parched voice finally gave out. A peaceful, if painful, contentment awaits those who know how to suffer in and with Jesus Christ. It is not that religion is the "opiate" of such people, but that the cross is an integral part of discipleship.

If suffering is the bumpy road, death is the dead end, but not an unhappy end. The term "happy death" is an unfamiliar one these days, probably because most people die in hospitals or institutions where the technical paraphernalia of healing overshadows the fact that we mortals must go through our own "passover" through death to new life. Even today the church's "Rite for the Commendation of the Dying" provides consolation for the person on the final curve of his or her life's road, as well for the family who gathers around the bed to watch and pray. We who are left behind with no clear idea of what lies ahead on this road do indeed suffer grief.

However, frequent reflection on death, not in a morbid vein, but rather a hopeful one, helps us focus on what lies beyond. We might want to write out a few notes about how we would like to see our funeral celebrated, listing those scripture readings and songs which express the kind of memorial we would like to have others give us. The example of, "O Happy Day," sung as the recessional song of the funeral of a woman whose deep belief in the risen Jesus had been evident to the entire community was indeed inspirational—there was not a dry eye in the church and each tear was a tear of joy.

Scripture As Our Road Map

Jesus has quite a bit to say about happiness; perhaps the most familiar passage being the Beatitudes: "Blessed [happy] are you . . ." (Lk 6:20–23). The beatitudes are just that, "be-attitudes", attitudes of being. Just as Moses went up to the mountain to receive the Ten Commandments, so Jesus, the New Moses, went up the mountain to preach the Beatitudes, not as laws to be observed, but as a way of life leading to happiness with the Father. Some look upon the Beatitudes as a progression in the spiritual life, from being poor in spirit to offering one's life as a martyr. Others suggest that Jesus was perhaps making observations about people who were truly happy and commented on the causes of their joy. Whatever the case, the Beatitudes provide a simple and beautiful answer to the question, "What is necessary to be happy?"

Since we have subtitled this book, "A Scriptural Approach to Adult Spiritual Formation," the idea of scripture as a road map should come as no surprise. All through our "Calls" we have drawn from scripture, in the stylized prayer ritual we developed, in the introductory sections to the lesson, and in the practical applications we have tried to develop. Just as roads snake across a map in a variety of seemingly unplanned patterns, we know as we traverse them that the pattern comes from the terrain they trace. Likewise, the patterns of scripture come from the stories they tell about the people and communities into whose lives God came. As we read these stories and learn more about the people and their times, we can identify ourselves in the plan of God; we can get on the road to happiness. "Happy are they who hear the word of God and keep it." Anyone who has read a love letter knows the joy of that experience. And that is precisely what sacred scripture is—God's love letters to us.

At the end of a course such as this, to a certain extent we feel weary and glad to be finished. But on the other hand, we know there are other roads that beckon. We need to pause and celebrate. We need to take time for recuperative leisure. Then, hopefully, we need to pick up the map again and plan another trip. As authors who have endeavored to bring the scriptures before you, we recommend an in-depth study of the scriptures themselves, either an introductory overview, or a book-at-a-time approach. The more familiar we become with God's word, the closer we come to God.

DISCUSSION

1. Write a brief response to **one** of these questions:
   a. What is the difference between pleasure and happiness? Give examples of each from your own experience.
   b. Like most maps, all the roads to happiness weren't listed in this chapter. Which "roads" have you found most helpful in living a happy life? Why have they led to happiness for you?
2. Form groups of four and share your responses.

BREAK

Enjoy refreshments and each other's company. Make this a real celebration!

WRAP-UP

Participate in the Closing Prayer.

DURING THE WEEK

If you haven't seen *Babette's Feast,* rent a copy from your local video store and watch it with your family and friends. If you have seen it, prepare a feast of your own for those you love. Better, think about all the lonely and homeless people who usually get attention only at Thanksgiving or Christmas. Could you prepare some type of feast for them?

BACK TO THE FUTURE

1. Look for a Bible-study class or group and join it.
2. Set aside time to go over all the "During the Week" sections that you didn't have time to do while your group was meeting regularly.
3. Review the "Twenty minutes of prayer" presented in chapter 9; spend some time practicing this method.

Appendix: The Passover Meal*

THE SEDER (ORDER)

Lighting of the Festival Lights

Kiddush—The Blessing of the Feast
The Cup of Thanksgiving
The Washing of Hands
The Karpas (Green Herbs)
The Matzos (Unleavened Bread)
(Hiding of the Aphikomon or "After-Meal")

Haggadah—The Story of Deliverance
The Four Questions
The Narrative
The Symbolism of the Foods
The Hallel (Psalm 113)

The Meal
The Cup of Deliverance
Blessing of the Bread
Sharing of the Meal
Partaking of the Aphikomon

Grace after the Meal
Grace
The Cup of Redemption

* Because the Passover has been celebrated all over the world for thousands of years, a great variety of customs have arisen around the basic seder ("Order"). The service which follows is drawn from the sources listed at the end.

The Great Hallel (Psalm 136)
The Cup of Blessing

Preparation for the Meal

The foods which are used all have a special meaning, as the rite itself explains. We as Christians will recognize the roots of our own eucharist as we celebrate. It was during such a Passover meal that Jesus instituted the eucharist, and the early Christians borrowed many Jewish customs as they developed their weekly liturgical celebration. Depending on the time available to the group, the service may be lengthened (by extending the meal itself, or adding appropriate songs) or shortened (by omitting the actual meal or some of the prayers). The following careful preparations will be needed:

Host/Hostess: The table is set with best dishes on a tablecloth, with flowers and candles. A pitcher of water with a basin and a towel are set nearby. Become familiar with the directions for serving so all will move smoothly.

Ceremonial Foods
Wine
Matzos (special crackers or unleavened bread)
Karpas (parsley or watercress)
Moror (bitter herb, such as horseradish)
Haroses (chopped apples, chopped nuts, cinnamon mixed with
  dressing)
Salt water
Roasted lamb (or cabrito)

Leader: Studies the directions and knows what is to be done so as to move the service along with ease.

Readers: Prepare parts (Youngest, Mother, Reader).

THE SEDER MEAL

Leader: The purpose of the celebration of the seder meal is to assist each member of the community to look on himself or herself as one who came forth out of Egypt. Let us pause a moment to allow this thought to be uppermost in our minds.

Lighting of the Festival Lights

Mother: (*as she lights the candles*) Blessed art Thou, O Lord our God, King of the universe, Who hast sanctified us by Thy commandments and commanded us to kindle the festival lights. Blessed art Thou, O Lord our God, King of the universe, Who hast kept us alive and sustained us and brought us to this season. May our home be consecrated, O God, by the light of Thy countenance, shining upon us in blessing and bringing us peace.

All: Amen.

Kiddush—the Blessing of the Feast

All are seated. On the table before each participant is a small dish of salt water and a plate containing matzo, horseradish or other bitter herb, haroses and Karpas (sprigs of some green herb such as parsley). Placed before the leader is a large goblet or bowl of wine.

The Cup of Thanksgiving

Leader: Blessed art Thou, O Lord our God, King of the universe, Who hast chosen us above all people, and hast exalted us above all tongues, and hast hallowed us with Thy commandments. In love hast Thou given us, O Lord our God, seasons for gladness, holy days, and times for rejoicing. This is the day of the feast of the unleavened bread, the time of our freedom, and the assembly day of holiness, a memorial to the Exodus from Egypt. Blessed art Thou, O Lord, Who dost sanctify Israel and the festivals. *The first cup of wine is poured.*

All: Blessed art Thou, O Lord our God, King of the universe, Who dost create the fruit of the vine. *All drink the first cup of wine.*

The Washing of Hands

The server presents a basin, pitcher and napkin to the leader, who washes his or her hands while saying:

Leader: Blessed art Thou, O Lord our God, King of the universe, Who hast hallowed us with Thy commandments and hast commanded us concerning the washing of hands.

The Karpas

All take up from their plates the Karpas, or green herbs, dip the herb in the salt water, symbolic of tears and sorrow, and say together:

All: Blessed art Thou, O Lord our God, King of the universe, Who dost create the fruit of the soil. *All eat the green herb.*

The Matzos

The server brings to the leader a plate on which are three large matzos wrapped in a napkin. The leader breaks the middle piece, then wraps the larger half in a napkin, setting it aside for the aphikomon or "after-meal." Then the leader raises the plate and prays:

Leader: Behold! This is the bread of affliction which our ancestors ate in the land of Egypt. Let all who are hungry come and eat. Let all who are in want come and celebrate the Passover with us. May it be God's will to redeem us from all evil and from all servitude. This year we are here; next year may we be in the land of Israel. This year we are slaves. Next year may we be free! *The leader replaces the dish on the table. If young children are present, the server takes the aphikomon and hides it.*

Haggadah—The Story of Deliverance

The Four Questions

Youngest: Why is this night different from all other nights? On all other nights we eat either leavened or unleavened bread. Why on this night do we eat only unleavened bread?

On all other nights we eat all kinds of herbs. Why on this night do we eat especially bitter herbs?

On all other nights we do not dip herbs in any condiment. Why on this night do we dip them in salt water and haroses?

On all other nights we eat without special festivities. Why on this night do we hold this Passover service?

The Narrative of Deliverance

Reader: It is well for all of us, whether young or old, to consider how God's help has been our unfailing stay and support through ages of trial and persecution. Ever since God called our father Abraham from the bondage of idolatry to the service of truth, this same God has been our Guardian; for not in one country alone nor in one age have violent men risen up against us, but in every generation and in every land, tyrants have sought to destroy us; and the Holy One, blessed be God, has delivered us from their hands.

The Torah tells us that when Jacob our father was a homeless wanderer, he went down into Egypt, and sojourned there with the seventy members of his household. And Joseph was already in Egypt as governor over the land. And Joseph cared for his father and his brothers, and gave them a dwelling, as Pharaoh had commanded. And Israel dwelt in the land of Goshen, where they got possessions, and were fruitful, and multiplied exceedingly.

And Joseph died, and all his brothers, and all that generation. Now there arose a new king over Egypt, who knew not Joseph. And he said to his people: "Behold, the people of the children of Israel are too many and too mighty for us; come let us deal wisely with them, lest they multiply, and it came to pass, that if we are attacked in war, they also join themselves with our enemies, and fight against us, and drive us out of the land." Therefore they set over them taskmasters to afflict them with burdens. And our ancestors built for Pharaoh whole cities. But the more the Egyptians afflicted them, the more the Israelites multiplied and the more they spread abroad.

And the Egyptians dealt ill with us, and afflicted us, and laid upon us cruel bondage. And we cried unto the Lord, the God of our ancestors, and the Lord heard our voice and saw our affliction and our toil and our oppression. And the Lord brought us forth out of Egypt, with a mighty hand and with an outstretched arm and with great terror and with signs and with wonders. God sent before us Moses and Aaron and Miriam, and brought forth His people with joy, His chosen ones with singing. And God guided them in the wilderness, as a shepherd his flock.

Therefore the Most High commanded us to observe the Passover in its season, from year to year, that God's law shall be in our mouths, and that we shall declare unto our children God's might, God's salvation to all generations.

All: Who is like unto Thee, O Lord, among the mighty?
Who is like unto Thee, glorious in holiness, fearful
in praises, doing wonders?
The Lord shall reign for ever and ever.

The Symbolism of the Foods

The paschal lamb is brought in and placed before the leader at the head table. As the leader lifts the paschal lamb, the entire company asks:

All: What is the meaning of pesach? (pes-ak)?

Leader: Pesach means the paschal lamb which our ancestors sacrificed to the Lord in memory of that night when the Holy One passed over the houses of our ancestors in Egypt, as it is written: "When your children shall say to you, 'What is the meaning of this service?' you shall say to them: 'It is the victim of the passage of the Lord, when God passed over the houses of the children of Israel in Egypt, striking the Egyptians, and saving our houses' " (Ex 12:26–27). *The leader uncovers the upper piece of unleavened bread and holds it up.*

All: What is the meaning of matzo?

Leader: This is the bread of affliction which our ancestors took with them out of Egypt as it is written: "And they baked the meal, which a little before they had brought out of Egypt, in dough; and they made hearth cakes unleavened, for it could not be leavened since the Egyptians were pressing them to depart and not allowing any of them to stay. Neither did they think of preparing any meat" (Ex 12:39). *The leader lifts up the bitter herb, while all ask:*

All: What is the meaning of moror?

Leader: Moror means bitter herb. We eat moror to recall that the Egyptians embittered the lives of our fathers, as it is written: "And the Egyptians hated the children of Israel, and afflicted them and mocked them. And they made their life bitter with hard work in clay and brick, and with all manner of service wherewith they were over-charged in the works of the earth" (Ex 1:13–14).

In every generation, each Jew should regard himself or herself as one who is brought out of Egypt. Not our ancestors alone, but us also, did the Holy One redeem.

All lift up their cups of wine and say:

All: So it is our duty to thank, praise and glorify God, who brought us and our ancestors from slavery unto freedom, from sorrow to joy, from mourning to festive day, from darkness unto light. Let us therefore proclaim God's praise:

The Hallel

All replace their cups on the table, then stand to chant or recite Psalm 113.

All: Alleluia! Let us praise the Lord!

Leader: When Israel came forth from Egypt,
the house of Jacob from a people of alien tongue,

All: Judah became God's sanctuary, Israel God's domain.

Leader: The sea beheld and fled; Jordan turned back.

All: The mountains skipped like rams,
the hills like the lambs of the flock.

Leader: Before the face of the Lord, tremble, O earth,
before the face of the God of Jacob.

All: Who turned the rock into pools of water,
the flint into flowing springs.
Alleluia! Let us praise the Lord!

The Meal

The Cup of Deliverance

All are seated and lift up their cups of wine.

Leader: Blessed art thou, O Lord, our God, King of the universe, who hast redeemed us and hast redeemed our ancestors from Egypt, and hast brought us to this night, to eat unleavened bread and bitter herbs. So may the Lord our God bring us to other festivals and holy days, happy in the building of thy city and joyous in thy service. May thy will be done through Jacob, thy chosen servant, so that thy name shall be sanctified in the midst of all the earth, and that all peoples may be moved to worship Thee with one accord. Blessed art Thou, O Lord, Who dost redeem Israel.

The cups are filled for the second time; all lift their cups and say:

All: Blessed art Thou, O Lord our God, King of the universe, Who dost create the fruit of the vine.

All drink the second cup of wine.

Blessing of the Bread

The leader takes the upper matzo and blesses it:

Leader: Blessed art thou, O Lord our God, King of the universe, who brings forth bread from the earth.

The leader breaks the matzos into small pieces and distributes a piece to each one. Holding the matzo in their hands, all say:

All: Blessed art Thou, O Lord our God, King of the universe, Who hast sanctified us by the commandments and hast commanded us concerning the eating of unleavened bread. *All eat the matzo.*

Leader: Let us do as the rabbi Hillel did when the Holy Temple still stood; he used to combine unleavened bread and bitter herbs and eat them together, to fulfill that which is said: "They shall eat with unleavened bread and bitter herbs" (Num 9:11).

Each person places a piece of bitter herb and some haroses between two pieces of matzo, sandwich style, and say together:

All: Blessed art Thou, O Lord our God, King of the universe, Who hast sanctified us by Thy commandments and hast commanded us concerning the eating of bitter herbs.

Sharing the Meal

The meal is served in a festive manner and is taken in a joyous and leisurely manner.

Partaking of the Aphikomon

At the conclusion of the meal, the children are given an opportunity to find the Aphikomon, which they give to the leader, who distributes pieces of it to all present. After partaking of the Aphikomon, it is customary to eat nothing else.

Grace after the Meal

Grace

Leader: Let us say grace.

All: Let us bless God, of whose bounty we have partaken and through whose goodness we live.

Leader: Praised art Thou, O Lord our God, King of the universe, who sustains the world with goodness, with grace, and with infinite mercy. Thou givest food to every creature, for Thy mercy endures forever.

All: Through Thy great goodness, food has not failed us. May it never fail us at any time, for the sake of Thy great name.

The Cup of Redemption

The cups are filled for the third time.

All: Blessed art Thou, O Lord our God, King of the universe, who creates the fruit of the vine. *All drink the third cup of wine.*

The Great Hallel (Psalm 136)

Leader: Give thanks to the Lord who is good,
　　　　　Give thanks to the God of gods,
　　　　　Give thanks to the Lord of lords,
All: God's mercy endures forever.
Leader: Who alone does great wonders,
　　　　　Who made the heavens in wisdom,
　　　　　Who spread out the earth upon the waters,
　　　　　Who made the great lights, the sun to rule over the day,
　　　　　　　the moon and the stars to rule over the night,
All: God's mercy endures forever.
Leader: Who smote the Egyptians in their first-born,
　　　　　And brought out Israel from their midst,
　　　　　With a mighty hand and an outstretched arm,
All: God's mercy endures forever.
Leader: Who led the people through the wilderness,
　　　　　Who smote great kings and slew powerful kings,
　　　　　And made their land a heritage, the heritage of Israel,
All: God's mercy endures forever.
Leader: Who remembered us in our abjection, and freed us from
　　　　　our foes,
　　　　　Who gives food to all flesh.
　　　　　Give thanks to the God of heaven.
All: God's mercy endures forever.

The Cup of Blessing

The cups are filled for the fourth time. All lift up their cups of wine and say:

All: Blessed art Thou, O Lord our God, King of the universe, Creator of the fruit of the vine. *All drink the fourth cup.*

Leader: The festive service is now completed according to our Passover law and custom. With songs of praise, we have lifted up the cups symbolizing the divine promises of salvation, and have called upon the name of God. May the God who broke Pharaoh's yoke forever shatter all fetters of oppression, and hasten the day when swords shall at last be broken and wars ended. Soon may the Lord cause the glad tidings of redemption to be heard in all lands so that all of humankind may celebrate the universal Passover united in an eternal covenant. May we go forth to build the new Jerusalem!

The Lord bless you and keep you!

The Lord let his face shine upon you, and be gracious to you!

The Lord look upon you kindly and give you peace!

Persons may remain to enjoy traditional songs and stories.

REFERENCES

Schauss, Hayyim. *The Jewish Festivals.* New York: Union of American Hebrew Congregations, 1938.

The Passover Haggadah, Nahum N. Blatzer, Ed. New York: Schocken Books, 1969.

The Union Haggadah, edited and published by the Central Conference of American Rabbis, 1923.

The Paschal Meal, compiled by Grailville and published by Abbey Press, St. Meinrad, Indiana, 1974.

The Jewish Festivals, New York: Union of American Hebrew Congregation, 1938.

An excellent and inexpensive booklet which contains a contemporary Haggadah is recommended for groups who wish additional information and detail:

The Passover Celebration. Edited by Rabbi Leon Klenicki with Introduction by Gabe Huck. Obtain from: Liturgy Training Publications, 1800 North Hermitage Avenue, Chicago, IL 60622: (312) 486-7008

Bibliography

The purpose of this bibliography is to give credit to those authors whose works are quoted in the book, and also to those who were influential in forming our basic framework. Several popular scriptural titles are cited with the hope that the reader will develop a small library of handy references. The field of spirituality is remarkably open-ended, with any number of approaches, so we simply encourage the interested reader to visit a parish, diocesan, or university library, or a Catholic bookstore to browse. The call of the Spirit is different for each individual, as will be the category of assistance sought.

BOOKS QUOTED

Abbott, Walter, *The Documents of Vatican II.* New York: The America Press, 1966.

Bonhoeffer, Dietrich, *The Cost of Discipleship.* New York: The Macmillan Company, 1963.

Fromm, Erich, *The Art of Loving.* New York: Harper and Row, 1956.

Haughton, Rosemary, *The Transformation of Man.* Springfield, IL: Templegate Publishers, 1980.

Luft, Joseph, *Group Processes.* Palo Alto, CA: National Press Books, 1970.

National Conference of Catholic Bishops, *Economic Justice for All.* Washington, D.C.: United States Catholic Conference, 1986.

Nouwen, Henri J. M., *The Wounded Healer.* New York: Doubleday Image Books, 1972.

Pieper, Josef, *An Anthology.* San Francisco: Ignatius Press, 1989.

Pope John Paul II, *Christifideles Laici.* In *Origins,* the National Catholic Documentary Service, Vol. 18, No. 35 (February 9, 1989), pp. 561; 563–95.

Westmeyer, Sr. Nancy, *Parish Life: A Manual for Spiritual Leadership Formation.* Multnomah, NH: Paulist Press, 1983.

BOOKS FROM WHICH BASIC CONCEPTS WERE DEVELOPED

Dulles, Avery, *Models of the Church.* New York: Doubleday Image Books, 1978.
————, *A Church to Believe In.* New York: Crossroad, 1987.
Fromm, Erich, *The Art of Loving.* New York: Harper and Row Publishers, 1956.
Nemeck, Francis Kelly, and Marie Theresa Coombs, *Contemplation.* Wilmington, Del: Michael Glazier, Inc., 1982.
Nemeck, Francis Kelly, and Marie Theresa Coombs, *The Spiritual Journey.* Wilmington, Del: Michael Glazier, 1987.
Progoff, Ira, *The Practice of Process Meditation.* New York: Dialogue House Library, 1980.
Whitehead, Evelyn Eaton and James D. Whitehead, *Christian Life Patterns.* Garden City, NY: Doubleday Image Books, 1982.
Whitehead, Evelyn Eaton and James D. Whitehead, *Community of Faith.* New York: Seabury, 1982.

BIBLICAL REFERENCES

Boadt, Lawrence, *Reading the Old Testament.* New York: Paulist Press, 1984.
Perkins, Pheme, *Reading the New Testament,* Second Edition, New York: Paulist Press, 1988.
The Collegeville Bible Commentary:
    Bergant, Dianne, editor, Old Testament Series, 25 booklets.
    Karris, Robert J., editor, New Testament Series, 11 booklets.
    One-volume reference edition includes commentaries for Old and New Testaments.
The New World Dictionary-Concordance to the New American Bible. World Bible Publishers, 1970.